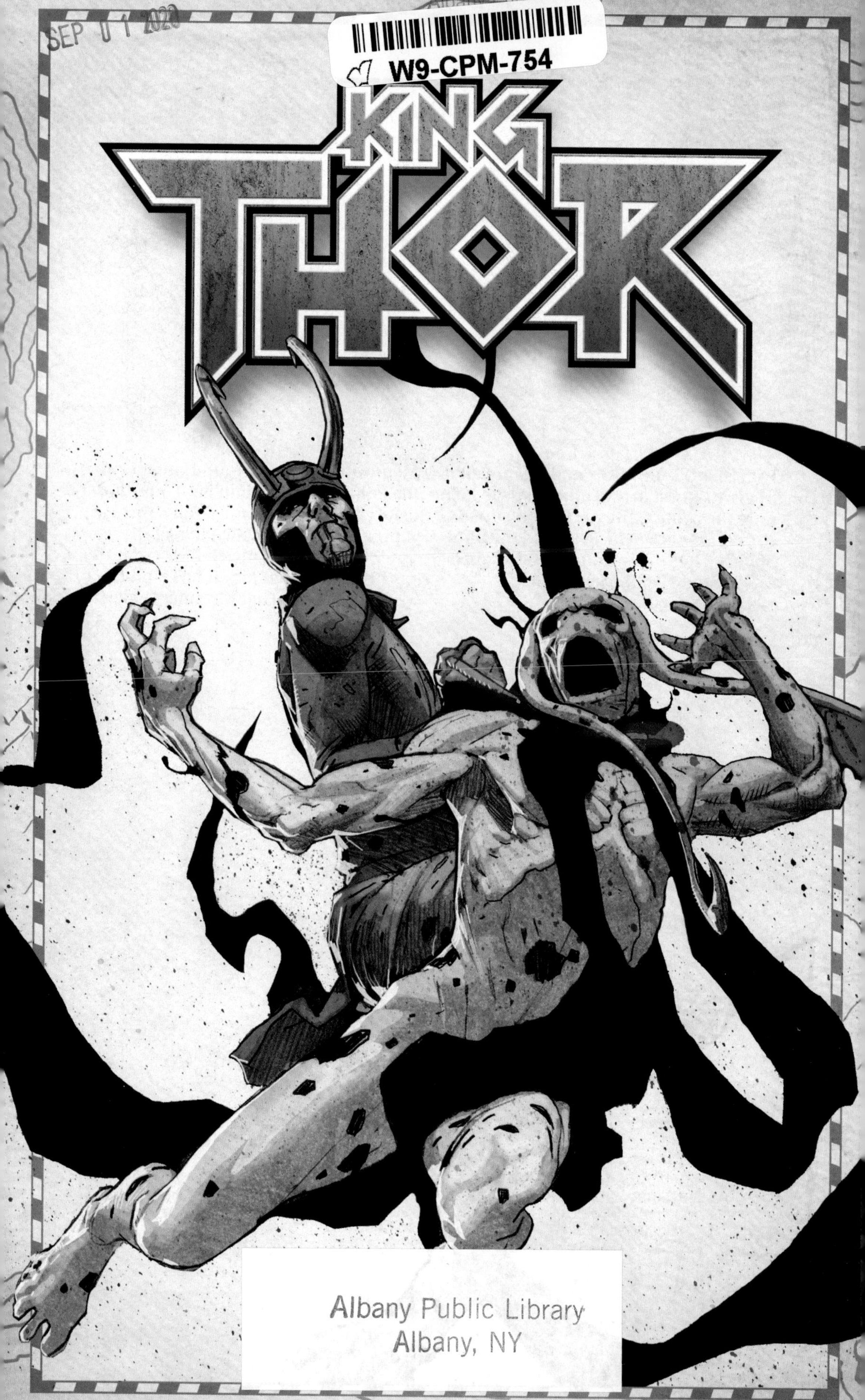
KING
THOR

THE GIRLS OF THUNDER
The sisters Frigg, Ellisiv and Atli are on a desperate quest to find other gods to help save the dying universe. The other gods are all thought to be dead, but the mad Shadrak has advised them to start their quest "at the beginning."

KING THOR
Meanwhile, the girls' grandfather is in the fight of his very long life. Eons ago, he faced an enemy named Gorr, wielder of an ancient force called the All-Black. After Gorr's death, the All-Black spent eons hiding out, but now it has found the ultimate host: Thor's brother Loki.

LOKI THE ALL-BUTCHER
...and he's here to end the universe.

COLLECTION EDITOR: JENNIFER GRÜNWALD • ASSISTANT MANAGING EDITOR: MAIA LOY
ASSISTANT MANAGING EDITOR: LISA MONTALBANO • EDITOR, SPECIAL PROJECTS: MARK D. BEAZLEY
VP PRODUCTION & SPECIAL PROJECTS: JEFF YOUNGQUIST • BOOK DESIGNER: JAY BOWEN
SVP PRINT, SALES & MARKETING: DAVID GABRIEL • EDITOR IN CHIEF: C.B. CEBULSKI

KING THOR. Contains material originally published in magazine form as KING THOR (2019) #1-4. First printing 2020. ISBN 978-1-302-92102-6. Published by MARVEL WORLDWIDE, INC., a subsidiary of MARVEL ENTERTAINMENT, LLC. OFFICE OF PUBLICATION: 1290 Avenue of the Americas, New York, NY 10104. © 2020 MARVEL No similarity between any of the names, characters, persons, and/or institutions in this magazine with those of any living or dead person or institution is intended, and any such similarity which may exist is purely coincidental. Printed in Canada. KEVIN FEIGE, Chief Creative Officer; DAN BUCKLEY, President, Marvel Entertainment; JOHN NEE, Publisher; JOE QUESADA, EVP & Creative Director; TOM BREVOORT, SVP of Publishing; DAVID BOGART, Associate Publisher & SVP of Talent Affairs; Publishing & Partnership; DAVID GABRIEL, VP of Print & Digital Publishing; JEFF YOUNGQUIST, VP of Production & Special Projects; DAN CARR, Executive Director of Publishing Technology; ALEX MORALES, Director of Publishing Operations; DAN EDINGTON, Managing Editor; SUSAN CRESPI, Production Manager; STAN LEE, Chairman Emeritus. For information regarding advertising in Marvel Comics or on Marvel.com, please contact Vit DeBellis, Custom Solutions & Integrated Advertising Manager, at vdebellis@marvel.com. For Marvel subscription inquiries, please call 888-511-5480. Manufactured between 1/24/2020 and 2/25/2020 by SOLISCO PRINTERS, SCOTT, QC, CANADA.

10 9 8 7 6 5 4 3 2 1

KING THOR

JASON AARON
WRITER

ESAD RIBIĆ
ARTIST

IVE SVORCINA
COLOR ARTIST

DAS PASTORAS
ADDITIONAL ART, #3

GABRIEL HERNANDEZ WALTA & CHRIS O'HALLORAN;
ANDREA SORRENTINO & DAVE STEWART; CHRIS BURNHAM
& NATHAN FAIRBAIRN; NICK PITARRA & MICHAEL GARLAND;
AARON KUDER & LAURA MARTIN; OLIVIER COIPEL &
LAURA MARTIN; RUSSELL DAUTERMAN &
MATTHEW WILSON; AND MIKE DEL MUNDO
ADDITIONAL ART, #4

VC's JOE SABINO
LETTERER

ESAD RIBIĆ
COVER ART

JAY BOWEN
LOGO

SARAH BRUNSTAD
ASSISTANT EDITOR

WIL MOSS
EDITOR

THOR CREATED BY
STAN LEE, LARRY LIEBER & JACK KIRBY

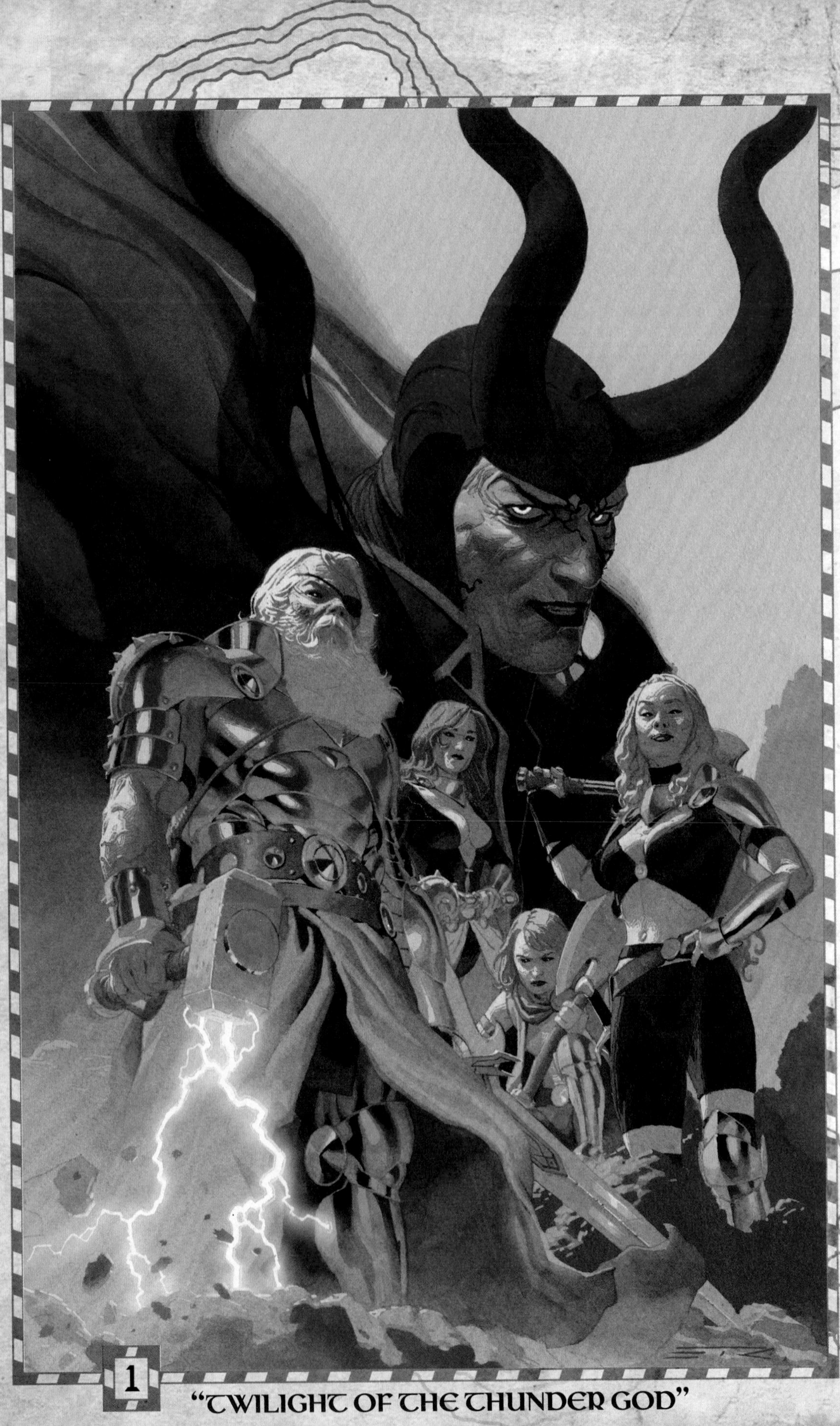

1

"TWILIGHT OF THE THUNDER GOD"

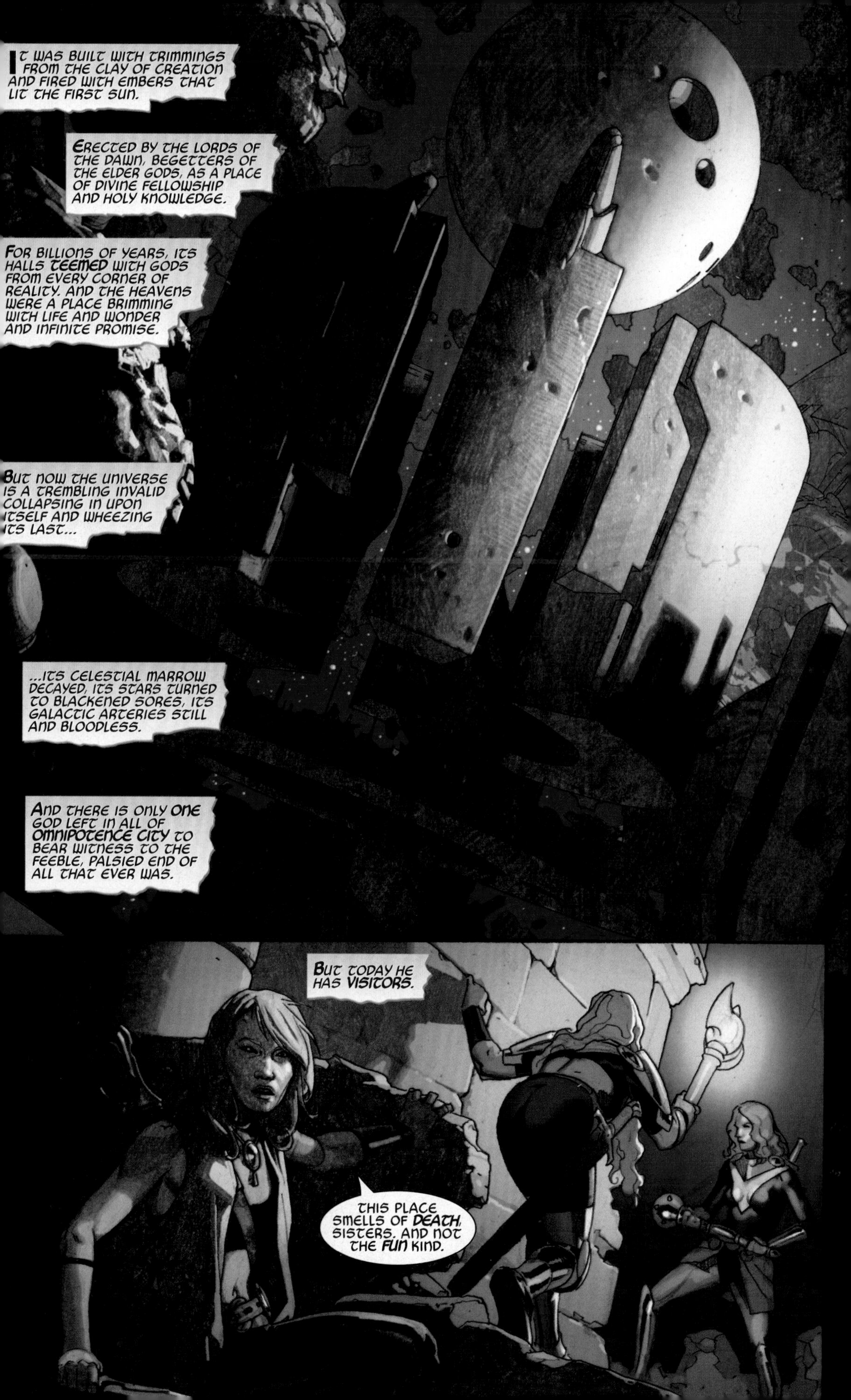
IT WAS BUILT WITH TRIMMINGS FROM THE CLAY OF CREATION AND FIRED WITH EMBERS THAT LIT THE FIRST SUN.
ERECTED BY THE LORDS OF THE DAWN, BEGETTERS OF THE ELDER GODS, AS A PLACE OF DIVINE FELLOWSHIP AND HOLY KNOWLEDGE.
FOR BILLIONS OF YEARS, ITS HALLS TEEMED WITH GODS FROM EVERY CORNER OF REALITY. AND THE HEAVENS WERE A PLACE BRIMMING WITH LIFE AND WONDER AND INFINITE PROMISE.
BUT NOW THE UNIVERSE IS A TREMBLING INVALID COLLAPSING IN UPON ITSELF AND WHEEZING ITS LAST...
...ITS CELESTIAL MARROW DECAYED, ITS STARS TURNED TO BLACKENED SORES, ITS GALACTIC ARTERIES STILL AND BLOODLESS.
AND THERE IS ONLY ONE GOD LEFT IN ALL OF OMNIPOTENCE CITY TO BEAR WITNESS TO THE FEEBLE, PALSIED END OF ALL THAT EVER WAS.
BUT TODAY HE HAS VISITORS.
THIS PLACE SMELLS OF DEATH, SISTERS. AND NOT THE FUN KIND.

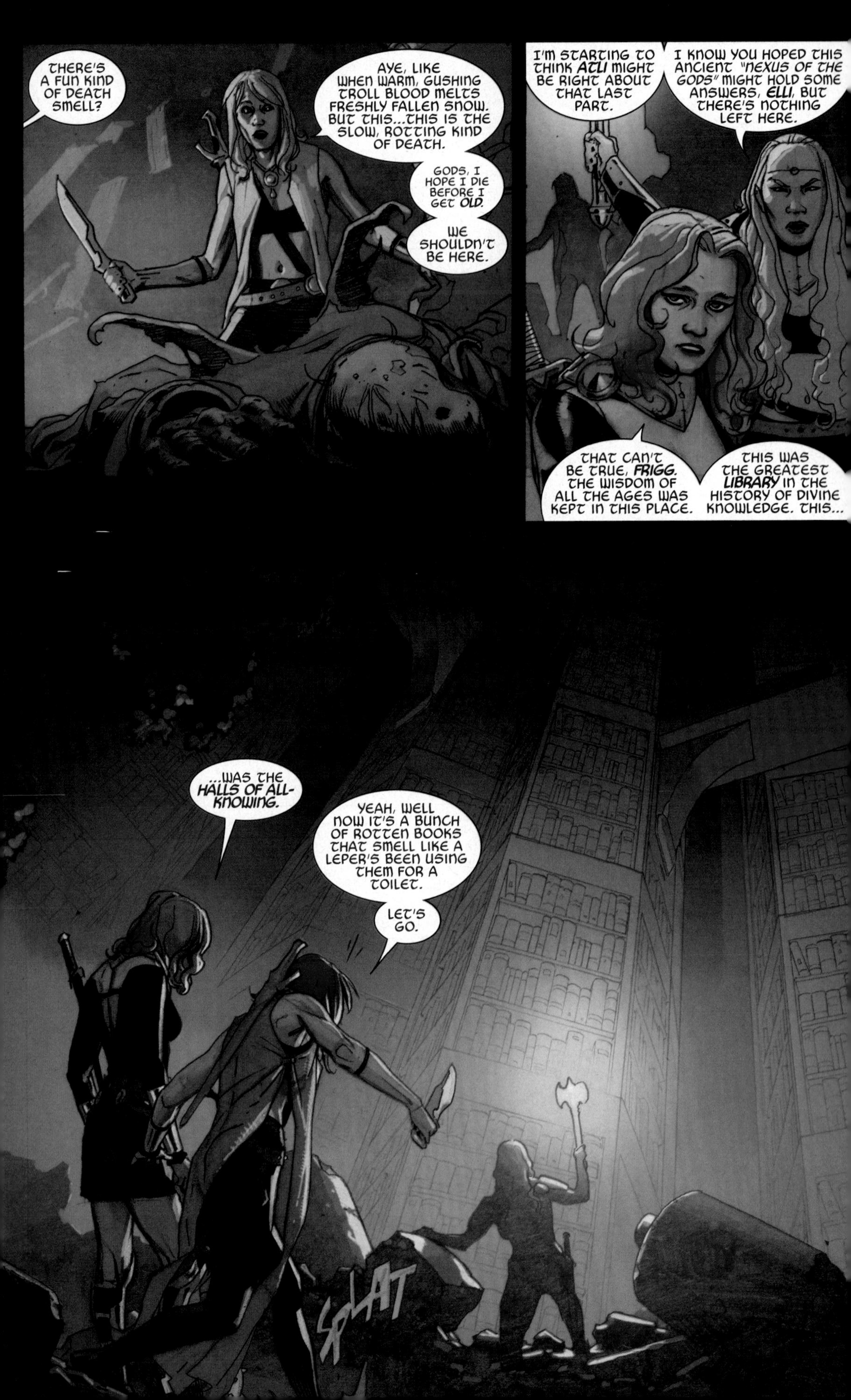
THERE'S A FUN KIND OF DEATH SMELL?
AYE, LIKE WHEN WARM, GUSHING TROLL BLOOD MELTS FRESHLY FALLEN SNOW. BUT THIS...THIS IS THE SLOW, ROTTING KIND OF DEATH.
GODS, I HOPE I DIE BEFORE I GET OLD.
WE SHOULDN'T BE HERE.
I'M STARTING TO THINK ATLI MIGHT BE RIGHT ABOUT THAT LAST PART.
I KNOW YOU HOPED THIS ANCIENT "NEXUS OF THE GODS" MIGHT HOLD SOME ANSWERS, ELLI, BUT THERE'S NOTHING LEFT HERE.
THAT CAN'T BE TRUE, FRIGG. THE WISDOM OF ALL THE AGES WAS KEPT IN THIS PLACE.
THIS WAS THE GREATEST LIBRARY IN THE HISTORY OF DIVINE KNOWLEDGE. THIS...
...WAS THE HALLS OF ALL-KNOWING.
YEAH, WELL NOW IT'S A BUNCH OF ROTTEN BOOKS THAT SMELL LIKE A LEPER'S BEEN USING THEM FOR A TOILET.
LET'S GO.
SPLAT

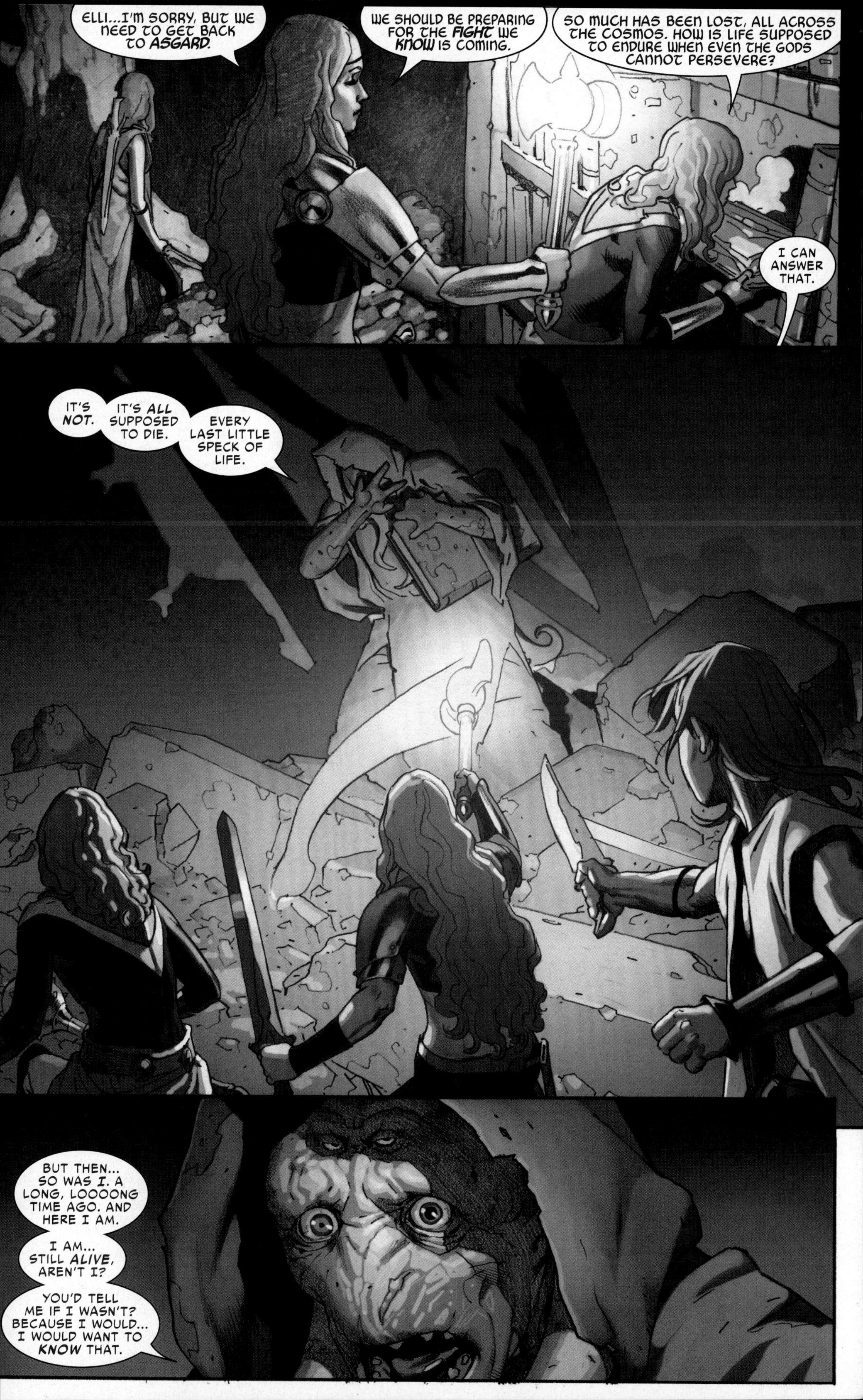

ELLI...I'M SORRY, BUT WE NEED TO GET BACK TO ASGARD.
WE SHOULD BE PREPARING FOR THE FIGHT WE KNOW IS COMING.
SO MUCH HAS BEEN LOST, ALL ACROSS THE COSMOS. HOW IS LIFE SUPPOSED TO ENDURE WHEN EVEN THE GODS CANNOT PERSEVERE?
I CAN ANSWER THAT.
IT'S NOT.
IT'S ALL SUPPOSED TO DIE.
EVERY LAST LITTLE SPECK OF LIFE.
BUT THEN... SO WAS I. A LONG, LOOOONG TIME AGO. AND HERE I AM.
I AM... STILL ALIVE, AREN'T I?
YOU'D TELL ME IF I WASN'T? BECAUSE I WOULD... I WOULD WANT TO KNOW THAT.

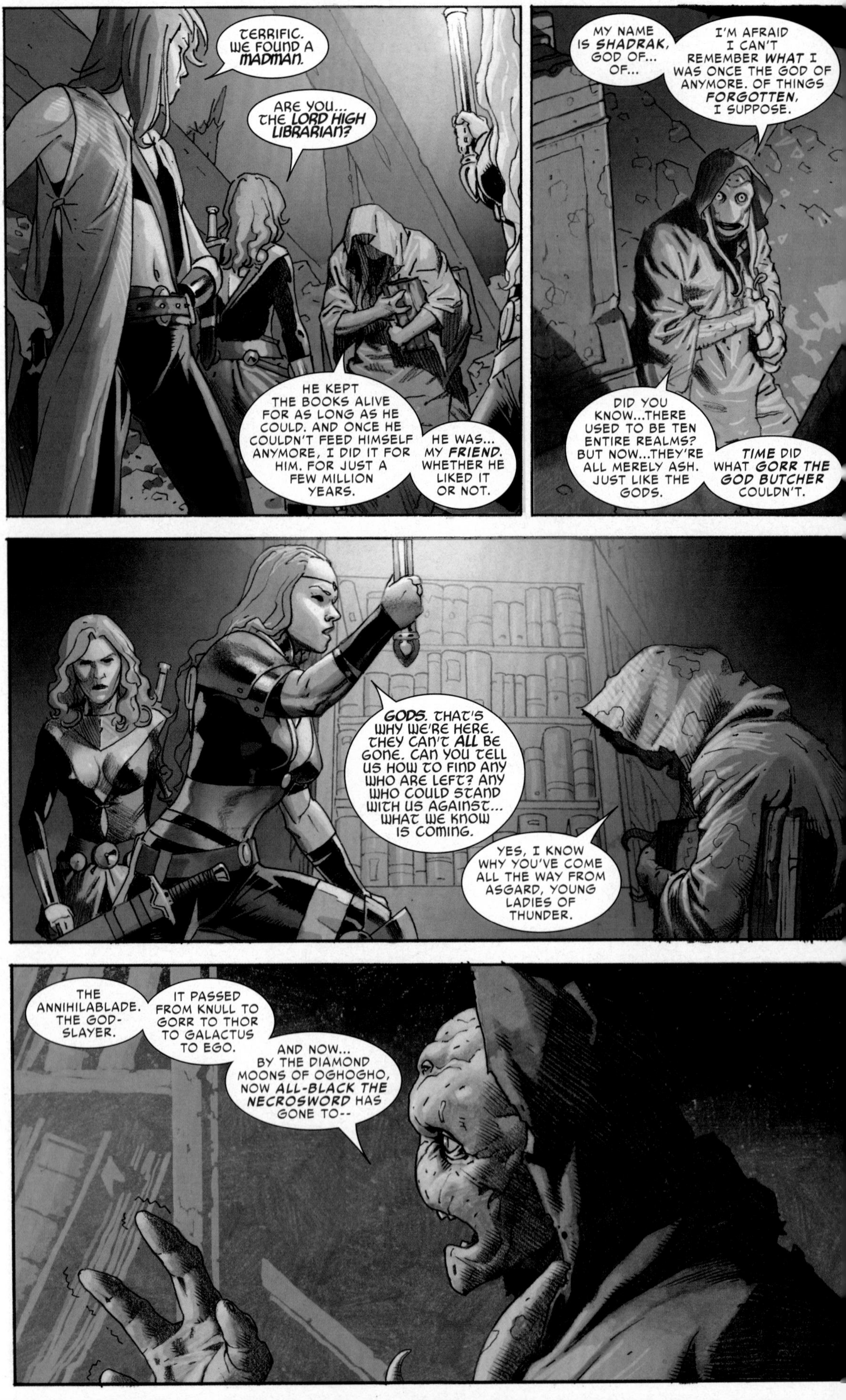

TERRIFIC. WE FOUND A MADMAN.
ARE YOU... THE LORD HIGH LIBRARIAN?
HE KEPT THE BOOKS ALIVE FOR AS LONG AS HE COULD. AND ONCE HE COULDN'T FEED HIMSELF ANYMORE, I DID IT FOR HIM. FOR JUST A FEW MILLION YEARS.
HE WAS... MY FRIEND. WHETHER HE LIKED IT OR NOT.
MY NAME IS SHADRAK, GOD OF... OF...
I'M AFRAID I CAN'T REMEMBER WHAT I WAS ONCE THE GOD OF ANYMORE. OF THINGS FORGOTTEN, I SUPPOSE.
DID YOU KNOW...THERE USED TO BE TEN ENTIRE REALMS? BUT NOW...THEY'RE ALL MERELY ASH. JUST LIKE THE GODS.
TIME DID WHAT GORR THE GOD BUTCHER COULDN'T.
GODS. THAT'S WHY WE'RE HERE. THEY CAN'T ALL BE GONE. CAN YOU TELL US HOW TO FIND ANY WHO ARE LEFT? ANY WHO COULD STAND WITH US AGAINST... WHAT WE KNOW IS COMING.
YES, I KNOW WHY YOU'VE COME ALL THE WAY FROM ASGARD, YOUNG LADIES OF THUNDER.
THE ANNIHILABLADE. THE GOD-SLAYER.
IT PASSED FROM KNULL TO GORR TO THOR TO GALACTUS TO EGO.
AND NOW... BY THE DIAMOND MOONS OF OGHOGHO, NOW ALL-BLACK THE NECROSWORD HAS GONE TO--

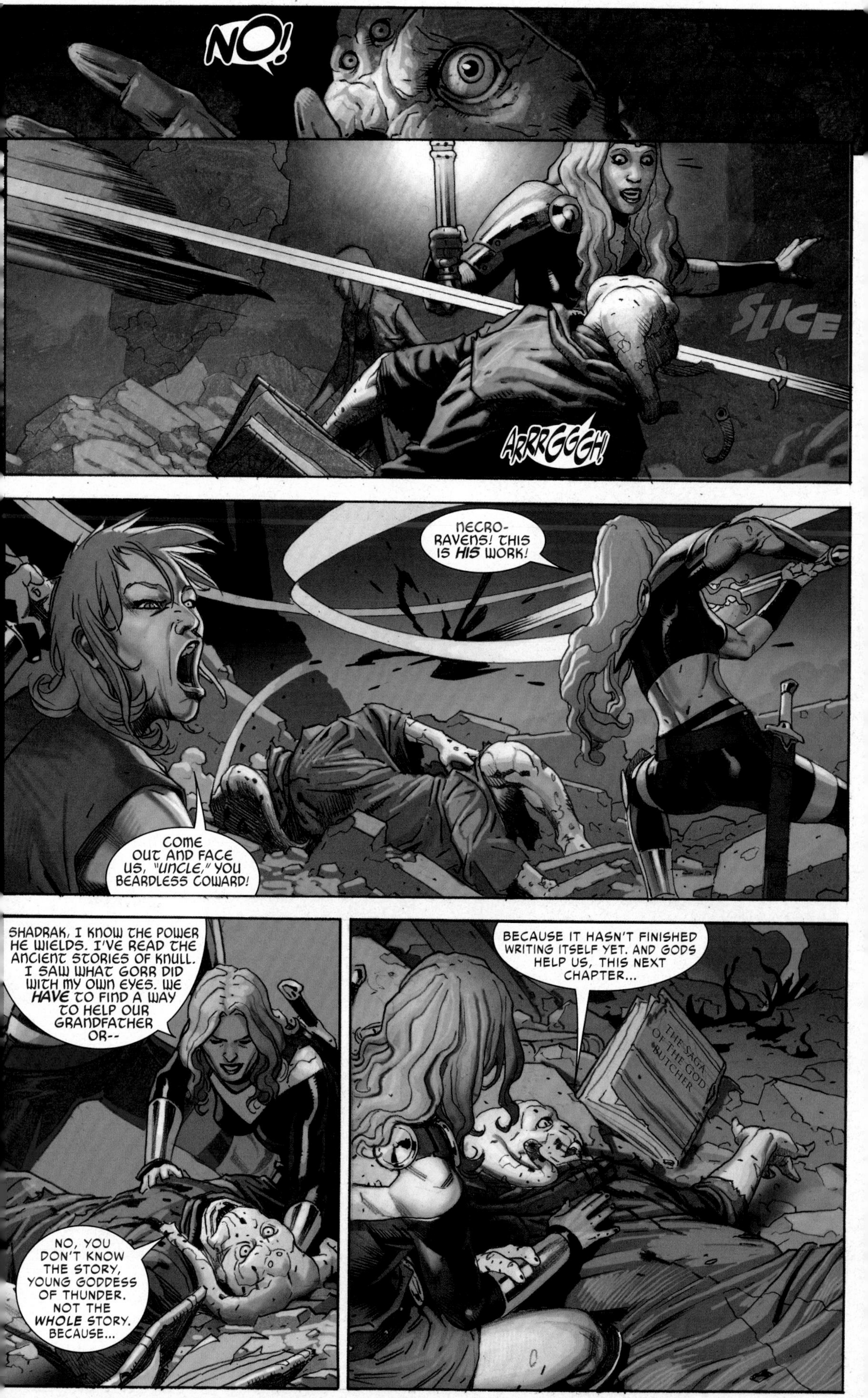
NO!
SLICE
ARRRGGGH!
NECRO-RAVENS! THIS IS HIS WORK!
COME OUT AND FACE US, "UNCLE," YOU BEARDLESS COWARD!
SHADRAK, I KNOW THE POWER HE WIELDS. I'VE READ THE ANCIENT STORIES OF KNULL. I SAW WHAT GORR DID WITH MY OWN EYES. WE HAVE TO FIND A WAY TO HELP OUR GRANDFATHER OR--
NO, YOU DON'T KNOW THE STORY, YOUNG GODDESS OF THUNDER. NOT THE WHOLE STORY. BECAUSE...
BECAUSE IT HASN'T FINISHED WRITING ITSELF YET. AND GODS HELP US, THIS NEXT CHAPTER...
THE SAGA OF THE GOD BUTCHER

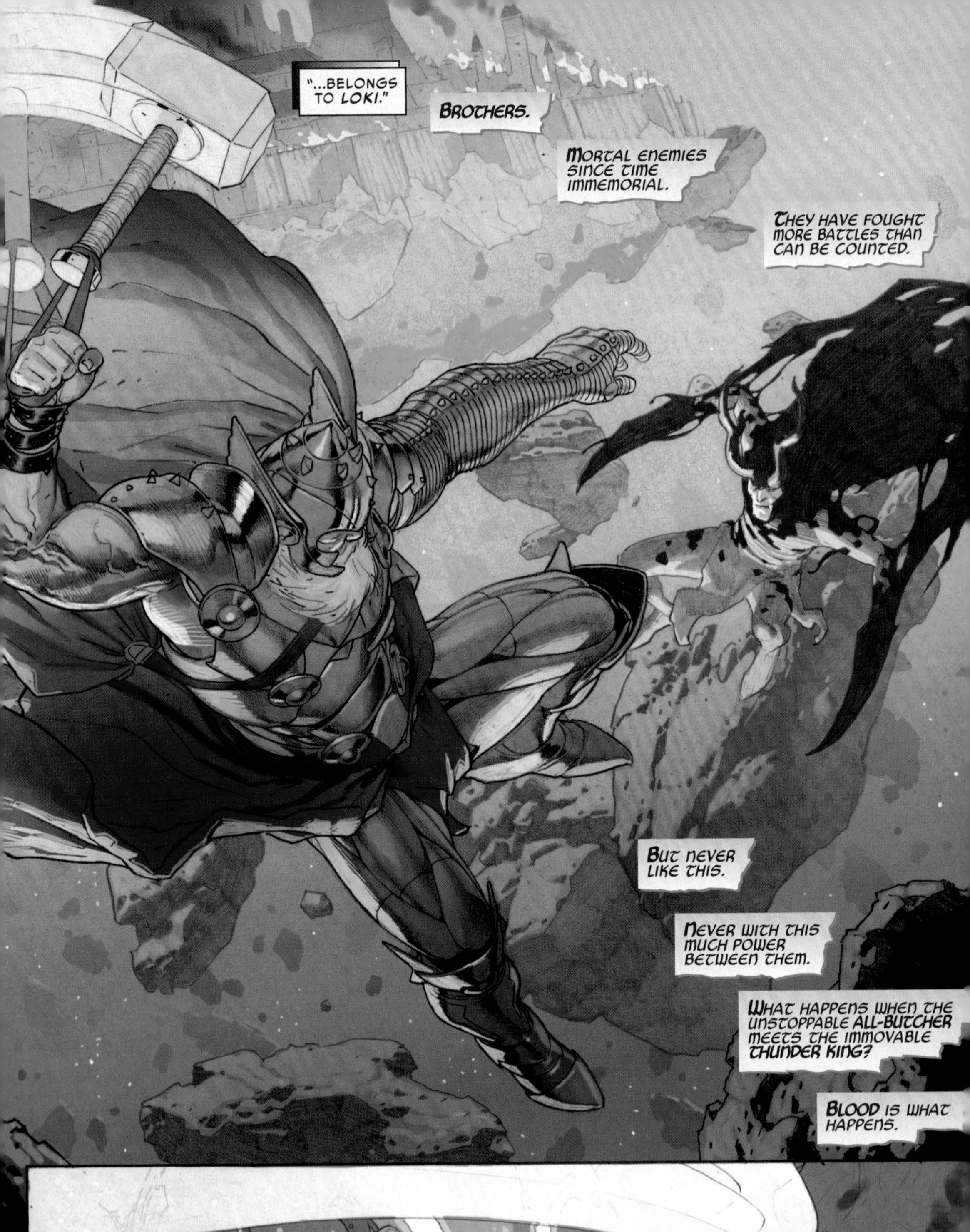
"...BELONGS TO LOKI."
BROTHERS.
MORTAL ENEMIES SINCE TIME IMMEMORIAL.
THEY HAVE FOUGHT MORE BATTLES THAN CAN BE COUNTED.
BUT NEVER LIKE THIS.
NEVER WITH THIS MUCH POWER BETWEEN THEM.
WHAT HAPPENS WHEN THE UNSTOPPABLE ALL-BUTCHER MEETS THE IMMOVABLE THUNDER KING?
BLOOD IS WHAT HAPPENS.
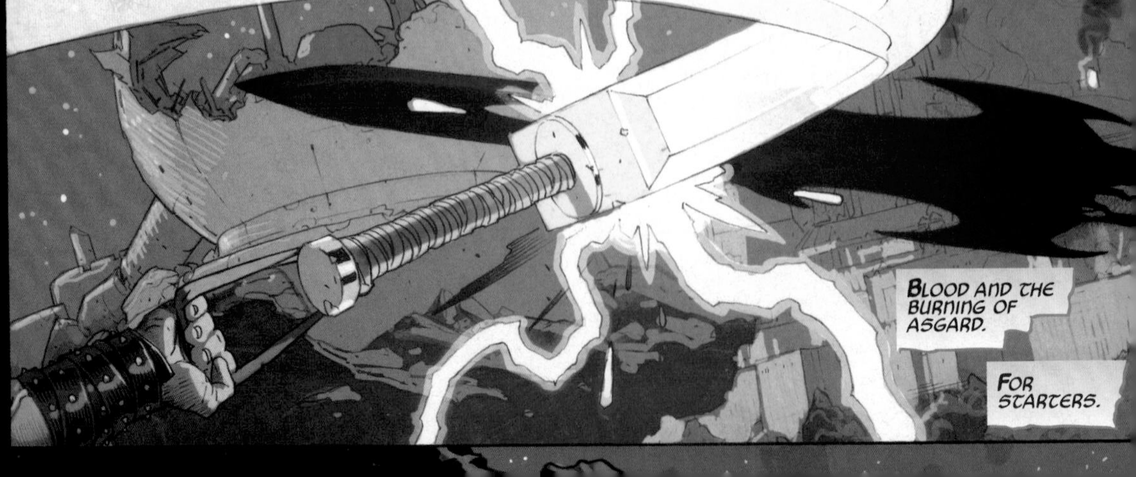
BLOOD AND THE BURNING OF ASGARD.
FOR STARTERS.

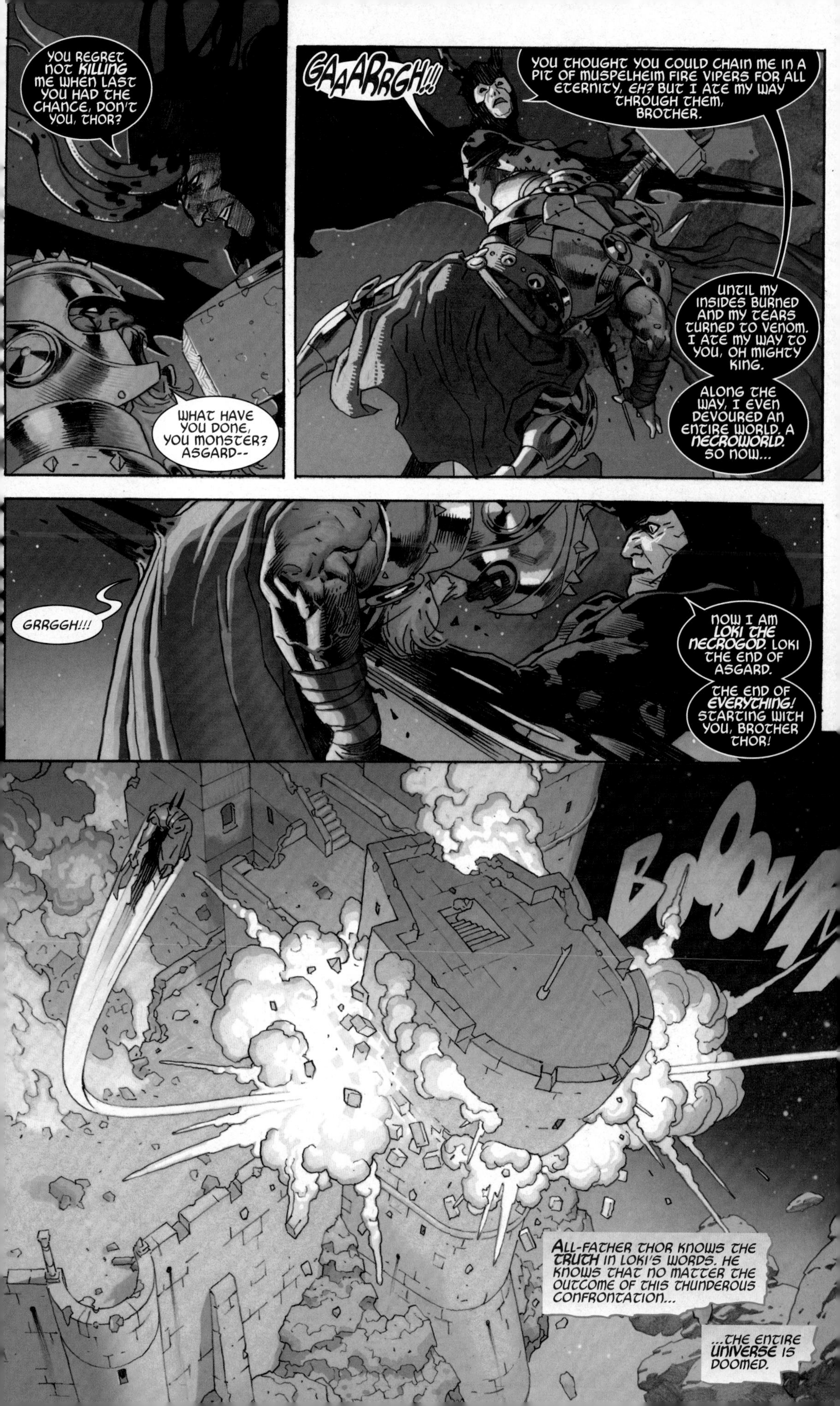
YOU REGRET NOT KILLING ME WHEN LAST YOU HAD THE CHANCE, DON'T YOU, THOR?
WHAT HAVE YOU DONE, YOU MONSTER? ASGARD--
GAAARRGH!!!
YOU THOUGHT YOU COULD CHAIN ME IN A PIT OF MUSPELHEIM FIRE VIPERS FOR ALL ETERNITY, EH? BUT I ATE MY WAY THROUGH THEM, BROTHER.
UNTIL MY INSIDES BURNED AND MY TEARS TURNED TO VENOM. I ATE MY WAY TO YOU, OH MIGHTY KING.
ALONG THE WAY, I EVEN DEVOURED AN ENTIRE WORLD. A NECROWORLD. SO NOW...
GRRGGH!!!
NOW I AM LOKI THE NECROGOD. LOKI THE END OF ASGARD.
THE END OF EVERYTHING! STARTING WITH YOU, BROTHER THOR!
ALL-FATHER THOR KNOWS THE TRUTH IN LOKI'S WORDS. HE KNOWS THAT NO MATTER THE OUTCOME OF THIS THUNDEROUS CONFRONTATION...
...THE ENTIRE UNIVERSE IS DOOMED.

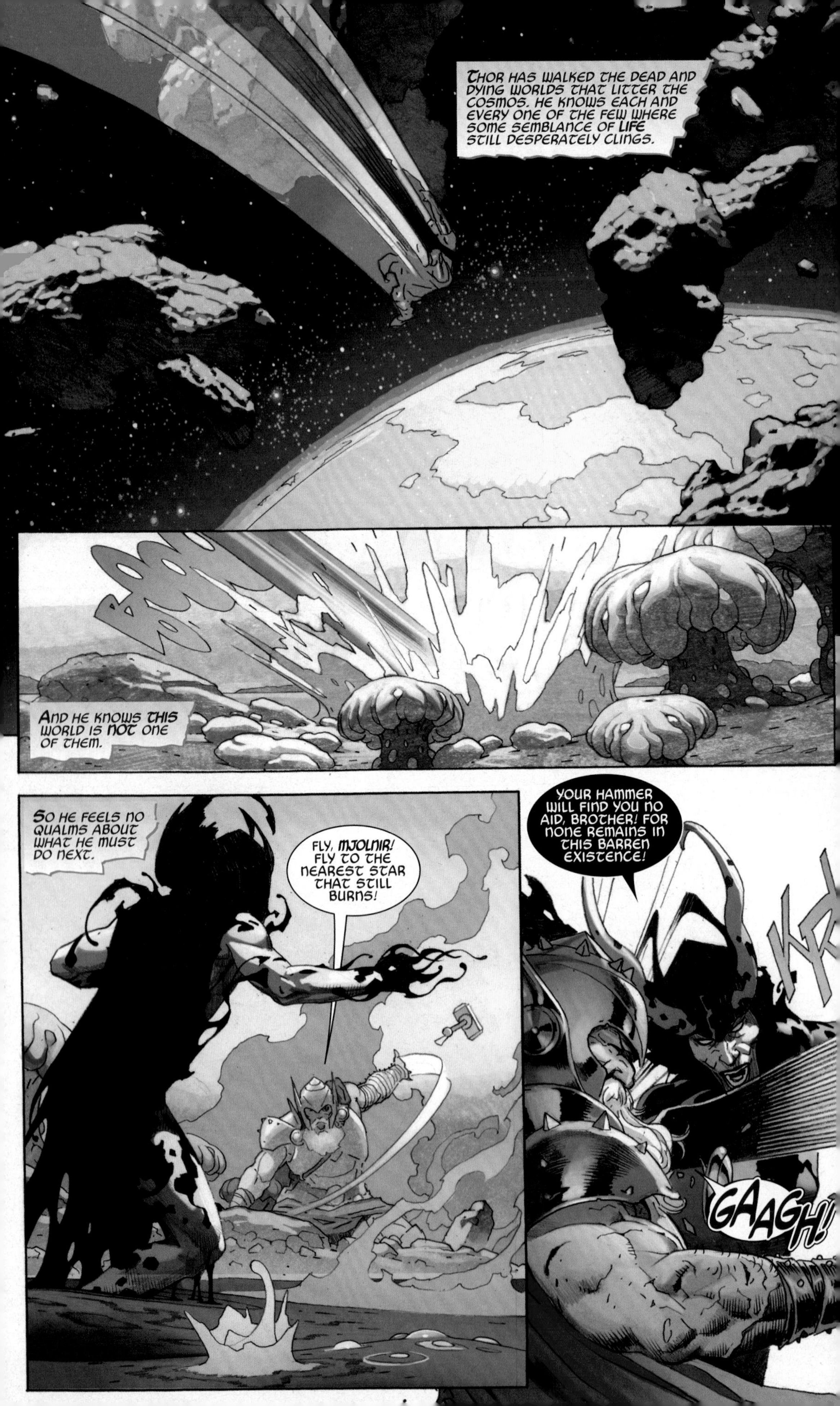
THOR HAS WALKED THE DEAD AND DYING WORLDS THAT LITTER THE COSMOS. HE KNOWS EACH AND EVERY ONE OF THE FEW WHERE SOME SEMBLANCE OF LIFE STILL DESPERATELY CLINGS.
BOOO
AND HE KNOWS THIS WORLD IS NOT ONE OF THEM.
SO HE FEELS NO QUALMS ABOUT WHAT HE MUST DO NEXT.
FLY, MJOLNIR! FLY TO THE NEAREST STAR THAT STILL BURNS!
YOUR HAMMER WILL FIND YOU NO AID, BROTHER! FOR NONE REMAINS IN THIS BARREN EXISTENCE!
GAAGH!

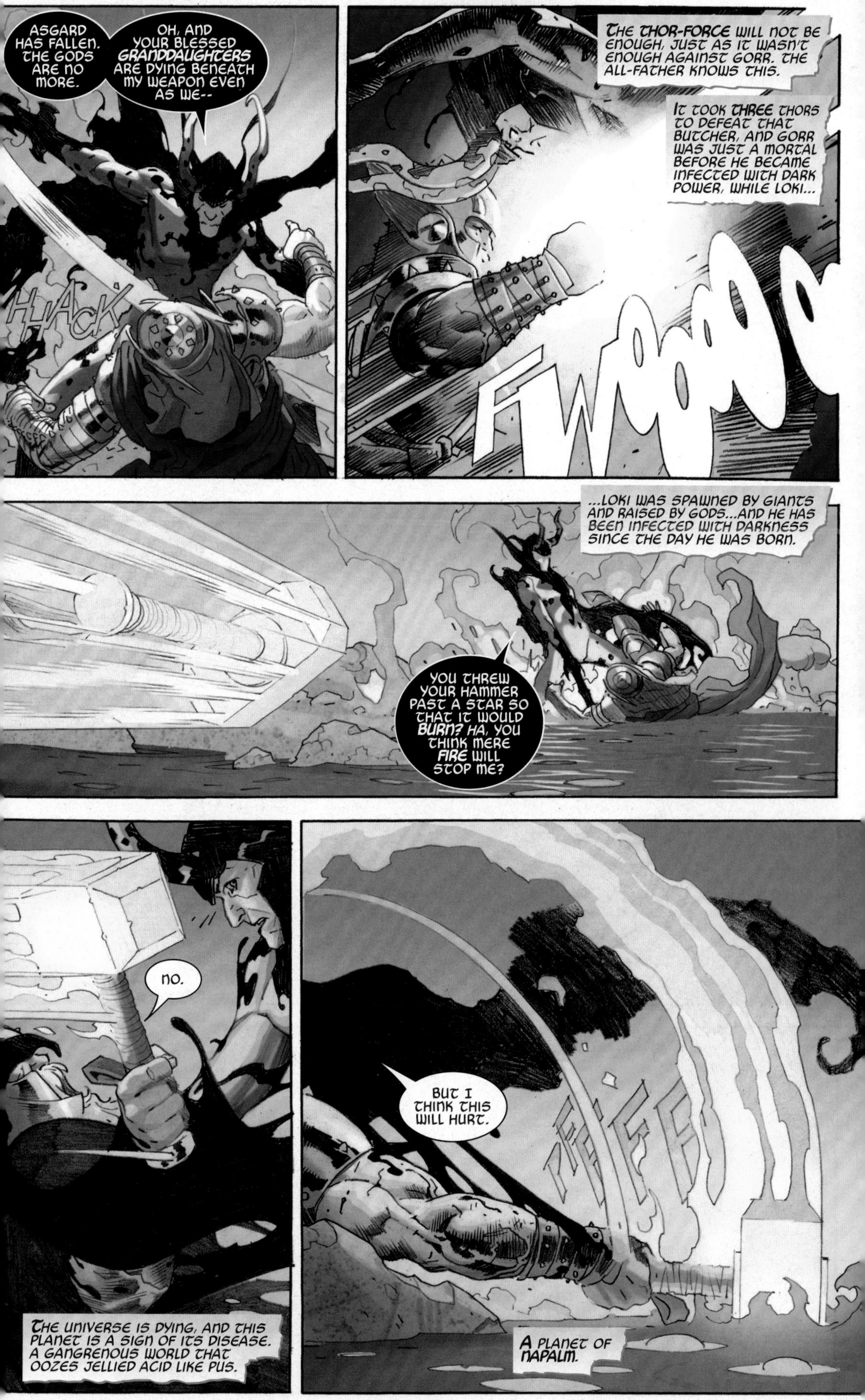

ASGARD HAS FALLEN. THE GODS ARE NO MORE.
OH, AND YOUR BLESSED GRANDDAUGHTERS ARE DYING BENEATH MY WEAPON EVEN AS WE--
HWACK
THE THOR-FORCE WILL NOT BE ENOUGH, JUST AS IT WASN'T ENOUGH AGAINST GORR. THE ALL-FATHER KNOWS THIS.
IT TOOK THREE THORS TO DEFEAT THAT BUTCHER, AND GORR WAS JUST A MORTAL BEFORE HE BECAME INFECTED WITH DARK POWER, WHILE LOKI...
...LOKI WAS SPAWNED BY GIANTS AND RAISED BY GODS...AND HE HAS BEEN INFECTED WITH DARKNESS SINCE THE DAY HE WAS BORN.
YOU THREW YOUR HAMMER PAST A STAR SO THAT IT WOULD BURN? HA, YOU THINK MERE FIRE WILL STOP ME?
no.
THE UNIVERSE IS DYING, AND THIS PLANET IS A SIGN OF ITS DISEASE. A GANGRENOUS WORLD THAT OOZES JELLIED ACID LIKE PUS.
BUT I THINK THIS WILL HURT.
A PLANET OF NAPALM.

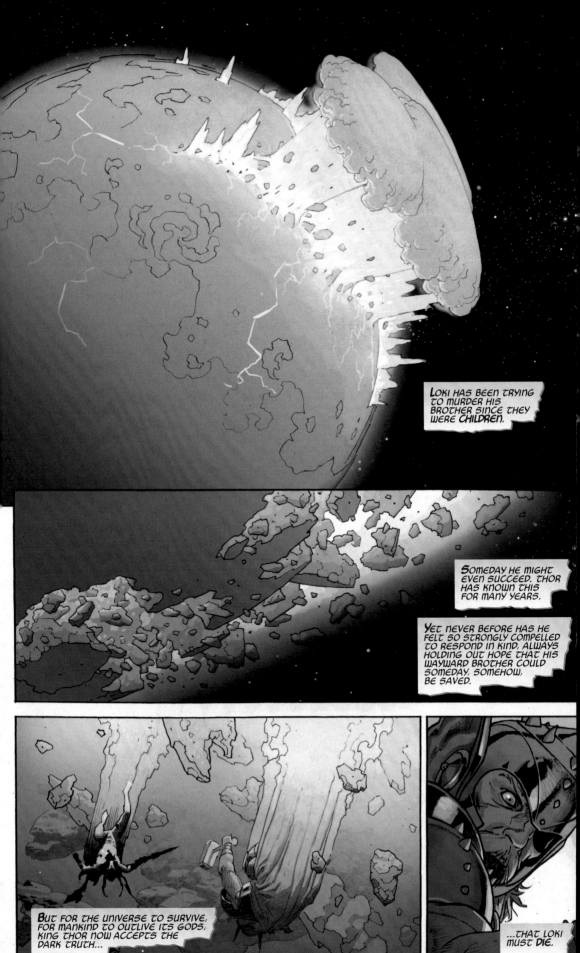

LOKI HAS BEEN TRYING TO MURDER HIS BROTHER SINCE THEY WERE *CHILDREN*.

SOMEDAY HE MIGHT EVEN SUCCEED. THOR HAS KNOWN THIS FOR MANY YEARS.

YET NEVER BEFORE HAS HE FELT SO STRONGLY COMPELLED TO RESPOND IN KIND, ALWAYS HOLDING OUT HOPE THAT HIS WAYWARD BROTHER COULD SOMEDAY, SOMEHOW, BE SAVED.

BUT FOR THE UNIVERSE TO SURVIVE, FOR MANKIND TO OUTLIVE ITS GODS, KING THOR NOW ACCEPTS THE DARK TRUTH...

...THAT LOKI MUST DIE.

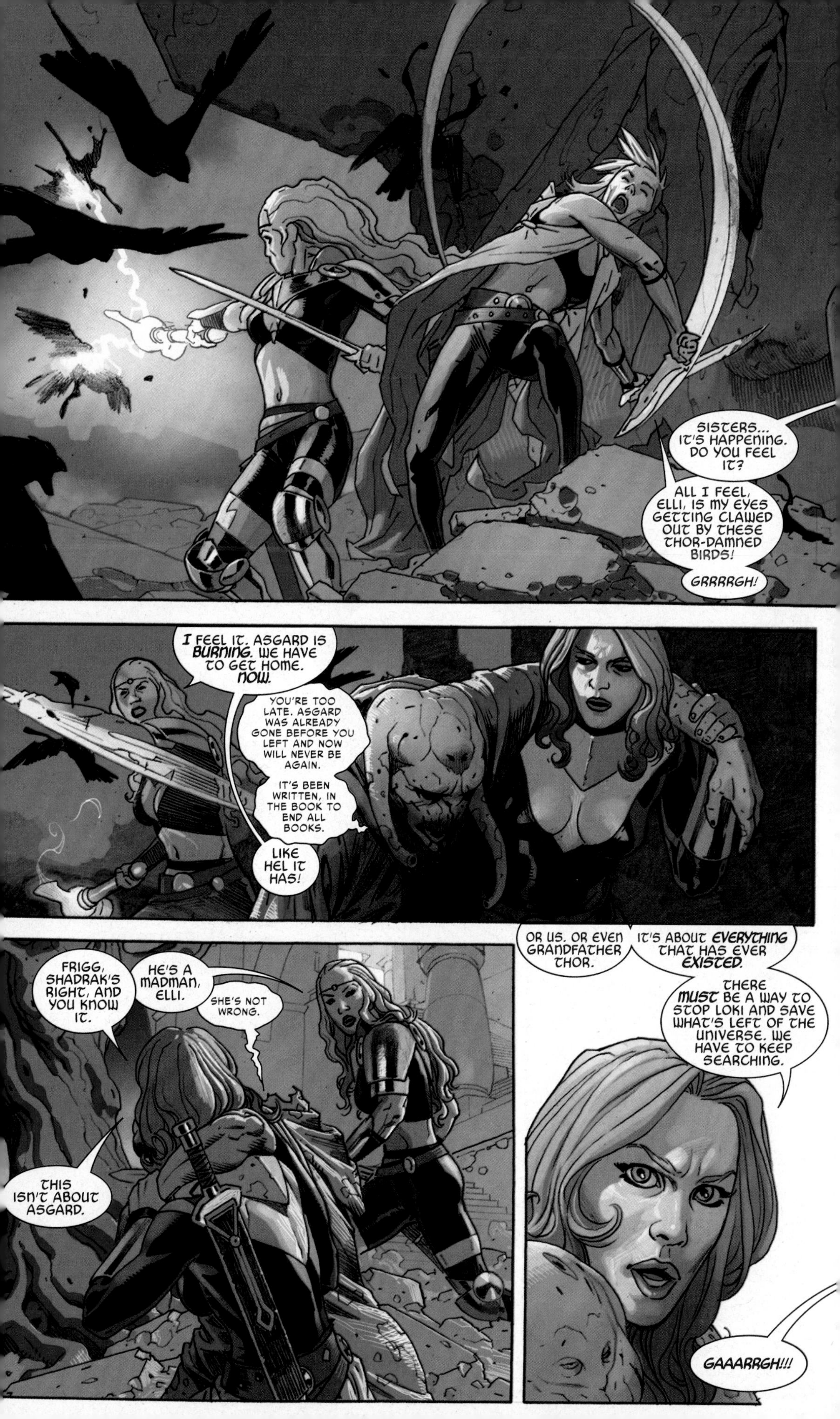
SISTERS... IT'S HAPPENING. DO YOU FEEL IT?
ALL I FEEL, ELLI, IS MY EYES GETTING CLAWED OUT BY THESE THOR-DAMNED BIRDS!
GRRRRGH!
I FEEL IT. ASGARD IS BURNING. WE HAVE TO GET HOME. NOW.
YOU'RE TOO LATE. ASGARD WAS ALREADY GONE BEFORE YOU LEFT AND NOW WILL NEVER BE AGAIN.
IT'S BEEN WRITTEN, IN THE BOOK TO END ALL BOOKS.
LIKE HEL IT HAS!
FRIGG, SHADRAK'S RIGHT, AND YOU KNOW IT.
HE'S A MADMAN, ELLI.
SHE'S NOT WRONG.
THIS ISN'T ABOUT ASGARD.
OR US. OR EVEN GRANDFATHER THOR.
IT'S ABOUT EVERYTHING THAT HAS EVER EXISTED.
THERE MUST BE A WAY TO STOP LOKI AND SAVE WHAT'S LEFT OF THE UNIVERSE. WE HAVE TO KEEP SEARCHING.
GAAARRGH!!!

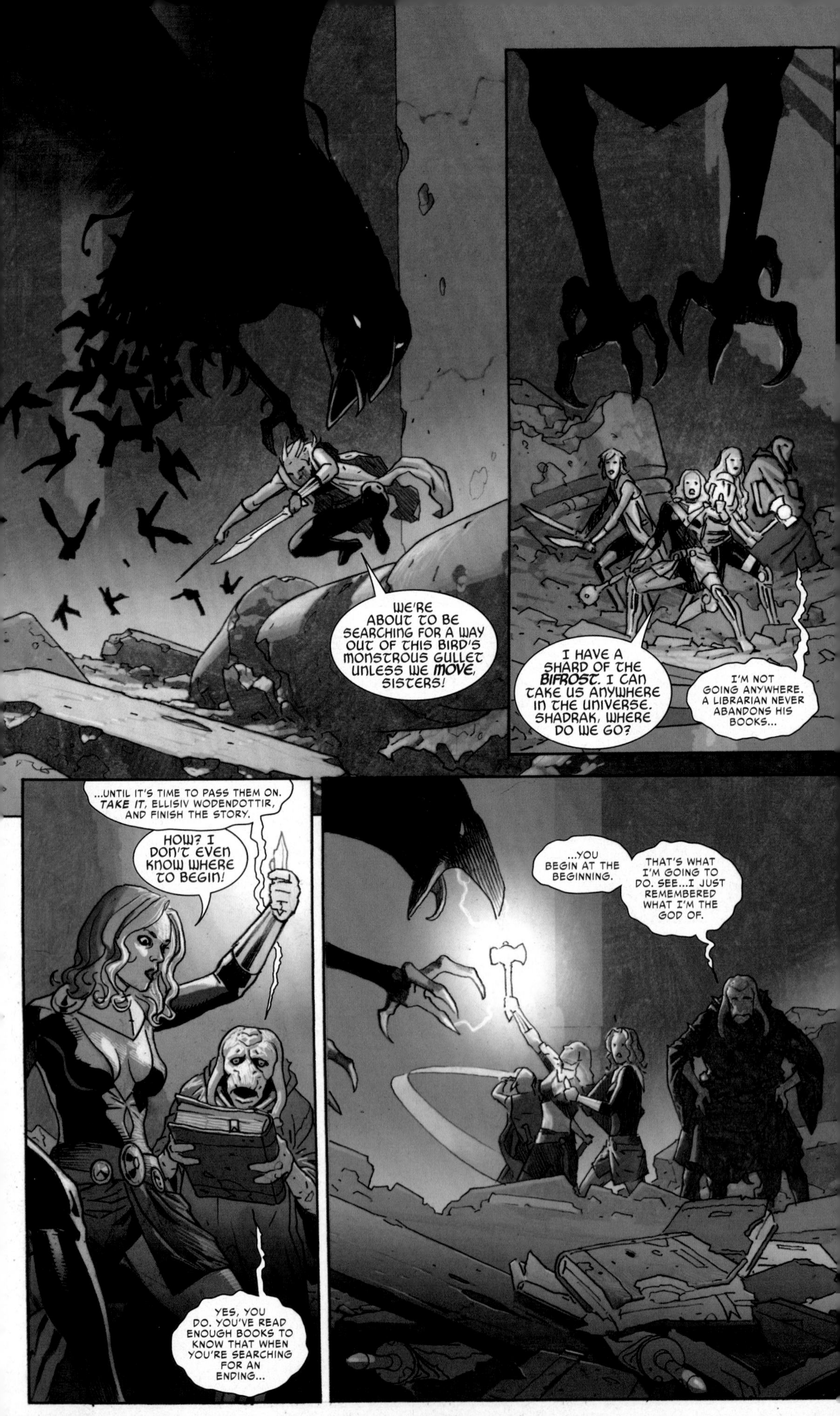
WE'RE ABOUT TO BE SEARCHING FOR A WAY OUT OF THIS BIRD'S MONSTROUS GULLET UNLESS WE *MOVE*, SISTERS!
I HAVE A SHARD OF THE *BIFROST*. I CAN TAKE US ANYWHERE IN THE UNIVERSE. SHADRAK, WHERE DO WE GO?
I'M NOT GOING ANYWHERE. A LIBRARIAN NEVER ABANDONS HIS BOOKS...
...UNTIL IT'S TIME TO PASS THEM ON. *TAKE IT*, ELLISIV WODENDOTTIR, AND FINISH THE STORY.
HOW? I DON'T EVEN KNOW WHERE TO BEGIN!
YES, YOU DO. YOU'VE READ ENOUGH BOOKS TO KNOW THAT WHEN YOU'RE SEARCHING FOR AN ENDING...
...YOU BEGIN AT THE BEGINNING.
THAT'S WHAT I'M GOING TO DO. SEE...I JUST REMEMBERED WHAT I'M THE GOD OF.

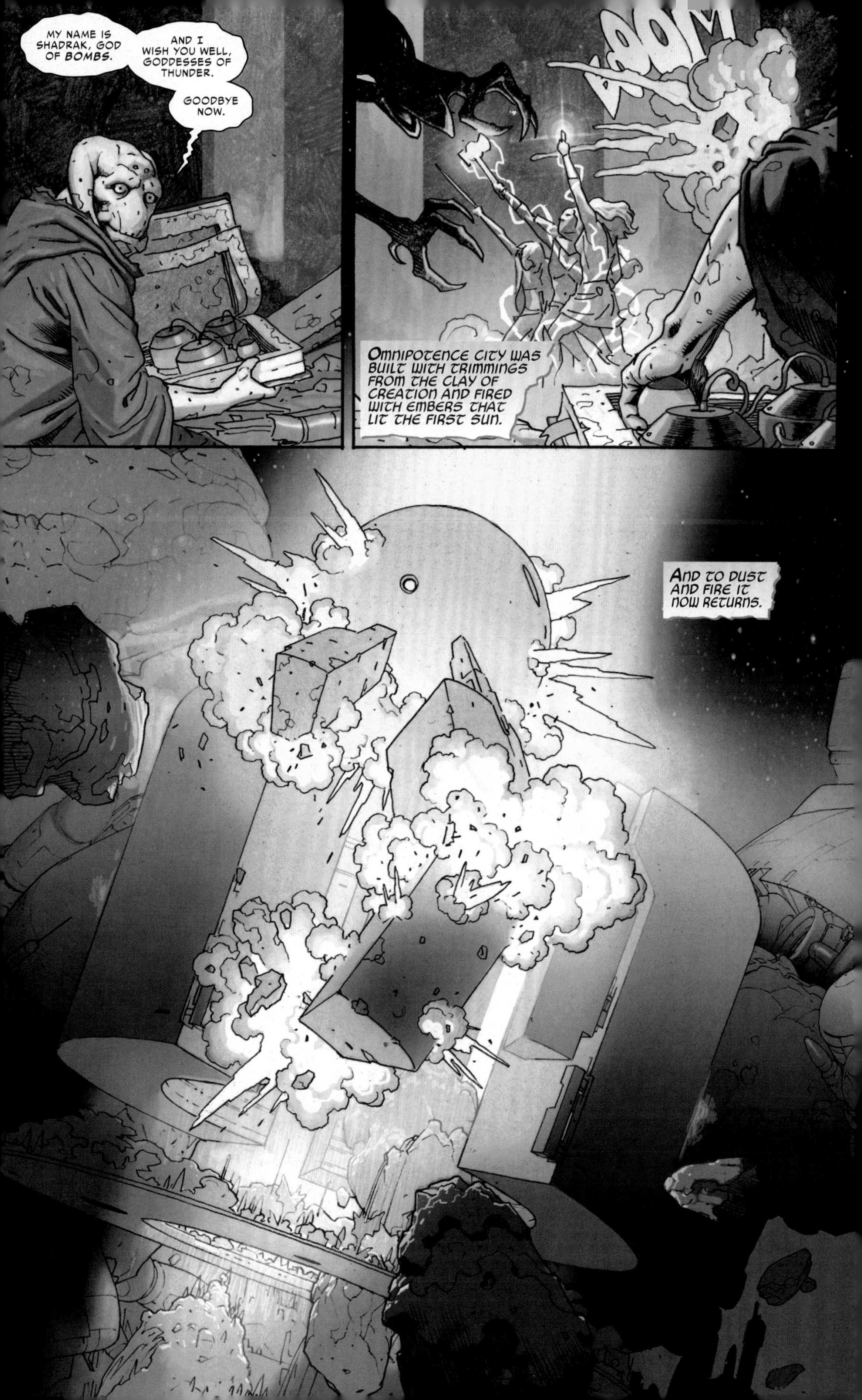
MY NAME IS SHADRAK, GOD OF *BOMBS*.
AND I WISH YOU WELL, GODDESSES OF THUNDER.
GOODBYE NOW.
OMNIPOTENCE CITY WAS BUILT WITH TRIMMINGS FROM THE CLAY OF CREATION AND FIRED WITH EMBERS THAT LIT THE FIRST SUN.
AND TO DUST AND FIRE IT NOW RETURNS.

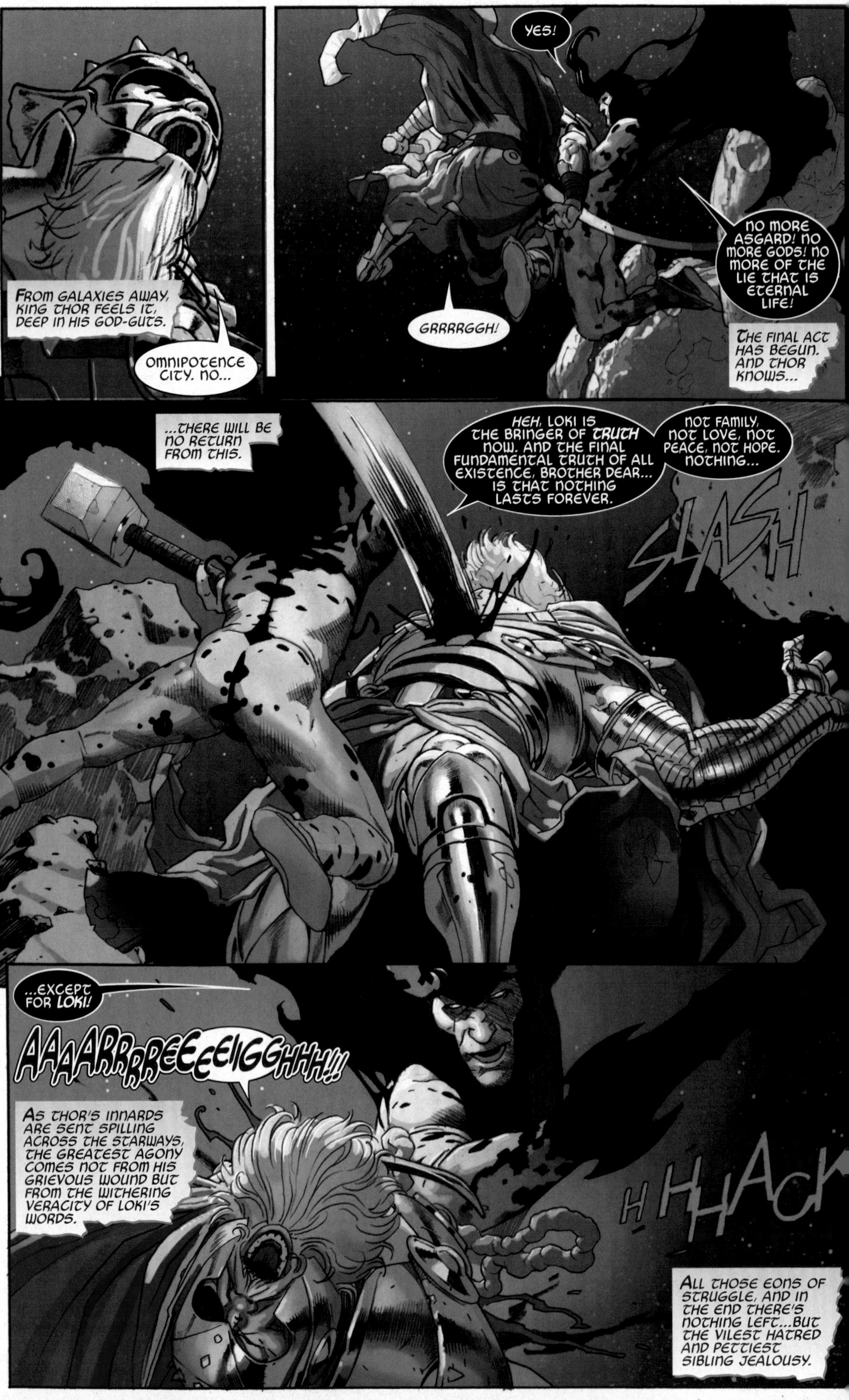

FROM GALAXIES AWAY, KING THOR FEELS IT, DEEP IN HIS GOD-GUTS.
OMNIPOTENCE CITY. NO...
YES!
GRRRRGGH!
NO MORE ASGARD! NO MORE GODS! NO MORE OF THE LIE THAT IS ETERNAL LIFE!
THE FINAL ACT HAS BEGUN. AND THOR KNOWS...
...THERE WILL BE NO RETURN FROM THIS.
HEH, LOKI IS THE BRINGER OF TRUTH NOW. AND THE FINAL FUNDAMENTAL TRUTH OF ALL EXISTENCE, BROTHER DEAR... IS THAT NOTHING LASTS FOREVER.
NOT FAMILY, NOT LOVE, NOT PEACE, NOT HOPE. NOTHING...
SLASH
...EXCEPT FOR LOKI!
AAAARRRRREEEEEIIGGHHH!!!
AS THOR'S INNARDS ARE SENT SPILLING ACROSS THE STARWAYS, THE GREATEST AGONY COMES NOT FROM HIS GRIEVOUS WOUND BUT FROM THE WITHERING VERACITY OF LOKI'S WORDS.
HHHACK
ALL THOSE EONS OF STRUGGLE, AND IN THE END THERE'S NOTHING LEFT...BUT THE VILEST HATRED AND PETTIEST SIBLING JEALOUSY.

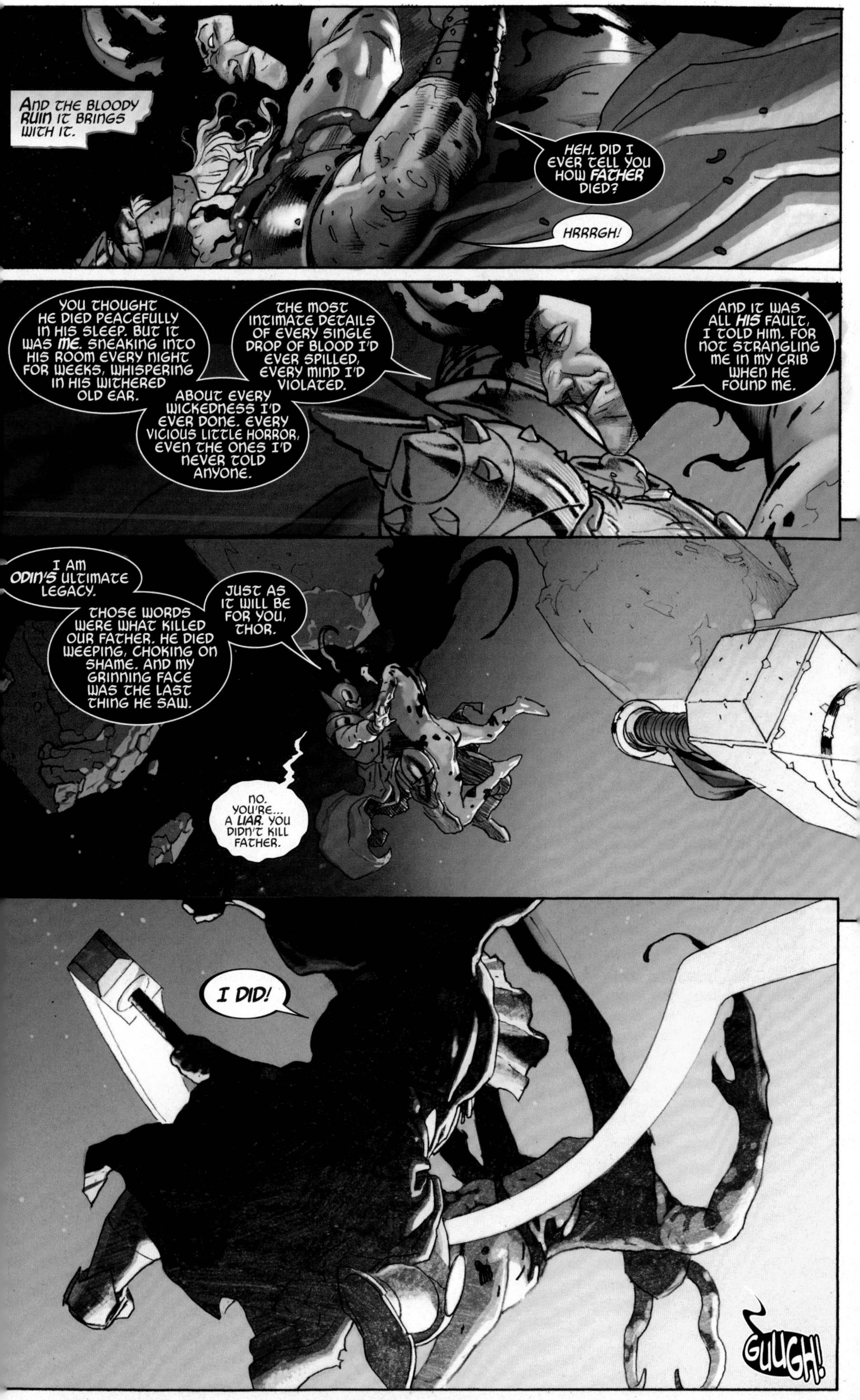
AND THE BLOODY RUIN IT BRINGS WITH IT.
HEH. DID I EVER TELL YOU HOW FATHER DIED?
HRRRGH!
YOU THOUGHT HE DIED PEACEFULLY IN HIS SLEEP. BUT IT WAS ME. SNEAKING INTO HIS ROOM EVERY NIGHT FOR WEEKS, WHISPERING IN HIS WITHERED OLD EAR.
ABOUT EVERY WICKEDNESS I'D EVER DONE. EVERY VICIOUS LITTLE HORROR, EVEN THE ONES I'D NEVER TOLD ANYONE.
THE MOST INTIMATE DETAILS OF EVERY SINGLE DROP OF BLOOD I'D EVER SPILLED, EVERY MIND I'D VIOLATED.
AND IT WAS ALL HIS FAULT, I TOLD HIM. FOR NOT STRANGLING ME IN MY CRIB WHEN HE FOUND ME.
I AM ODIN'S ULTIMATE LEGACY.
THOSE WORDS WERE WHAT KILLED OUR FATHER. HE DIED WEEPING, CHOKING ON SHAME. AND MY GRINNING FACE WAS THE LAST THING HE SAW.
JUST AS IT WILL BE FOR YOU, THOR.
NO. YOU'RE... A LIAR. YOU DIDN'T KILL FATHER.
I DID!
GUUGH!

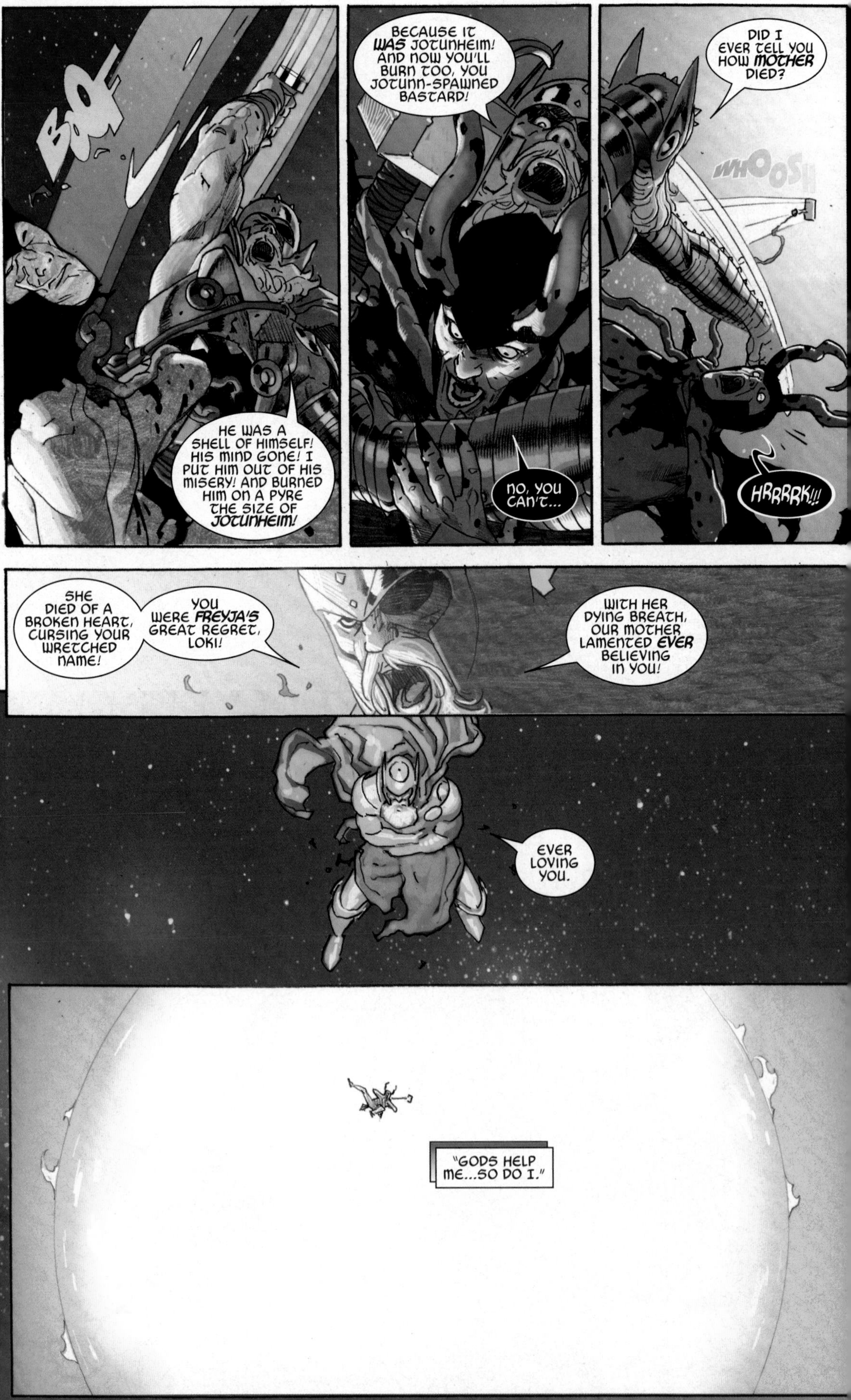
BOOM!
HE WAS A SHELL OF HIMSELF! HIS MIND GONE! I PUT HIM OUT OF HIS MISERY! AND BURNED HIM ON A PYRE THE SIZE OF JOTUNHEIM!
BECAUSE IT WAS JOTUNHEIM! AND NOW YOU'LL BURN TOO, YOU JOTUNN-SPAWNED BASTARD!
NO, YOU CAN'T...
DID I EVER TELL YOU HOW MOTHER DIED?
WHOOSH
HRRRRK!!!
SHE DIED OF A BROKEN HEART, CURSING YOUR WRETCHED NAME!
YOU WERE FREYJA'S GREAT REGRET, LOKI!
WITH HER DYING BREATH, OUR MOTHER LAMENTED EVER BELIEVING IN YOU!
EVER LOVING YOU.
"GODS HELP ME...SO DO I."

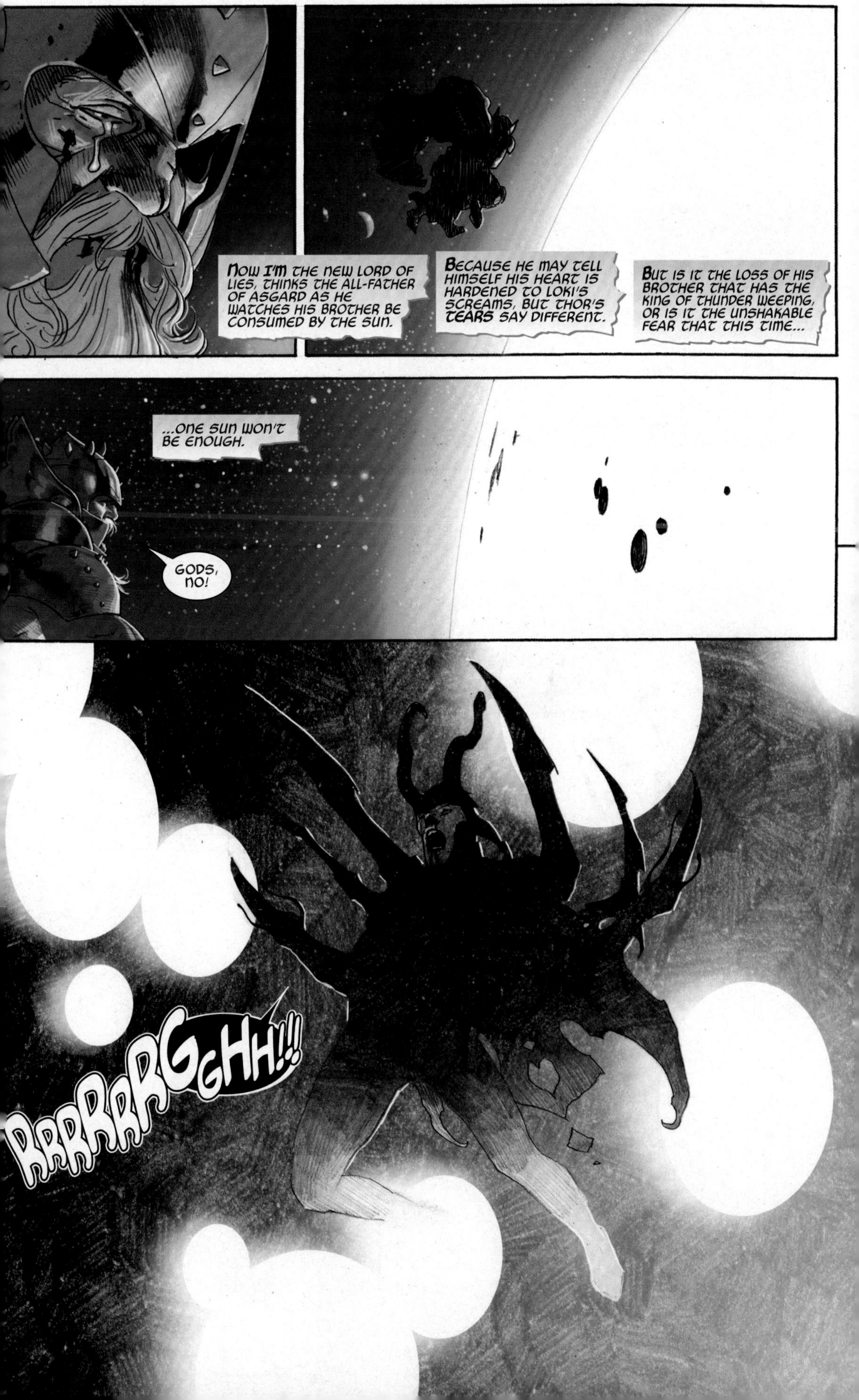
NOW I'M THE NEW LORD OF LIES, THINKS THE ALL-FATHER OF ASGARD AS HE WATCHES HIS BROTHER BE CONSUMED BY THE SUN.
BECAUSE HE MAY TELL HIMSELF HIS HEART IS HARDENED TO LOKI'S SCREAMS, BUT THOR'S TEARS SAY DIFFERENT.
BUT IS IT THE LOSS OF HIS BROTHER THAT HAS THE KING OF THUNDER WEEPING, OR IS IT THE UNSHAKABLE FEAR THAT THIS TIME...
...ONE SUN WON'T BE ENOUGH.
GODS, NO!
RRRRRRGHH!!!

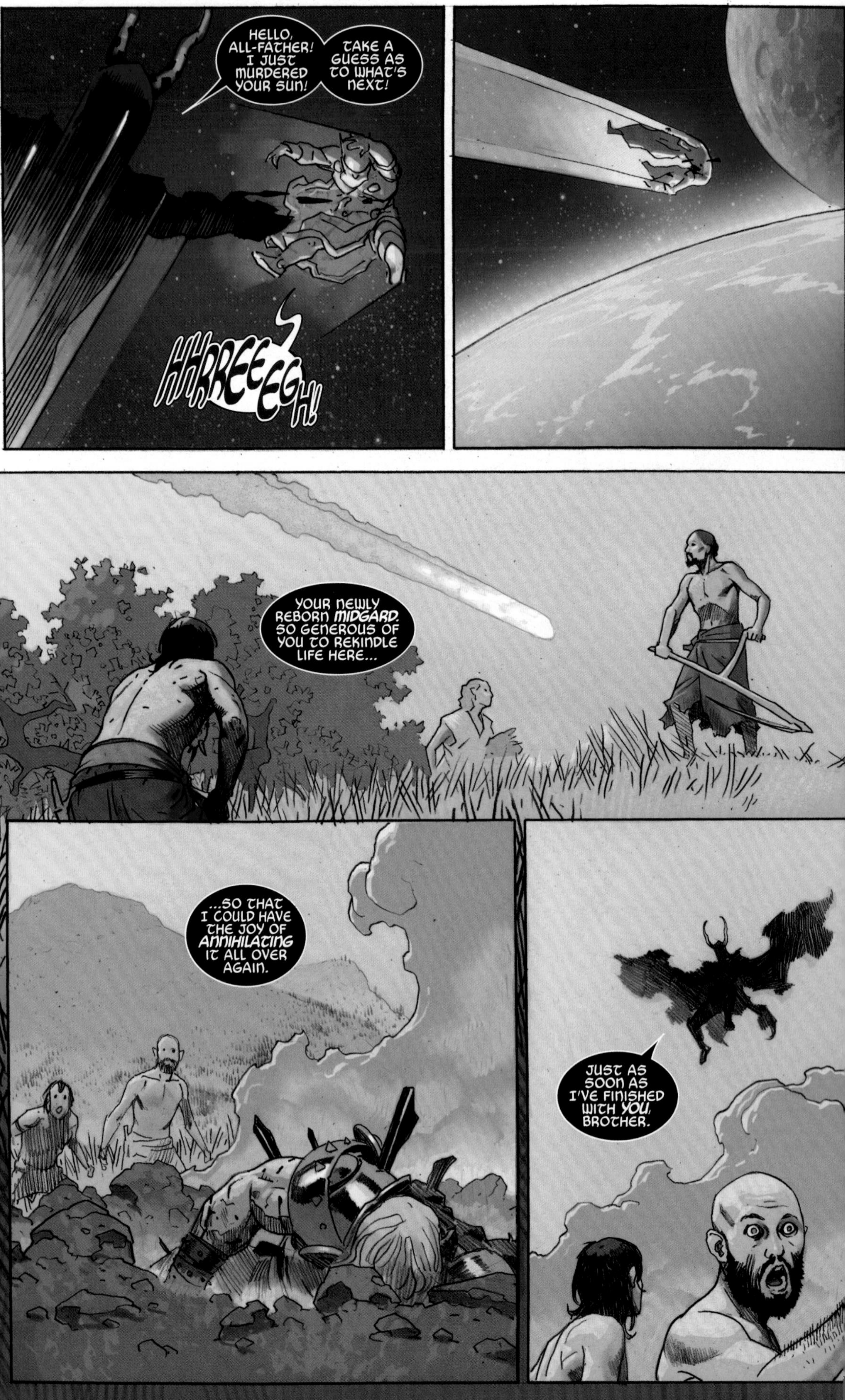
HELLO, ALL-FATHER! I JUST MURDERED YOUR SUN!
TAKE A GUESS AS TO WHAT'S NEXT!
HHRREEEGH!
YOUR NEWLY REBORN MIDGARD. SO GENEROUS OF YOU TO REKINDLE LIFE HERE...
...SO THAT I COULD HAVE THE JOY OF ANNIHILATING IT ALL OVER AGAIN.
JUST AS SOON AS I'VE FINISHED WITH YOU, BROTHER.

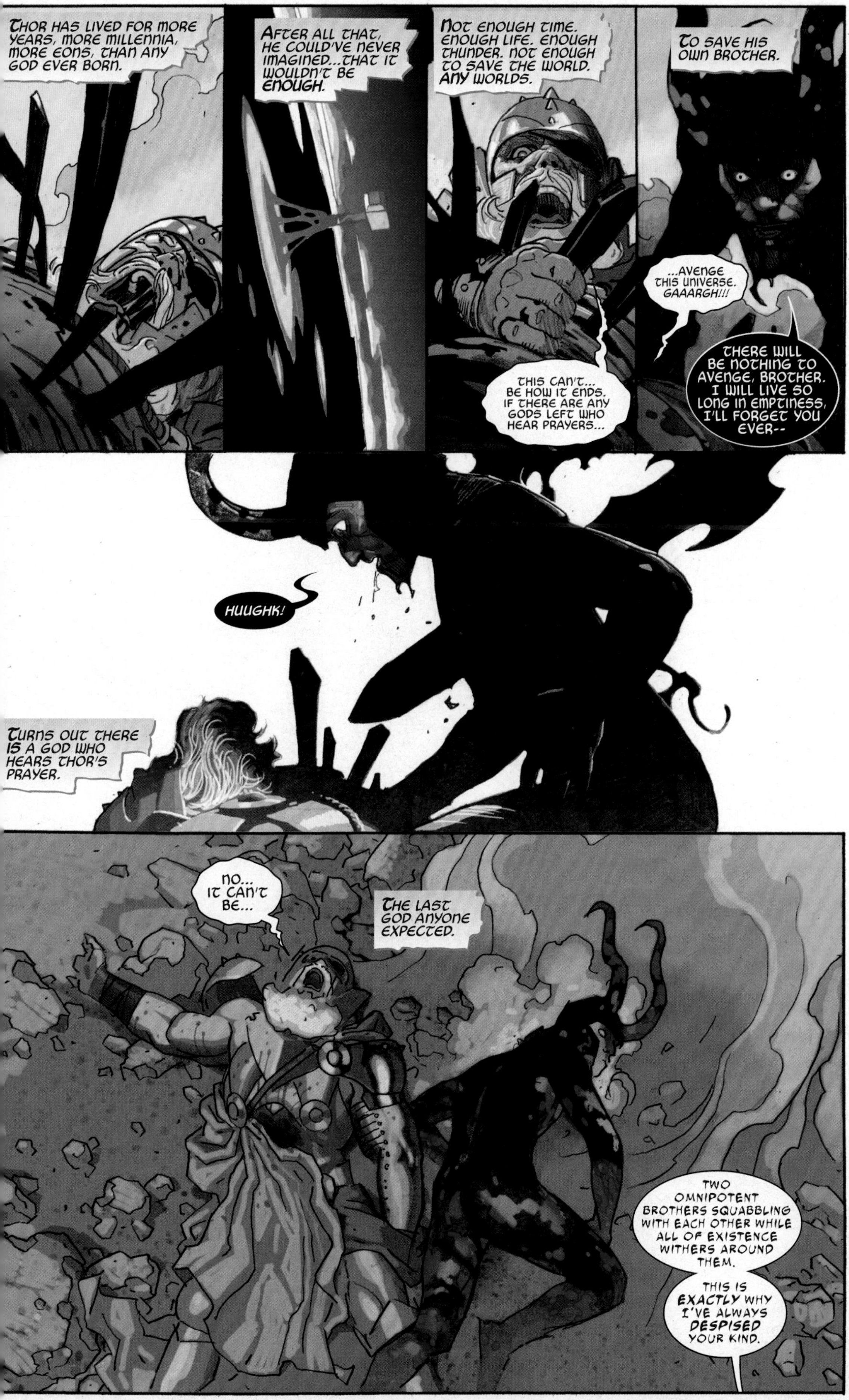
THOR HAS LIVED FOR MORE YEARS, MORE MILLENNIA, MORE EONS, THAN ANY GOD EVER BORN.
AFTER ALL THAT, HE COULD'VE NEVER IMAGINED...THAT IT WOULDN'T BE ENOUGH.
NOT ENOUGH TIME. ENOUGH LIFE. ENOUGH THUNDER. NOT ENOUGH TO SAVE THE WORLD. ANY WORLDS.
THIS CAN'T... BE HOW IT ENDS. IF THERE ARE ANY GODS LEFT WHO HEAR PRAYERS...
TO SAVE HIS OWN BROTHER.
...AVENGE THIS UNIVERSE. GAAARGH!!!
THERE WILL BE NOTHING TO AVENGE, BROTHER. I WILL LIVE SO LONG IN EMPTINESS, I'LL FORGET YOU EVER--
HUUGHK!
TURNS OUT THERE IS A GOD WHO HEARS THOR'S PRAYER.
NO... IT CAN'T BE...
THE LAST GOD ANYONE EXPECTED.
TWO OMNIPOTENT BROTHERS SQUABBLING WITH EACH OTHER WHILE ALL OF EXISTENCE WITHERS AROUND THEM.
THIS IS EXACTLY WHY I'VE ALWAYS DESPISED YOUR KIND.

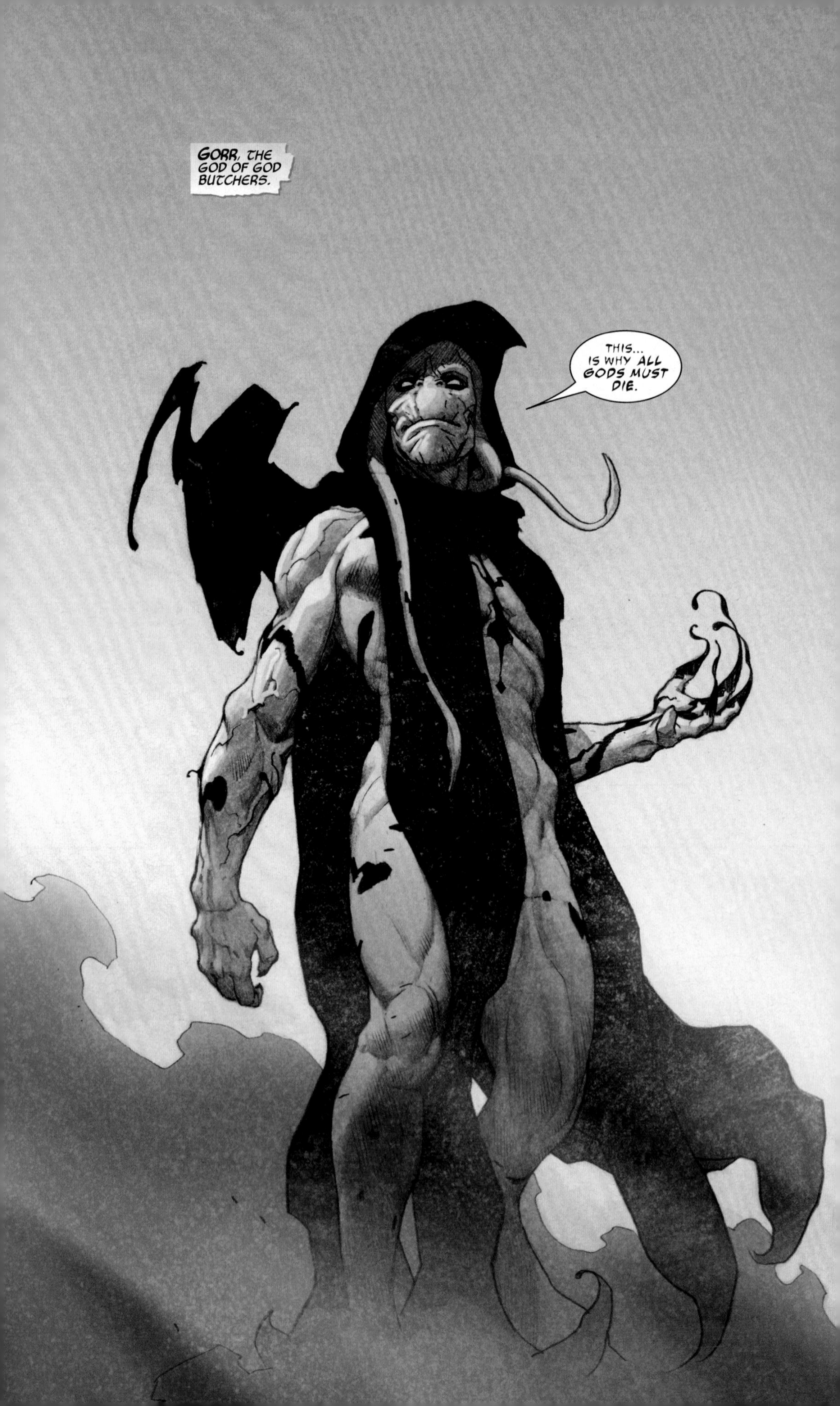
GORR, THE GOD OF GOD BUTCHERS.
THIS... IS WHY ALL GODS MUST DIE.

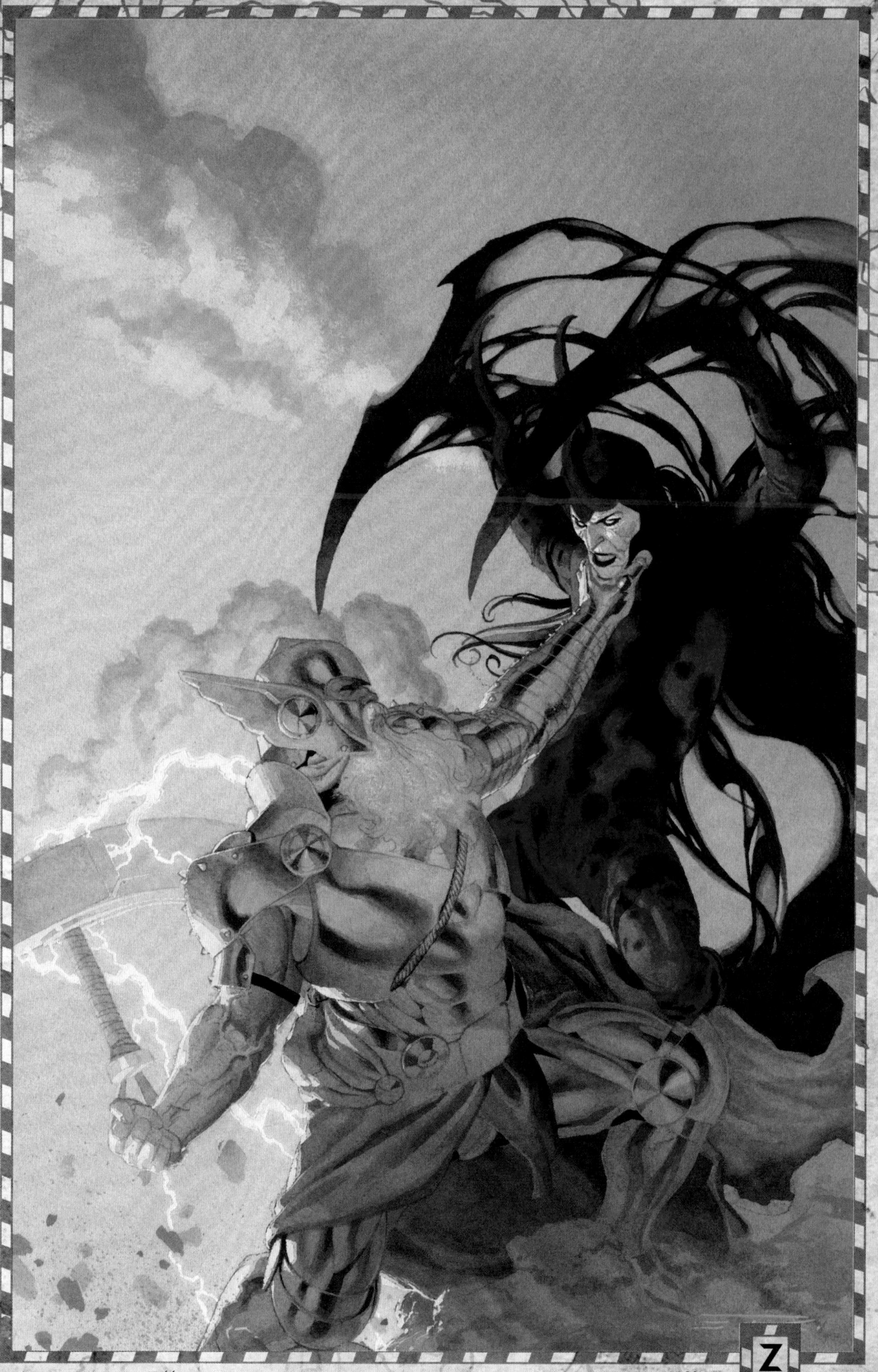
Z

"GORR AND THE LAST OF THE GODS"

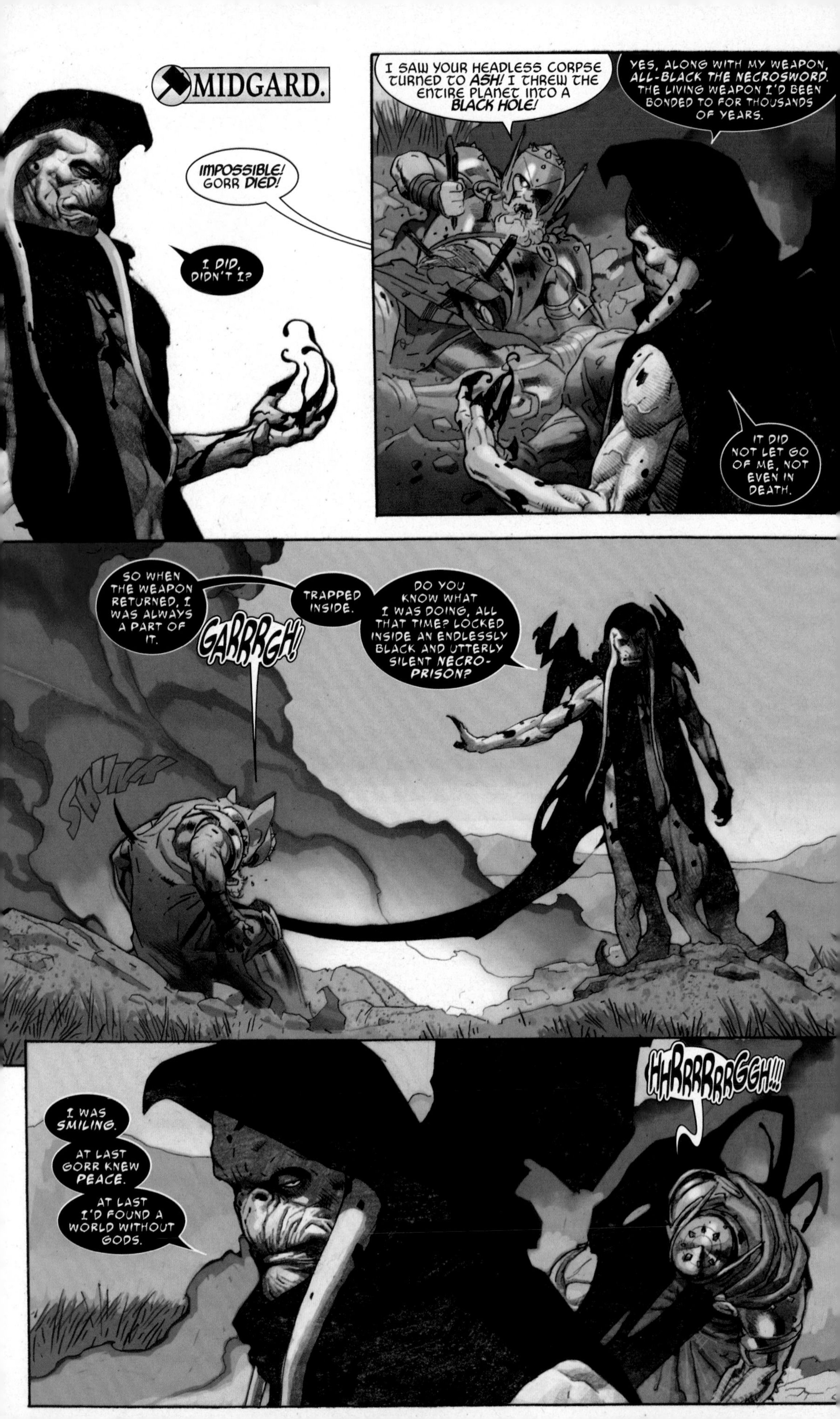
MIDGARD.
IMPOSSIBLE! GORR DIED!
I DID, DIDN'T I?
I SAW YOUR HEADLESS CORPSE TURNED TO ASH! I THREW THE ENTIRE PLANET INTO A BLACK HOLE!
YES, ALONG WITH MY WEAPON, ALL-BLACK THE NECROSWORD. THE LIVING WEAPON I'D BEEN BONDED TO FOR THOUSANDS OF YEARS.
IT DID NOT LET GO OF ME, NOT EVEN IN DEATH.
SO WHEN THE WEAPON RETURNED, I WAS ALWAYS A PART OF IT.
TRAPPED INSIDE.
DO YOU KNOW WHAT I WAS DOING, ALL THAT TIME? LOCKED INSIDE AN ENDLESSLY BLACK AND UTTERLY SILENT NECRO-PRISON?
GARRRGH!
I WAS SMILING.
AT LAST GORR KNEW PEACE.
AT LAST I'D FOUND A WORLD WITHOUT GODS.
HHRRRRRRGGH!!!

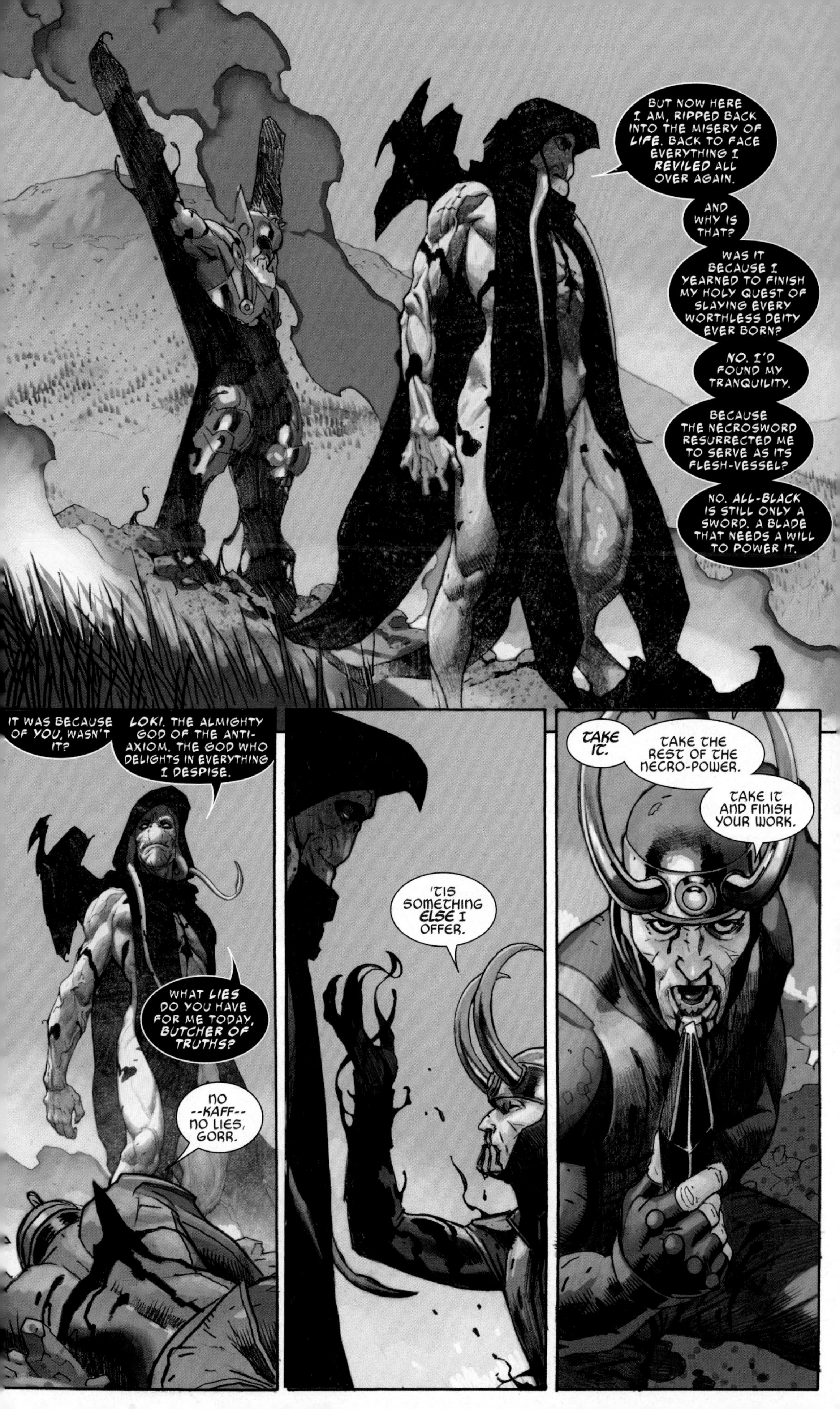

BUT NOW HERE I AM, RIPPED BACK INTO THE MISERY OF LIFE. BACK TO FACE EVERYTHING I REVILED ALL OVER AGAIN.
AND WHY IS THAT?
WAS IT BECAUSE I YEARNED TO FINISH MY HOLY QUEST OF SLAYING EVERY WORTHLESS DEITY EVER BORN?
NO. I'D FOUND MY TRANQUILITY.
BECAUSE THE NECROSWORD RESURRECTED ME TO SERVE AS ITS FLESH-VESSEL?
NO. ALL-BLACK IS STILL ONLY A SWORD. A BLADE THAT NEEDS A WILL TO POWER IT.
IT WAS BECAUSE OF YOU, WASN'T IT?
LOKI. THE ALMIGHTY GOD OF THE ANTI-AXIOM. THE GOD WHO DELIGHTS IN EVERYTHING I DESPISE.
WHAT LIES DO YOU HAVE FOR ME TODAY, BUTCHER OF TRUTHS?
NO --KAFF-- NO LIES, GORR.
'TIS SOMETHING ELSE I OFFER.
TAKE IT.
TAKE THE REST OF THE NECRO-POWER.
TAKE IT AND FINISH YOUR WORK.

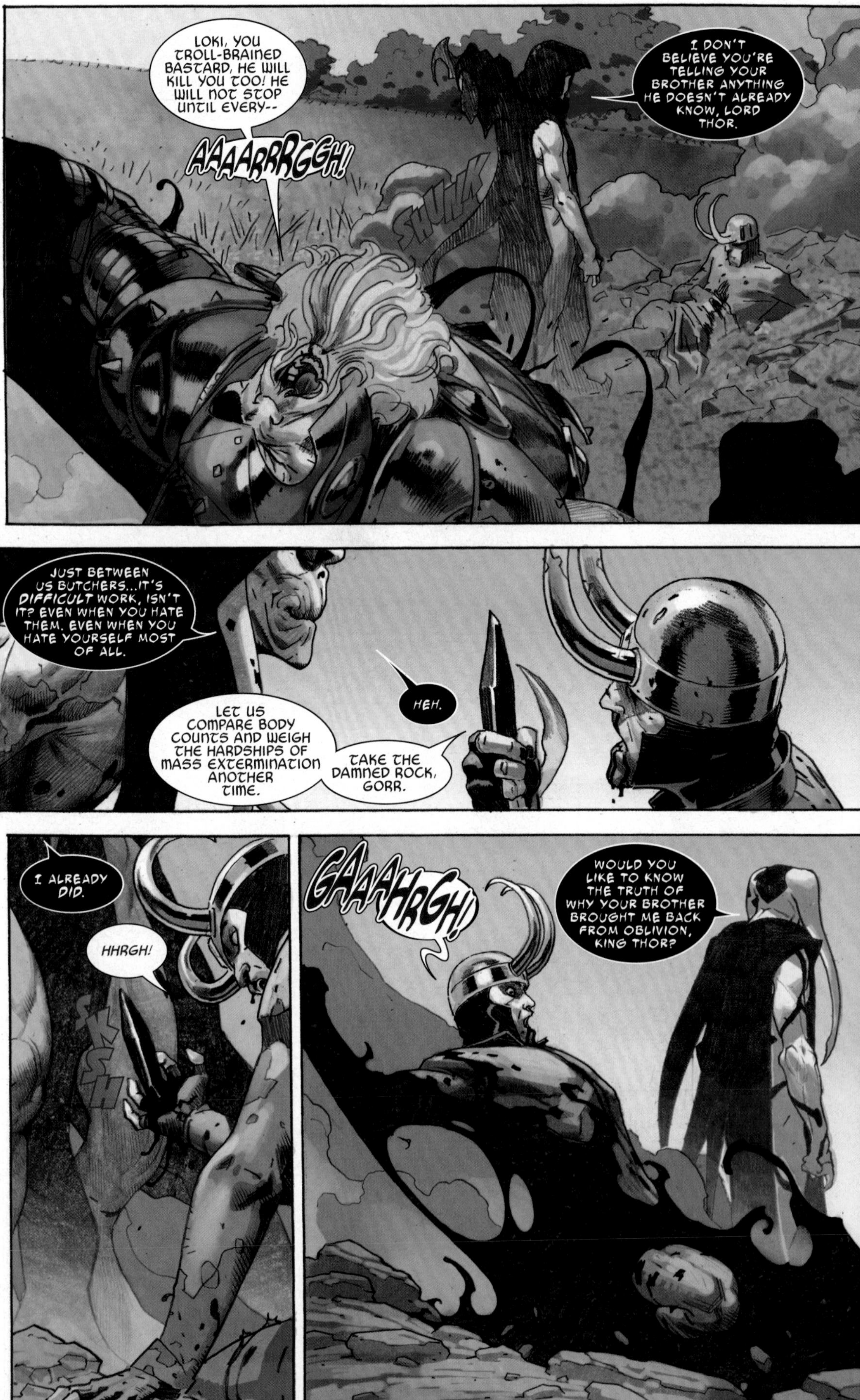
LOKI, YOU TROLL-BRAINED BASTARD, HE WILL KILL YOU TOO! HE WILL NOT STOP UNTIL EVERY--
AAAARRRGGH!
SHUNK
I DON'T BELIEVE YOU'RE TELLING YOUR BROTHER ANYTHING HE DOESN'T ALREADY KNOW, LORD THOR.
JUST BETWEEN US BUTCHERS...IT'S DIFFICULT WORK, ISN'T IT? EVEN WHEN YOU HATE THEM. EVEN WHEN YOU HATE YOURSELF MOST OF ALL.
HEH.
LET US COMPARE BODY COUNTS AND WEIGH THE HARDSHIPS OF MASS EXTERMINATION ANOTHER TIME.
TAKE THE DAMNED ROCK, GORR.
I ALREADY DID.
HHRGH!
SKSH
GAAAHRGH!
WOULD YOU LIKE TO KNOW THE TRUTH OF WHY YOUR BROTHER BROUGHT ME BACK FROM OBLIVION, KING THOR?

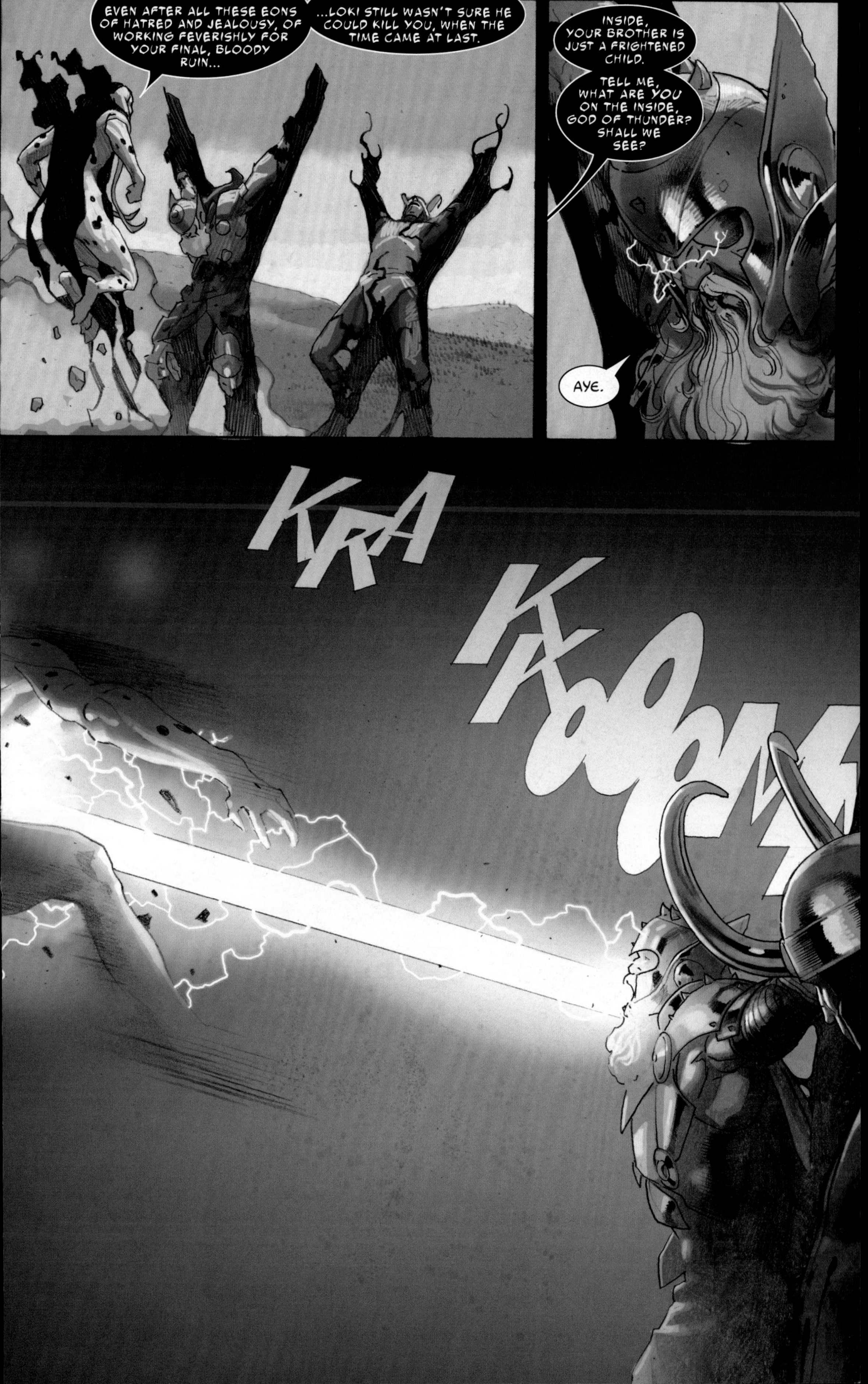
EVEN AFTER ALL THESE EONS OF HATRED AND JEALOUSY, OF WORKING FEVERISHLY FOR YOUR FINAL, BLOODY RUIN...
...LOKI STILL WASN'T SURE HE COULD KILL YOU, WHEN THE TIME CAME AT LAST.
INSIDE, YOUR BROTHER IS JUST A FRIGHTENED CHILD.
TELL ME, WHAT ARE YOU ON THE INSIDE, GOD OF THUNDER? SHALL WE SEE?
AYE.
KRA
KKOOOM

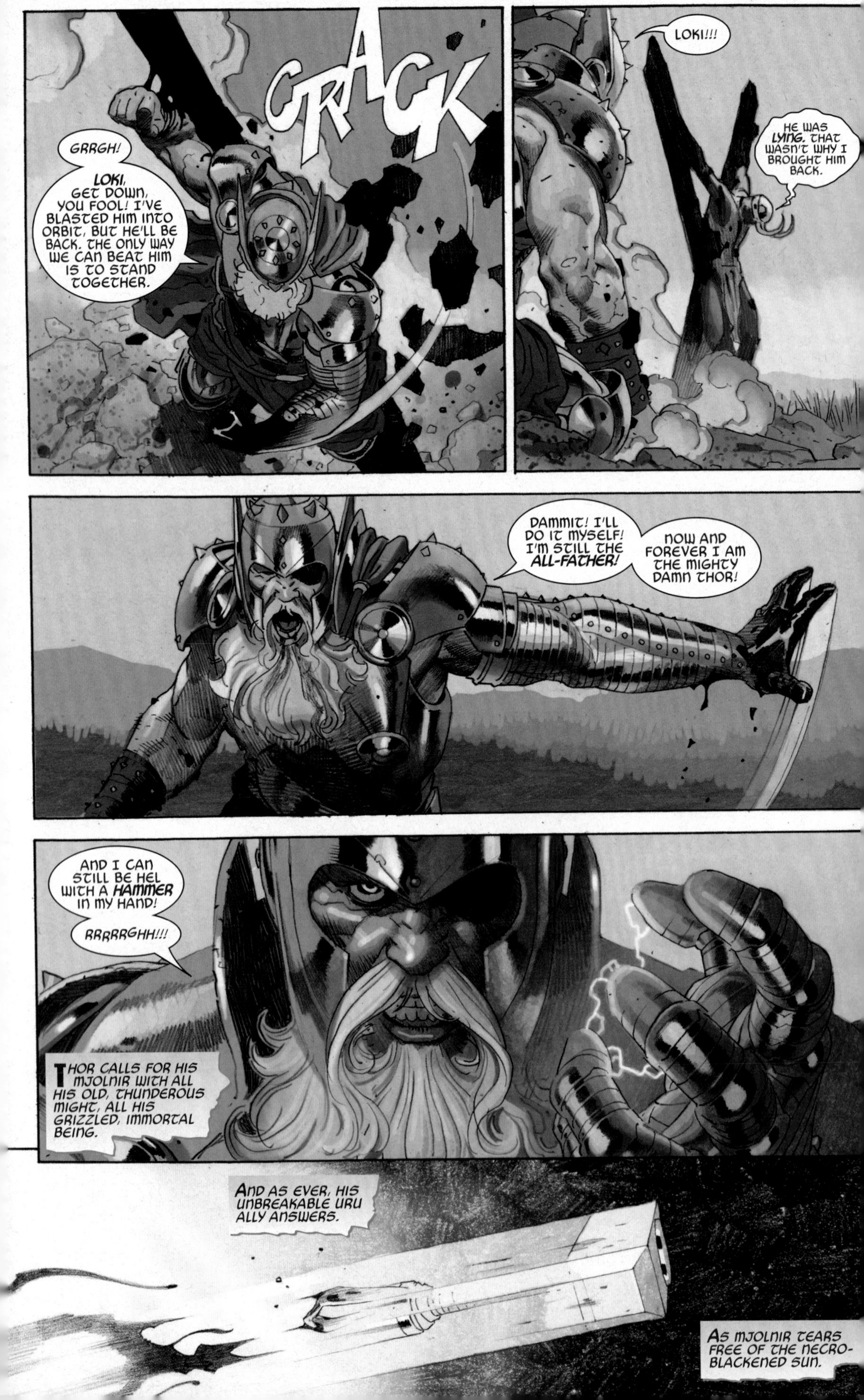

CRACK
GRRGH!
LOKI, GET DOWN, YOU FOOL! I'VE BLASTED HIM INTO ORBIT, BUT HE'LL BE BACK. THE ONLY WAY WE CAN BEAT HIM IS TO STAND TOGETHER.
LOKI!!!
HE WAS LYING. THAT WASN'T WHY I BROUGHT HIM BACK.
DAMMIT! I'LL DO IT MYSELF! I'M STILL THE ALL-FATHER!
NOW AND FOREVER I AM THE MIGHTY DAMN THOR!
AND I CAN STILL BE HEL WITH A HAMMER IN MY HAND!
RRRRRGHH!!!
THOR CALLS FOR HIS MJOLNIR WITH ALL HIS OLD, THUNDEROUS MIGHT, ALL HIS GRIZZLED, IMMORTAL BEING.
AND AS EVER, HIS UNBREAKABLE URU ALLY ANSWERS.
AS MJOLNIR TEARS FREE OF THE NECRO-BLACKENED SUN.

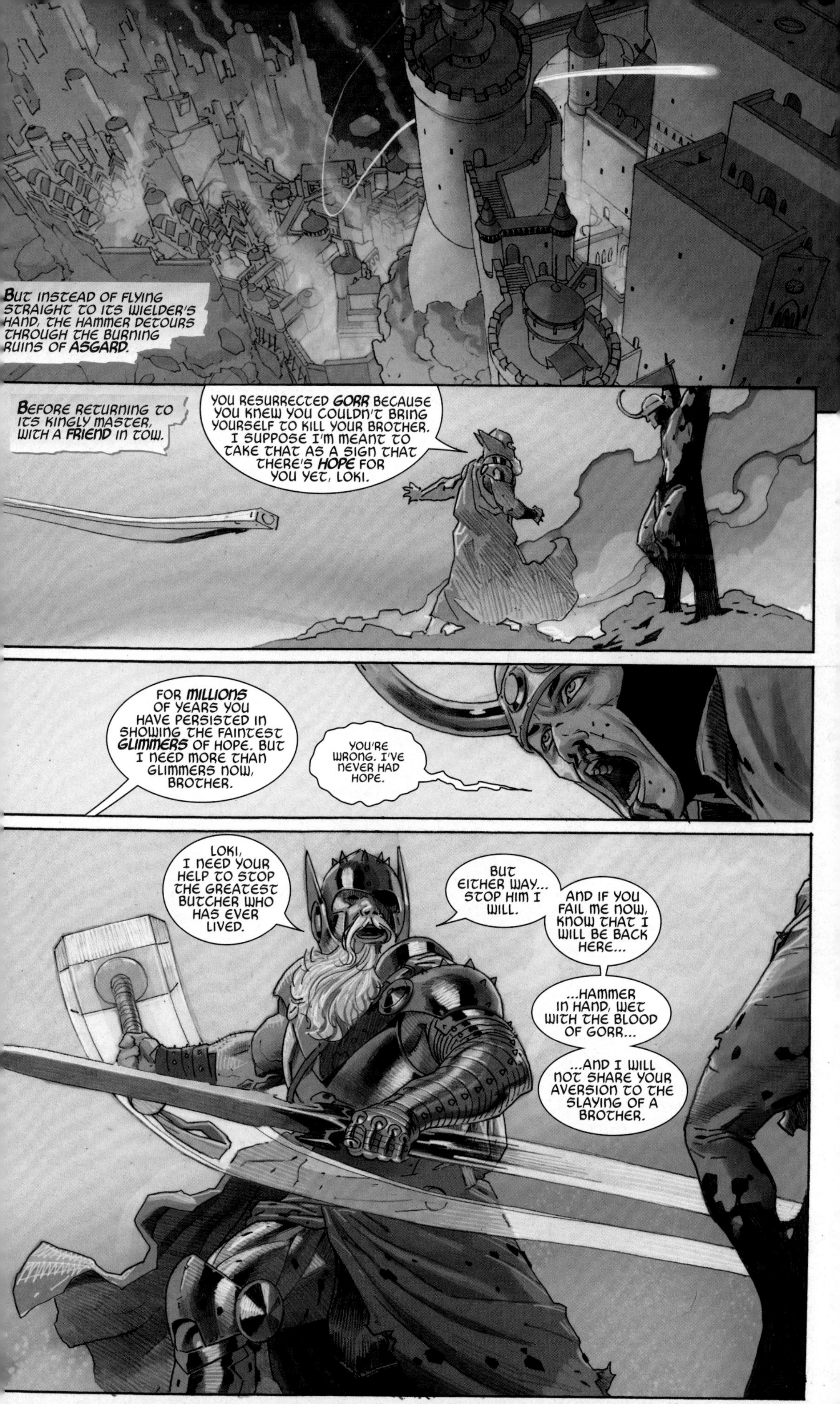
BUT INSTEAD OF FLYING STRAIGHT TO ITS WIELDER'S HAND, THE HAMMER DETOURS THROUGH THE BURNING RUINS OF ASGARD.
BEFORE RETURNING TO ITS KINGLY MASTER, WITH A FRIEND IN TOW.
YOU RESURRECTED GORR BECAUSE YOU KNEW YOU COULDN'T BRING YOURSELF TO KILL YOUR BROTHER. I SUPPOSE I'M MEANT TO TAKE THAT AS A SIGN THAT THERE'S HOPE FOR YOU YET, LOKI.
FOR MILLIONS OF YEARS YOU HAVE PERSISTED IN SHOWING THE FAINTEST GLIMMERS OF HOPE. BUT I NEED MORE THAN GLIMMERS NOW, BROTHER.
YOU'RE WRONG. I'VE NEVER HAD HOPE.
LOKI, I NEED YOUR HELP TO STOP THE GREATEST BUTCHER WHO HAS EVER LIVED.
BUT EITHER WAY... STOP HIM I WILL.
AND IF YOU FAIL ME NOW, KNOW THAT I WILL BE BACK HERE...
...HAMMER IN HAND, WET WITH THE BLOOD OF GORR...
...AND I WILL NOT SHARE YOUR AVERSION TO THE SLAYING OF A BROTHER.

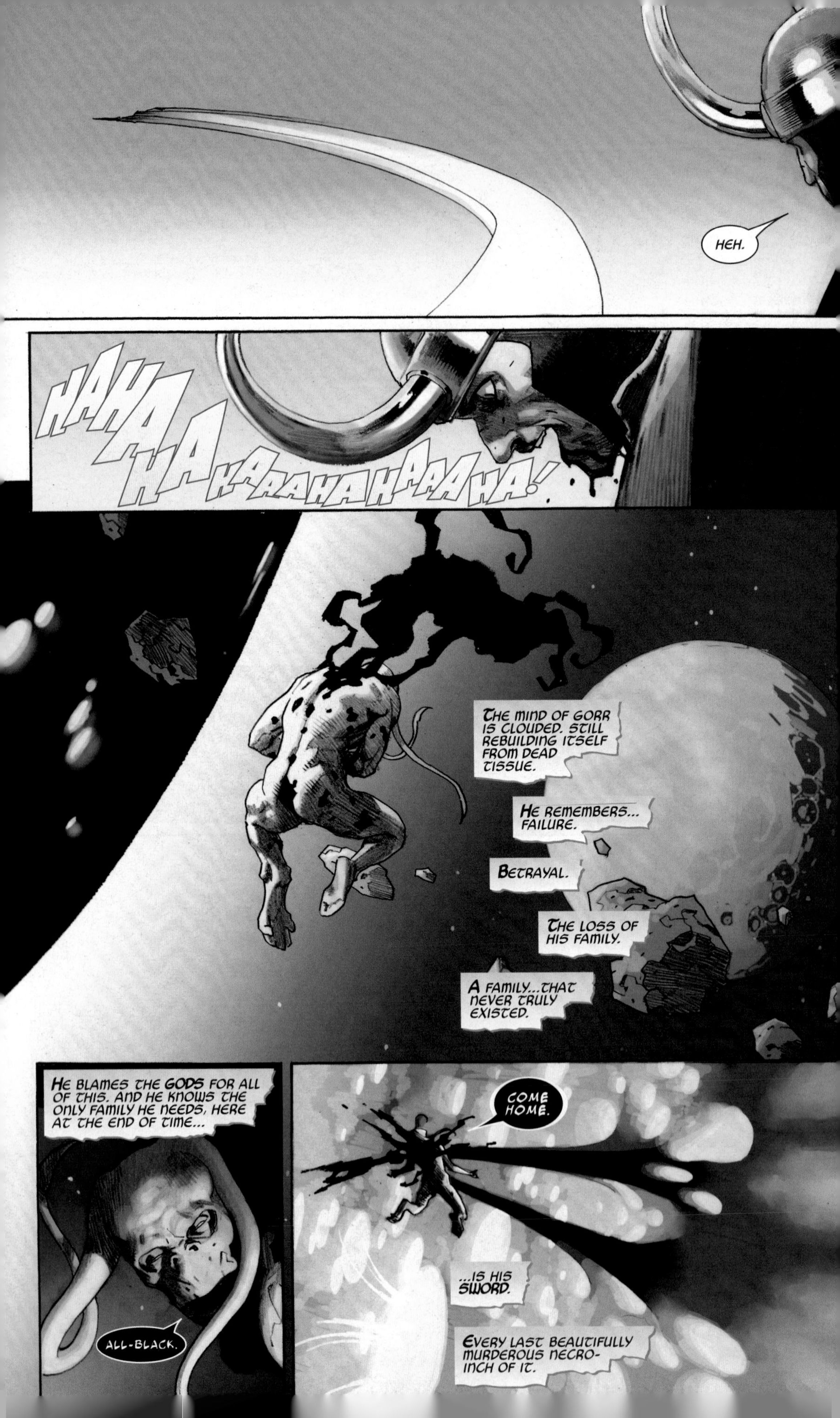
HEH.
HAHAHAHA KAAAHAHAHAAAAHA!
THE MIND OF GORR IS CLOUDED. STILL REBUILDING ITSELF FROM DEAD TISSUE.
HE REMEMBERS... FAILURE.
BETRAYAL.
THE LOSS OF HIS FAMILY.
A FAMILY...THAT NEVER TRULY EXISTED.
HE BLAMES THE GODS FOR ALL OF THIS. AND HE KNOWS THE ONLY FAMILY HE NEEDS, HERE AT THE END OF TIME...
ALL-BLACK.
COME HOME.
...IS HIS SWORD.
EVERY LAST BEAUTIFULLY MURDEROUS NECRO-INCH OF IT.

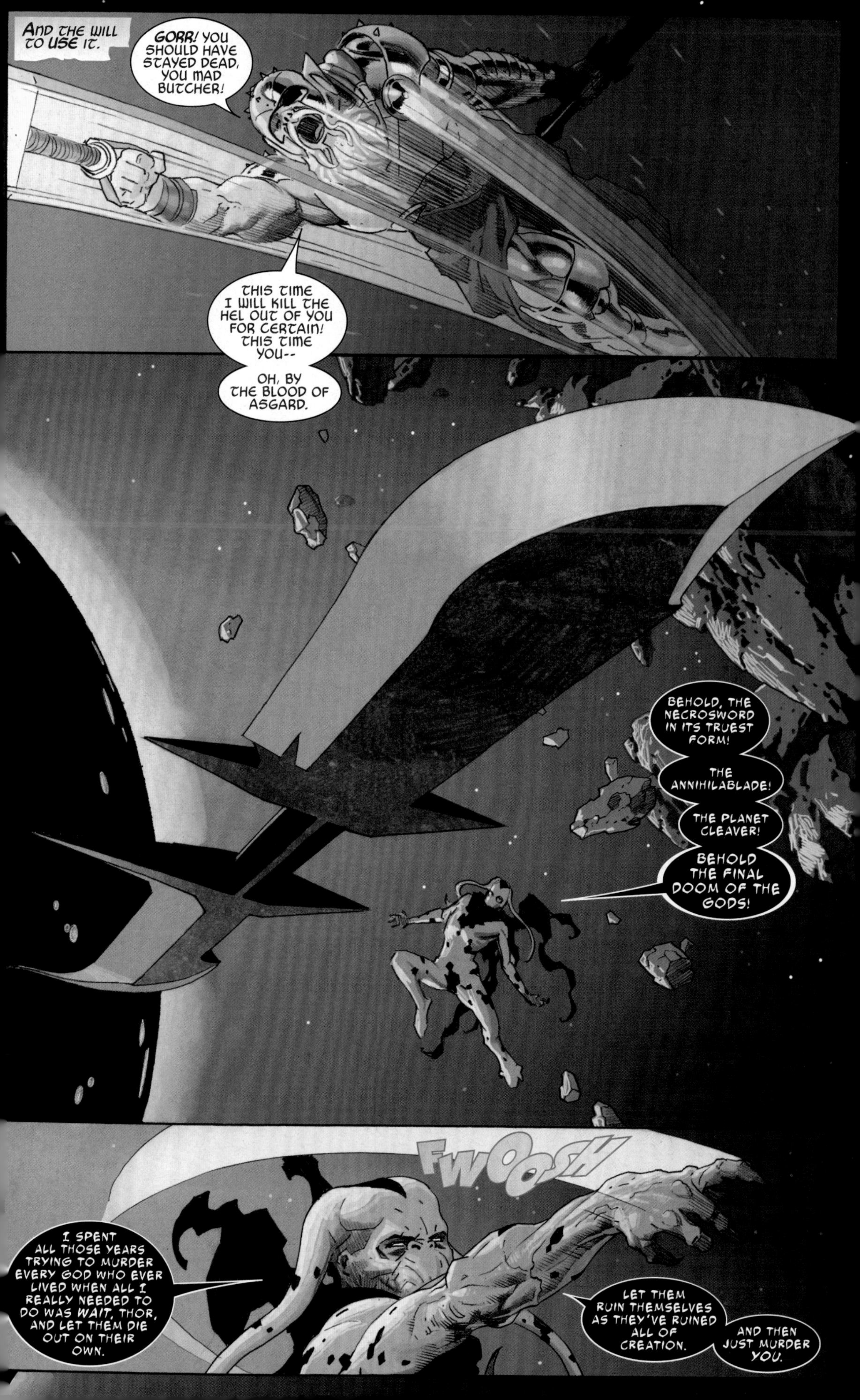
AND THE WILL TO USE IT.
GORR! YOU SHOULD HAVE STAYED DEAD, YOU MAD BUTCHER!
THIS TIME I WILL KILL THE HEL OUT OF YOU FOR CERTAIN! THIS TIME YOU--
OH, BY THE BLOOD OF ASGARD.
BEHOLD, THE NECROSWORD IN ITS TRUEST FORM!
THE ANNIHILABLADE!
THE PLANET CLEAVER!
BEHOLD THE FINAL DOOM OF THE GODS!
FWOOOSH
I SPENT ALL THOSE YEARS TRYING TO MURDER EVERY GOD WHO EVER LIVED WHEN ALL I REALLY NEEDED TO DO WAS WAIT, THOR, AND LET THEM DIE OUT ON THEIR OWN.
LET THEM RUIN THEMSELVES AS THEY'VE RUINED ALL OF CREATION.
AND THEN JUST MURDER YOU.

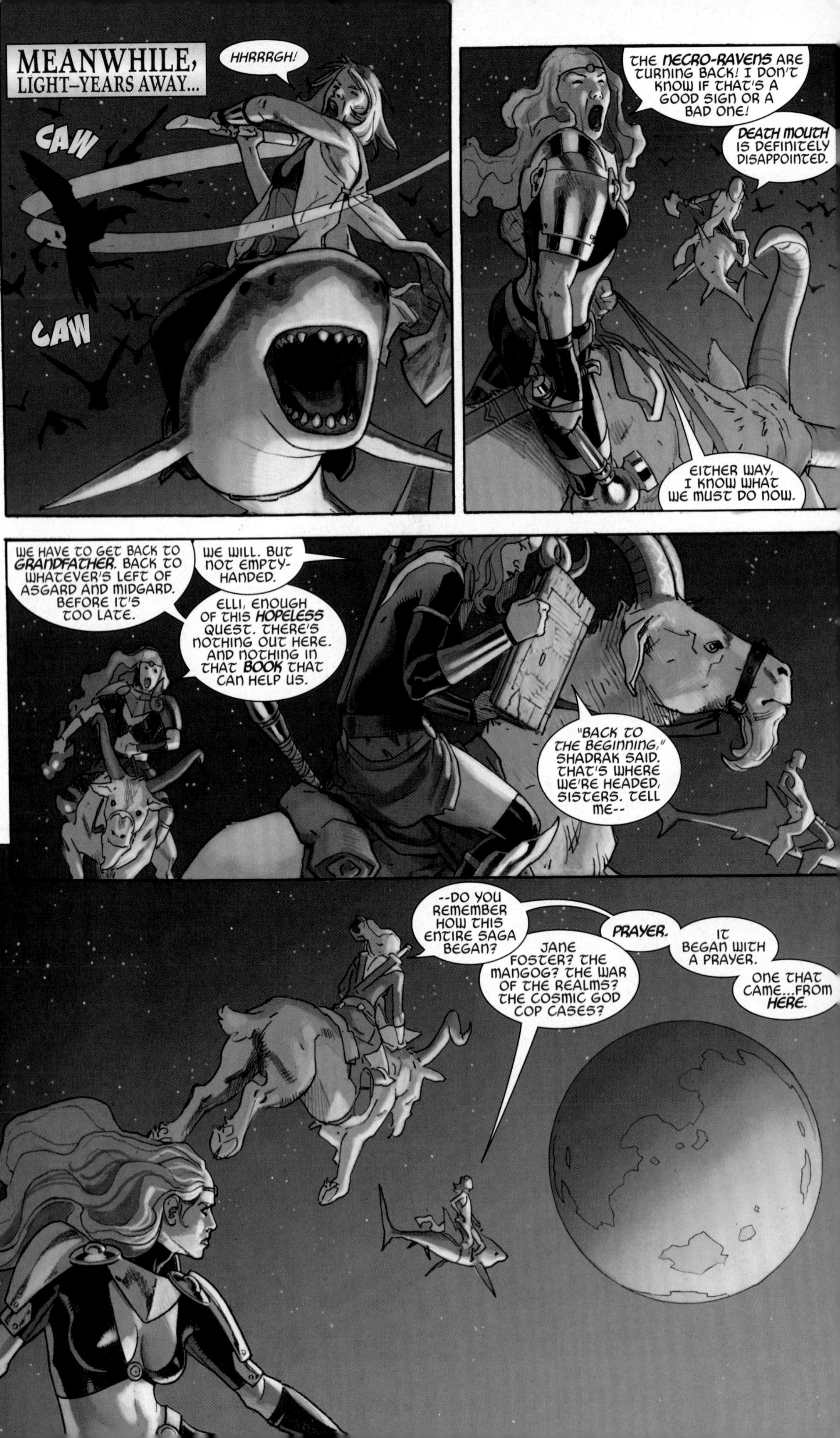
MEANWHILE, LIGHT-YEARS AWAY...
HHRRRGH!
CAW
CAW
THE NECRO-RAVENS ARE TURNING BACK! I DON'T KNOW IF THAT'S A GOOD SIGN OR A BAD ONE!
DEATH MOUTH IS DEFINITELY DISAPPOINTED.
EITHER WAY, I KNOW WHAT WE MUST DO NOW.
WE HAVE TO GET BACK TO GRANDFATHER. BACK TO WHATEVER'S LEFT OF ASGARD AND MIDGARD. BEFORE IT'S TOO LATE.
WE WILL. BUT NOT EMPTY-HANDED.
ELLI, ENOUGH OF THIS HOPELESS QUEST. THERE'S NOTHING OUT HERE. AND NOTHING IN THAT BOOK THAT CAN HELP US.
"BACK TO THE BEGINNING," SHADRAK SAID. THAT'S WHERE WE'RE HEADED, SISTERS. TELL ME--
--DO YOU REMEMBER HOW THIS ENTIRE SAGA BEGAN?
JANE FOSTER? THE MANGOG? THE WAR OF THE REALMS? THE COSMIC GOD COP CASES?
PRAYER.
IT BEGAN WITH A PRAYER.
ONE THAT CAME...FROM HERE.

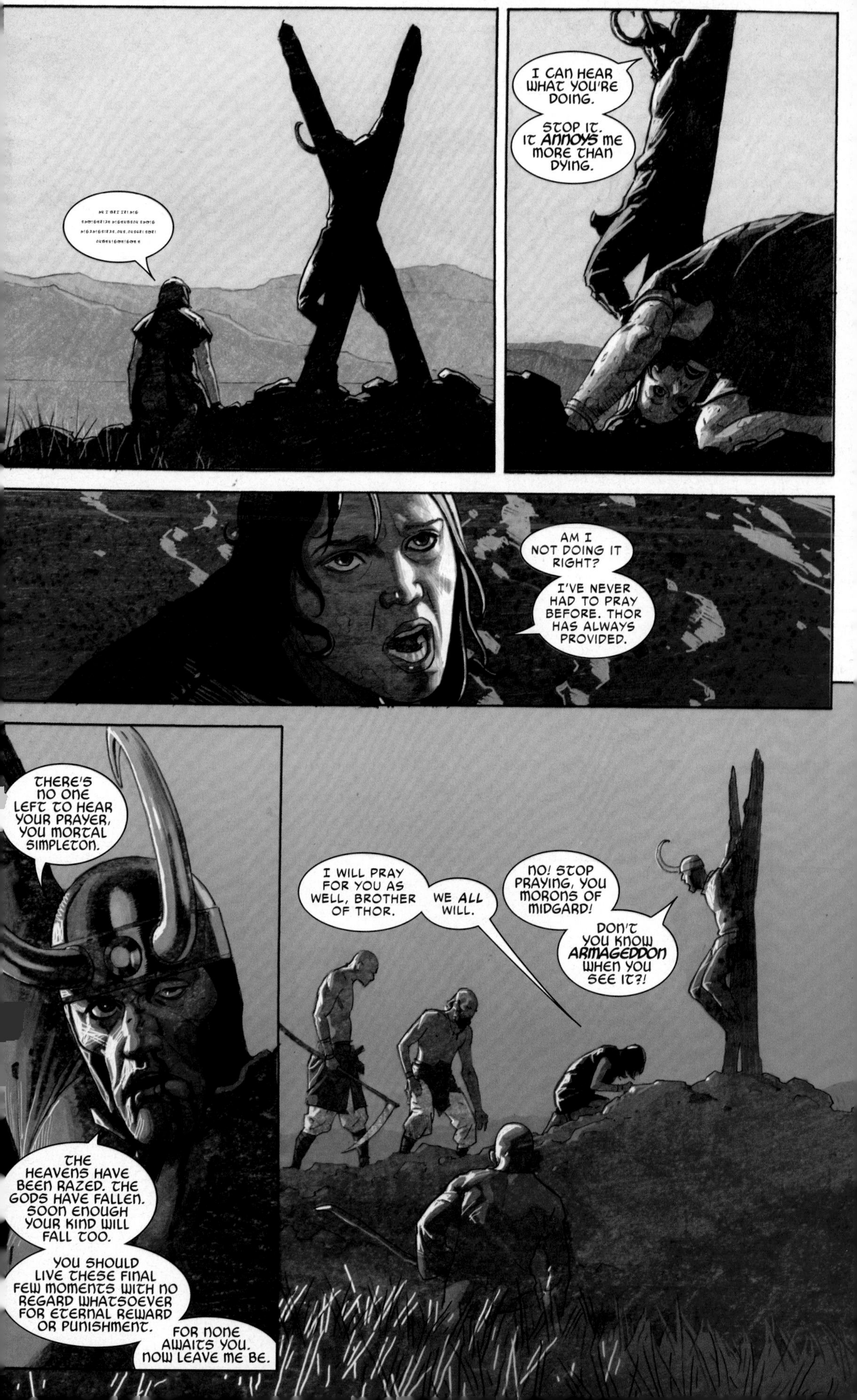
I CAN HEAR WHAT YOU'RE DOING.
STOP IT. IT ANNOYS ME MORE THAN DYING.
AM I NOT DOING IT RIGHT?
I'VE NEVER HAD TO PRAY BEFORE. THOR HAS ALWAYS PROVIDED.
THERE'S NO ONE LEFT TO HEAR YOUR PRAYER, YOU MORTAL SIMPLETON.
I WILL PRAY FOR YOU AS WELL, BROTHER OF THOR.
WE ALL WILL.
NO! STOP PRAYING, YOU MORONS OF MIDGARD!
DON'T YOU KNOW ARMAGEDDON WHEN YOU SEE IT?!
THE HEAVENS HAVE BEEN RAZED. THE GODS HAVE FALLEN. SOON ENOUGH YOUR KIND WILL FALL TOO.
YOU SHOULD LIVE THESE FINAL FEW MOMENTS WITH NO REGARD WHATSOEVER FOR ETERNAL REWARD OR PUNISHMENT.
FOR NONE AWAITS YOU. NOW LEAVE ME BE.

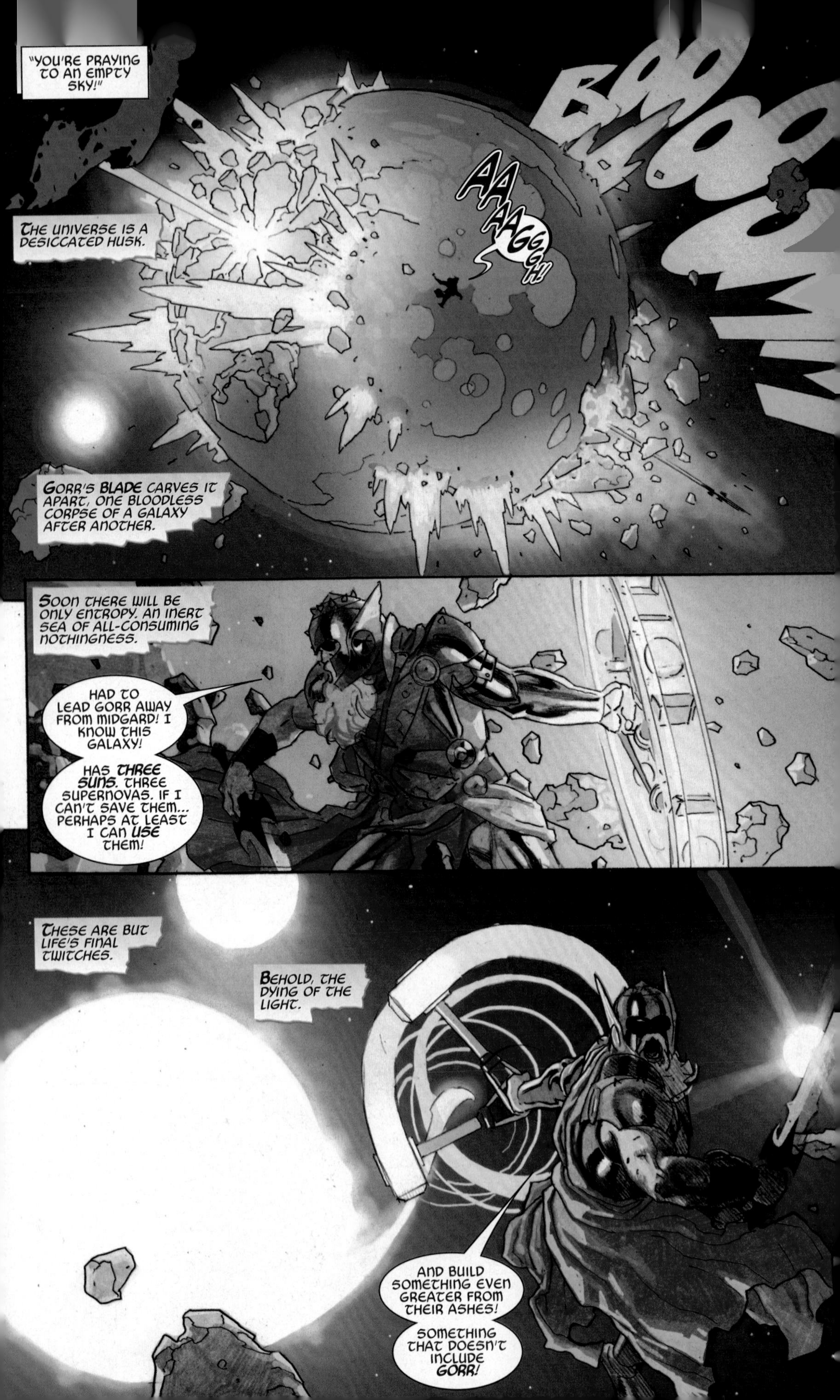

"YOU'RE PRAYING TO AN EMPTY SKY!"
BOOOOOM
THE UNIVERSE IS A DESICCATED HUSK.
AAAAGGGH!
GORR'S BLADE CARVES IT APART, ONE BLOODLESS CORPSE OF A GALAXY AFTER ANOTHER.
SOON THERE WILL BE ONLY ENTROPY. AN INERT SEA OF ALL-CONSUMING NOTHINGNESS.
HAD TO LEAD GORR AWAY FROM MIDGARD! I KNOW THIS GALAXY!
HAS THREE SUNS. THREE SUPERNOVAS. IF I CAN'T SAVE THEM... PERHAPS AT LEAST I CAN USE THEM!
THESE ARE BUT LIFE'S FINAL TWITCHES.
BEHOLD, THE DYING OF THE LIGHT.
AND BUILD SOMETHING EVEN GREATER FROM THEIR ASHES!
SOMETHING THAT DOESN'T INCLUDE GORR!

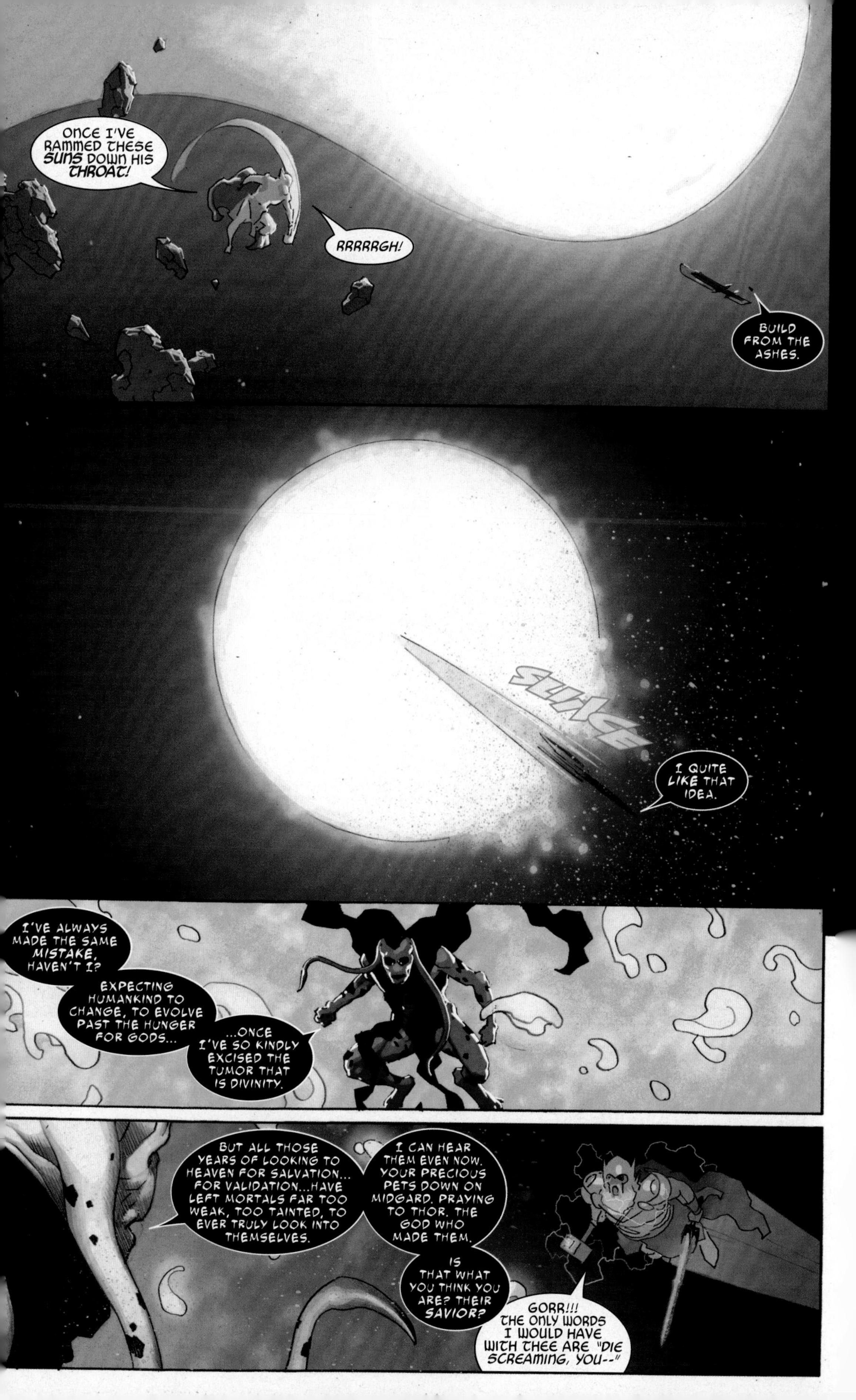
ONCE I'VE RAMMED THESE SUNS DOWN HIS THROAT!
RRRRRGH!
BUILD FROM THE ASHES.
SLICE
I QUITE LIKE THAT IDEA.
I'VE ALWAYS MADE THE SAME MISTAKE, HAVEN'T I?
EXPECTING HUMANKIND TO CHANGE, TO EVOLVE PAST THE HUNGER FOR GODS...
...ONCE I'VE SO KINDLY EXCISED THE TUMOR THAT IS DIVINITY.
BUT ALL THOSE YEARS OF LOOKING TO HEAVEN FOR SALVATION... FOR VALIDATION...HAVE LEFT MORTALS FAR TOO WEAK, TOO TAINTED, TO EVER TRULY LOOK INTO THEMSELVES.
I CAN HEAR THEM EVEN NOW. YOUR PRECIOUS PETS DOWN ON MIDGARD. PRAYING TO THOR. THE GOD WHO MADE THEM.
IS THAT WHAT YOU THINK YOU ARE? THEIR SAVIOR?
GORR!!! THE ONLY WORDS I WOULD HAVE WITH THEE ARE "DIE SCREAMING, YOU--"

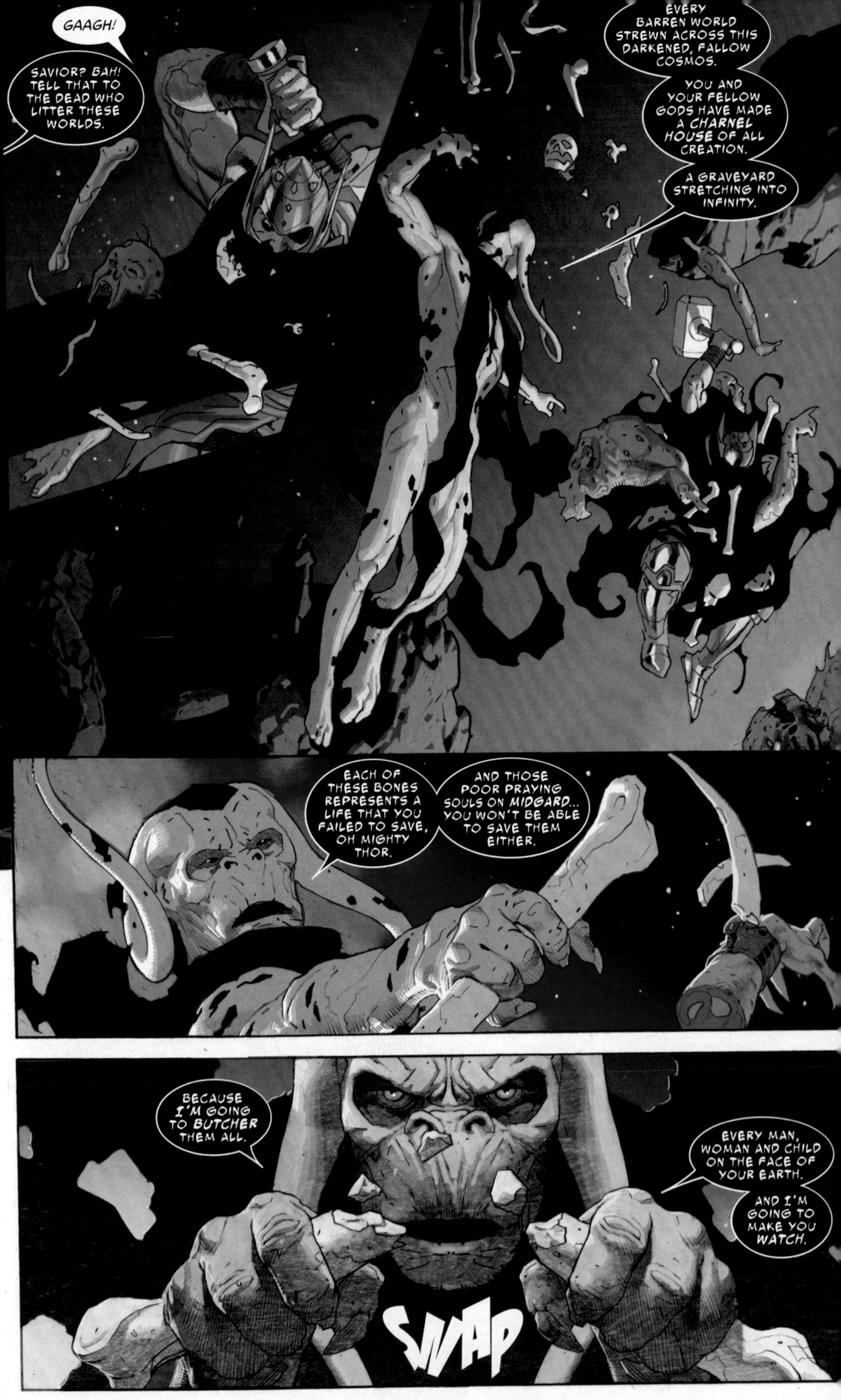
GAAGH!
SAVIOR? BAH! TELL THAT TO THE DEAD WHO LITTER THESE WORLDS.
EVERY BARREN WORLD STREWN ACROSS THIS DARKENED, FALLOW COSMOS.
YOU AND YOUR FELLOW GODS HAVE MADE A CHARNEL HOUSE OF ALL CREATION.
A GRAVEYARD STRETCHING INTO INFINITY.
EACH OF THESE BONES REPRESENTS A LIFE THAT YOU FAILED TO SAVE, OH MIGHTY THOR.
AND THOSE POOR PRAYING SOULS ON MIDGARD... YOU WON'T BE ABLE TO SAVE THEM EITHER.
BECAUSE I'M GOING TO BUTCHER THEM ALL.
EVERY MAN, WOMAN AND CHILD ON THE FACE OF YOUR EARTH.
AND I'M GOING TO MAKE YOU WATCH.
SNAP

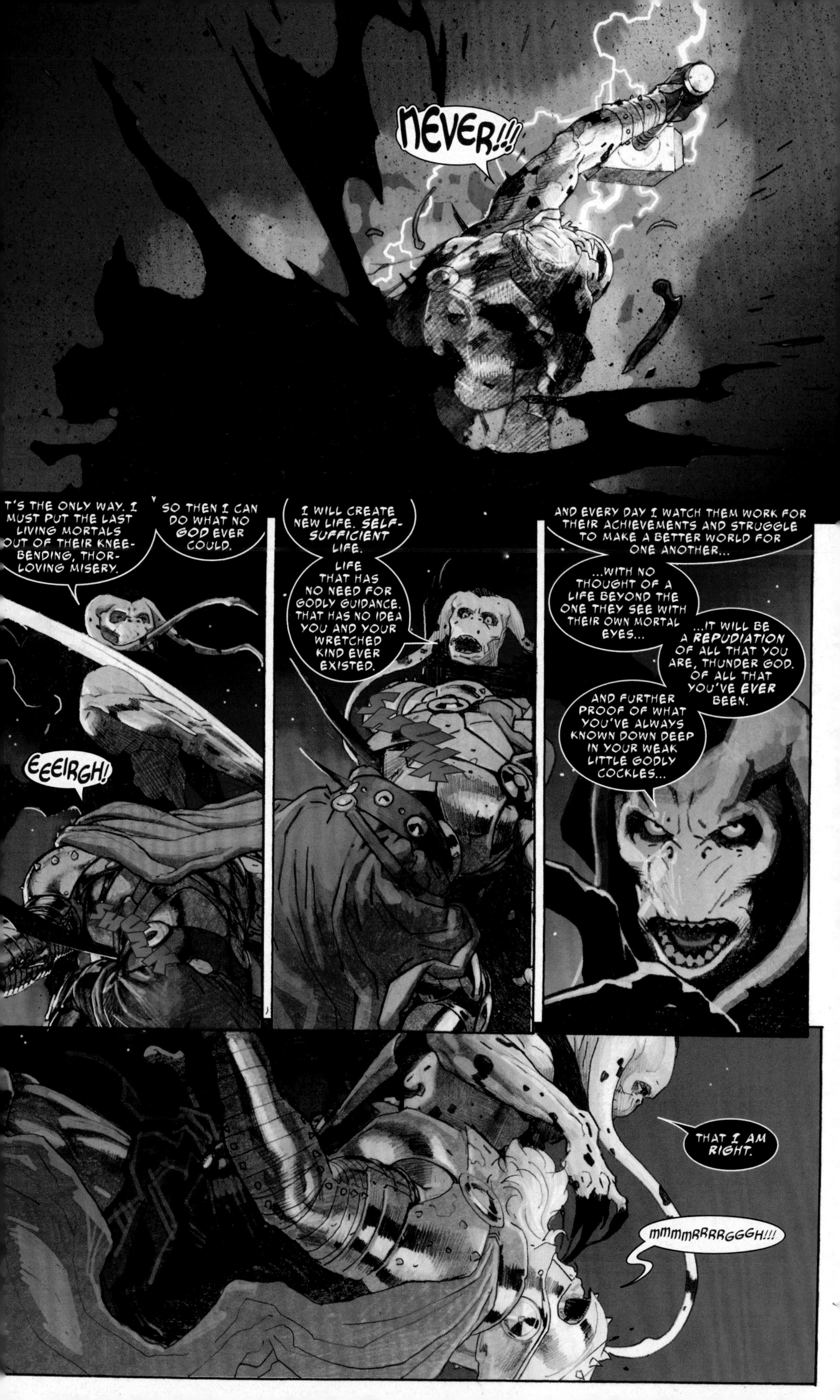
NEVER!!!
T'S THE ONLY WAY. I MUST PUT THE LAST LIVING MORTALS OUT OF THEIR KNEE-BENDING, THOR-LOVING MISERY.
SO THEN I CAN DO WHAT NO GOD EVER COULD.
EEEIRGH!
SHUNK
I WILL CREATE NEW LIFE. SELF-SUFFICIENT LIFE.
LIFE THAT HAS NO NEED FOR GODLY GUIDANCE. THAT HAS NO IDEA YOU AND YOUR WRETCHED KIND EVER EXISTED.
SHUNK
AND EVERY DAY I WATCH THEM WORK FOR THEIR ACHIEVEMENTS AND STRUGGLE TO MAKE A BETTER WORLD FOR ONE ANOTHER...
...WITH NO THOUGHT OF A LIFE BEYOND THE ONE THEY SEE WITH THEIR OWN MORTAL EYES...
...IT WILL BE A REPUDIATION OF ALL THAT YOU ARE, THUNDER GOD. OF ALL THAT YOU'VE EVER BEEN.
AND FURTHER PROOF OF WHAT YOU'VE ALWAYS KNOWN DOWN DEEP IN YOUR WEAK LITTLE GODLY COCKLES...
THAT I AM RIGHT.
MMMMRRRRGGGH!!!

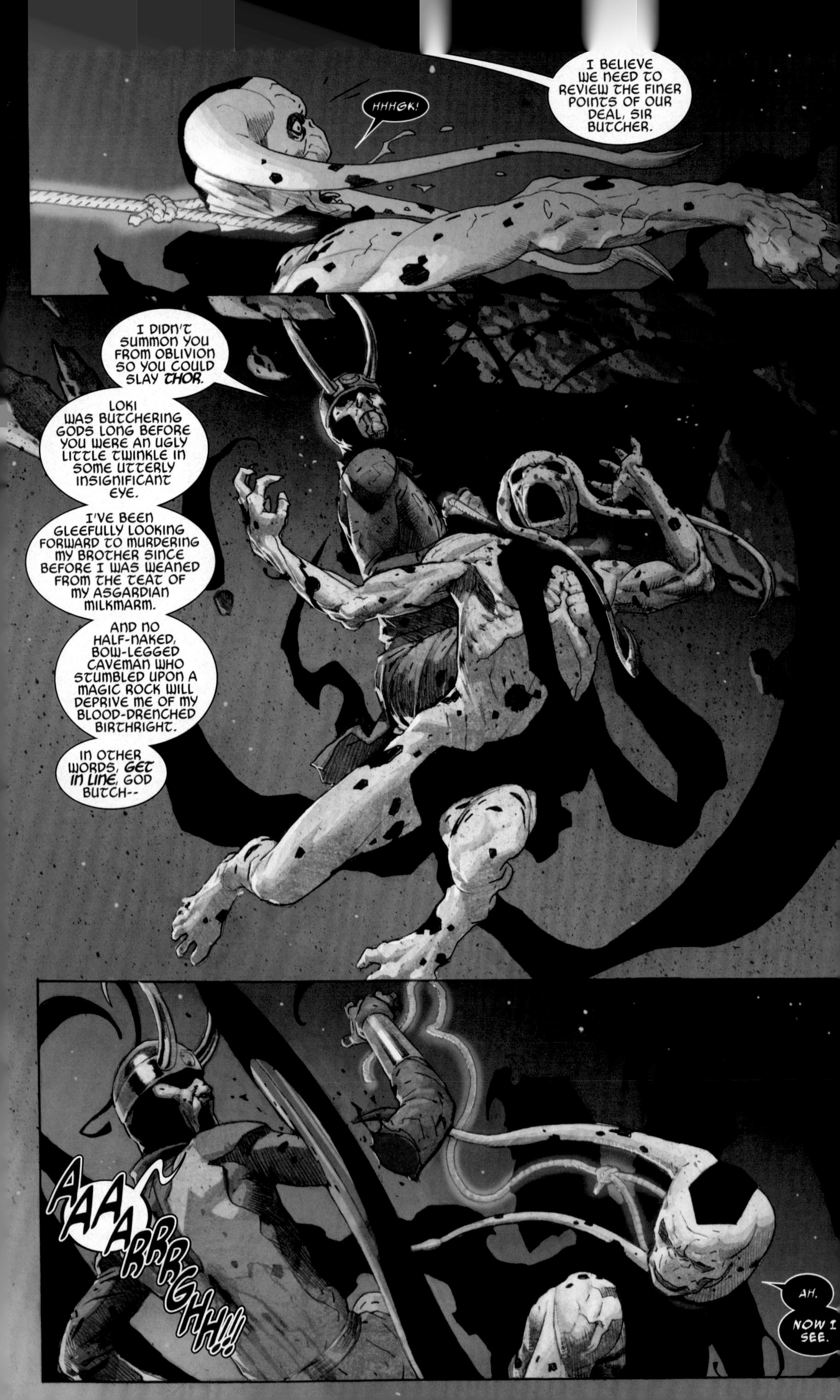
I BELIEVE WE NEED TO REVIEW THE FINER POINTS OF OUR DEAL, SIR BUTCHER.
HHHGK!
I DIDN'T SUMMON YOU FROM OBLIVION SO YOU COULD SLAY THOR.
LOKI WAS BUTCHERING GODS LONG BEFORE YOU WERE AN UGLY LITTLE TWINKLE IN SOME UTTERLY INSIGNIFICANT EYE.
I'VE BEEN GLEEFULLY LOOKING FORWARD TO MURDERING MY BROTHER SINCE BEFORE I WAS WEANED FROM THE TEAT OF MY ASGARDIAN MILKMARM.
AND NO HALF-NAKED, BOW-LEGGED CAVEMAN WHO STUMBLED UPON A MAGIC ROCK WILL DEPRIVE ME OF MY BLOOD-DRENCHED BIRTHRIGHT.
IN OTHER WORDS, GET IN LINE, GOD BUTCH--
AAAARRRGHH!!
AH.
NOW I SEE.

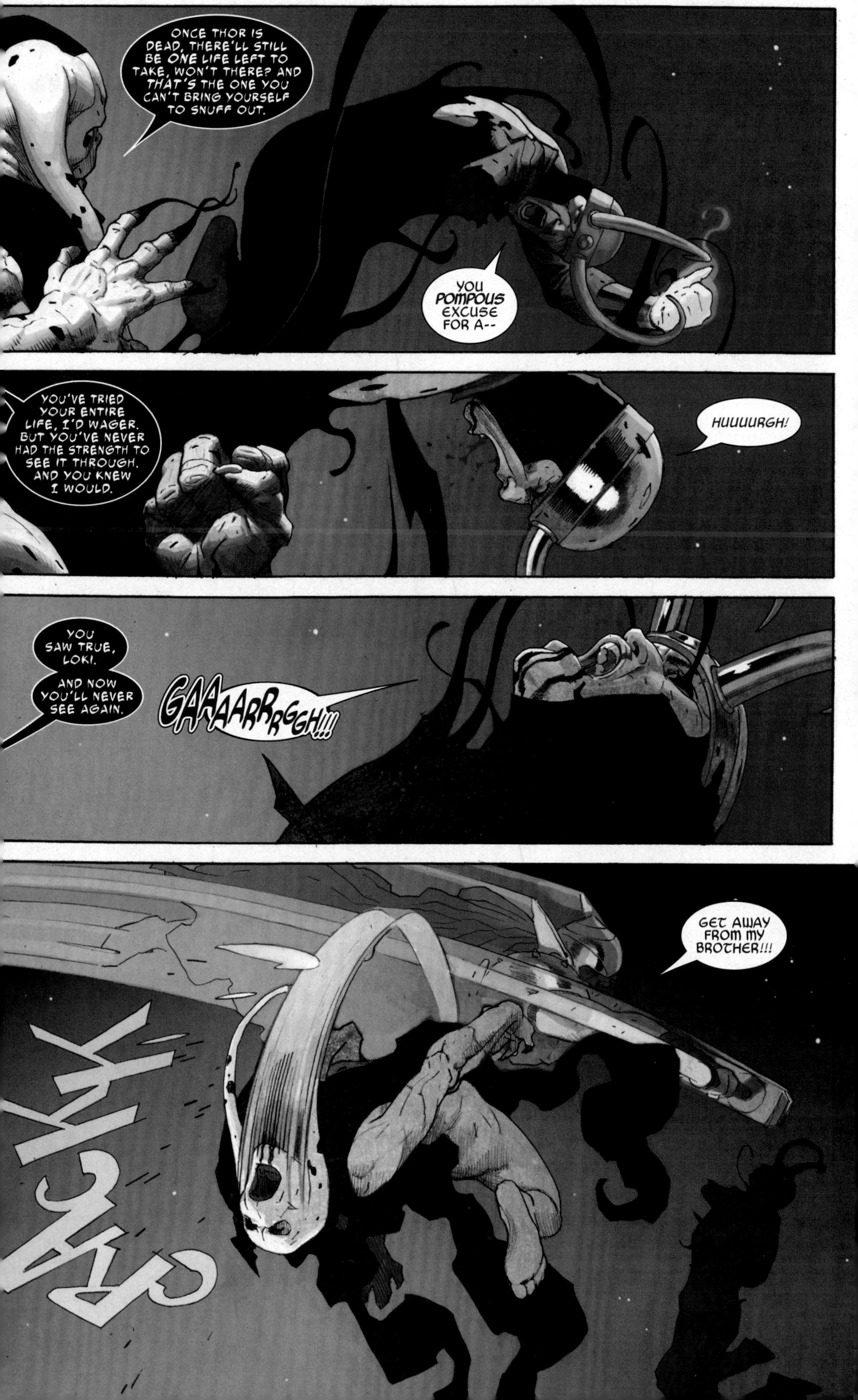
ONCE THOR IS DEAD, THERE'LL STILL BE ONE LIFE LEFT TO TAKE, WON'T THERE? AND THAT'S THE ONE YOU CAN'T BRING YOURSELF TO SNUFF OUT.
YOU POMPOUS EXCUSE FOR A--
YOU'VE TRIED YOUR ENTIRE LIFE, I'D WAGER. BUT YOU'VE NEVER HAD THE STRENGTH TO SEE IT THROUGH. AND YOU KNEW I WOULD.
HUUUURGH!
YOU SAW TRUE, LOKI.
AND NOW YOU'LL NEVER SEE AGAIN.
GAAAARRRGGH!!!
GET AWAY FROM MY BROTHER!!!
CRACK

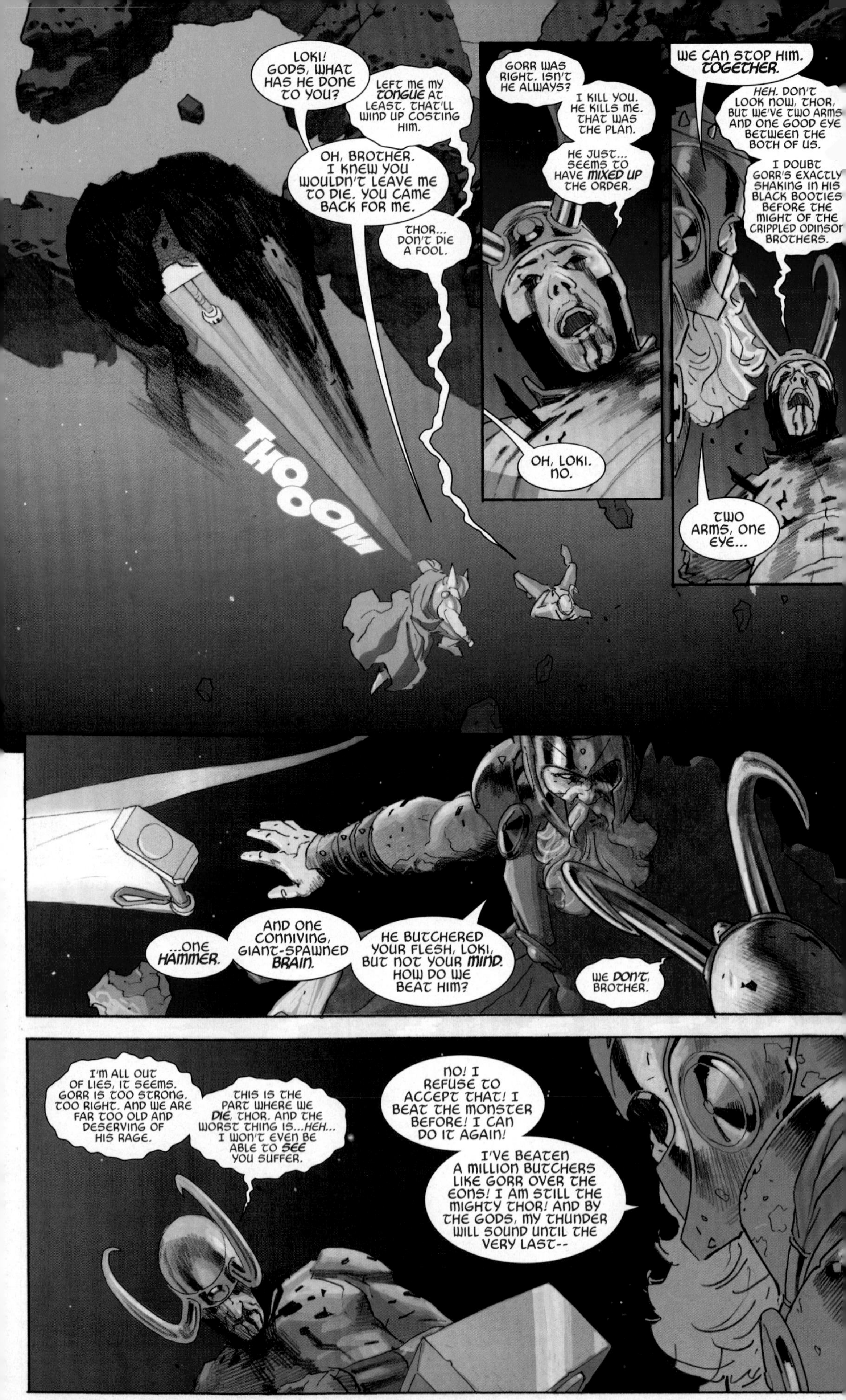
LOKI! GODS, WHAT HAS HE DONE TO YOU?
LEFT ME MY TONGUE AT LEAST. THAT'LL WIND UP COSTING HIM.
OH, BROTHER. I KNEW YOU WOULDN'T LEAVE ME TO DIE. YOU CAME BACK FOR ME.
THOR... DON'T DIE A FOOL.
THOOOM
GORR WAS RIGHT. ISN'T HE ALWAYS?
I KILL YOU. HE KILLS ME. THAT WAS THE PLAN.
HE JUST... SEEMS TO HAVE MIXED UP THE ORDER.
OH, LOKI. NO.
WE CAN STOP HIM. TOGETHER.
HEH. DON'T LOOK NOW, THOR, BUT WE'VE TWO ARMS AND ONE GOOD EYE BETWEEN THE BOTH OF US.
I DOUBT GORR'S EXACTLY SHAKING IN HIS BLACK BOOTIES BEFORE THE MIGHT OF THE CRIPPLED ODINSON BROTHERS.
TWO ARMS, ONE EYE...
...ONE HAMMER.
AND ONE CONNIVING, GIANT-SPAWNED BRAIN.
HE BUTCHERED YOUR FLESH, LOKI, BUT NOT YOUR MIND. HOW DO WE BEAT HIM?
WE DON'T, BROTHER.
I'M ALL OUT OF LIES, IT SEEMS. GORR IS TOO STRONG. TOO RIGHT. AND WE ARE FAR TOO OLD AND DESERVING OF HIS RAGE.
THIS IS THE PART WHERE WE DIE, THOR. AND THE WORST THING IS...HEH... I WON'T EVEN BE ABLE TO SEE YOU SUFFER.
NO! I REFUSE TO ACCEPT THAT! I BEAT THE MONSTER BEFORE! I CAN DO IT AGAIN!
I'VE BEATEN A MILLION BUTCHERS LIKE GORR OVER THE EONS! I AM STILL THE MIGHTY THOR! AND BY THE GODS, MY THUNDER WILL SOUND UNTIL THE VERY LAST--

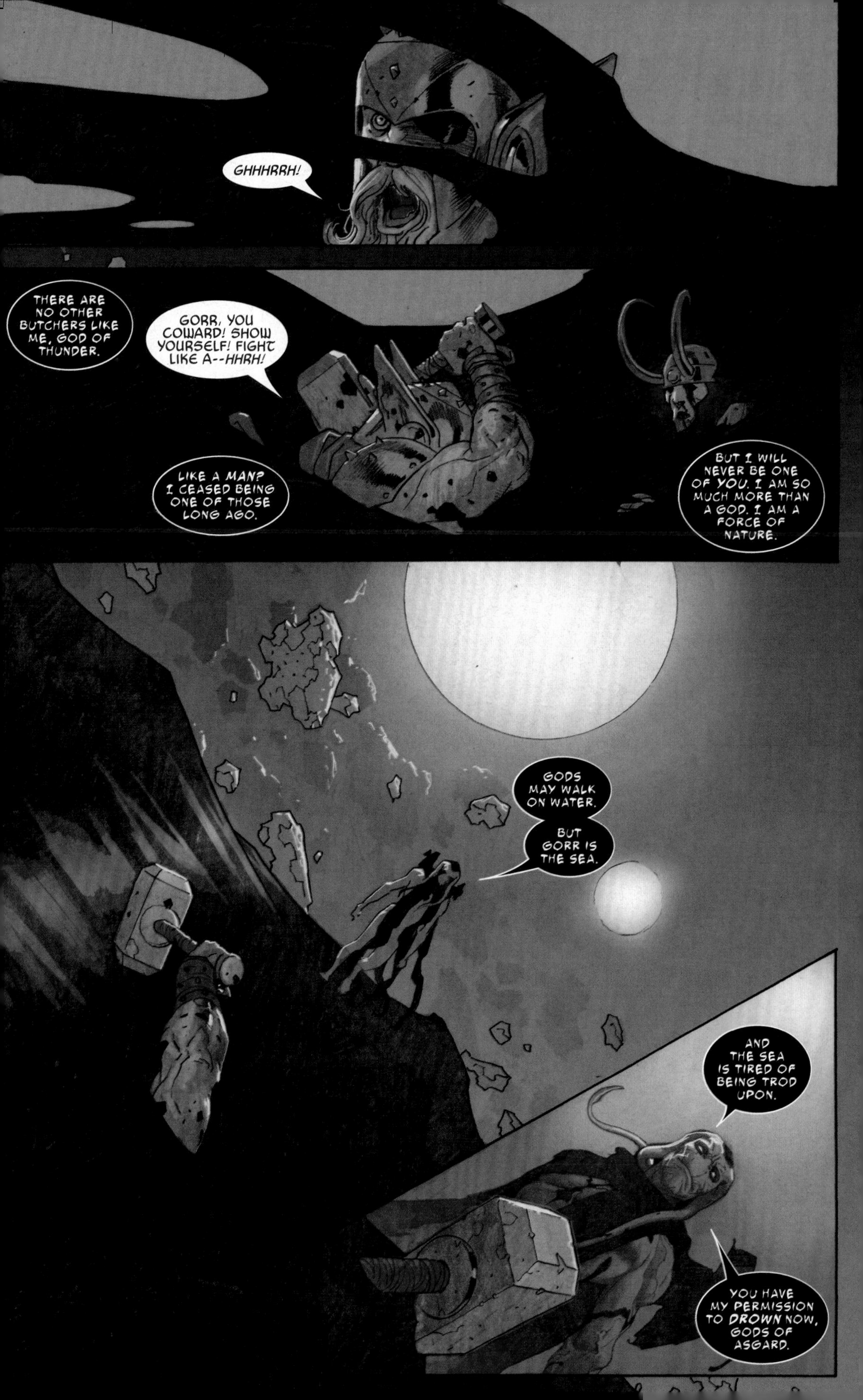
GHHHRRH!
THERE ARE NO OTHER BUTCHERS LIKE ME, GOD OF THUNDER.
GORR, YOU COWARD! SHOW YOURSELF! FIGHT LIKE A--HHRH!
LIKE A MAN? I CEASED BEING ONE OF THOSE LONG AGO.
BUT I WILL NEVER BE ONE OF YOU. I AM SO MUCH MORE THAN A GOD. I AM A FORCE OF NATURE.
GODS MAY WALK ON WATER.
BUT GORR IS THE SEA.
AND THE SEA IS TIRED OF BEING TROD UPON.
YOU HAVE MY PERMISSION TO DROWN NOW, GODS OF ASGARD.

HRRRRRRGH!!!

LOKI! I CAN'T HOLD BACK THE DARKNESS!

I NEVER ASKED YOU TO! LET ME DIE, DAMMIT!

JUST AS LONG AS OUR FATHER'S BLOODLINE DIES RIGHT BY MY SIDE!

IF THIS IS IT, BROTHER...I WANT YOU TO KNOW...

I LIED.

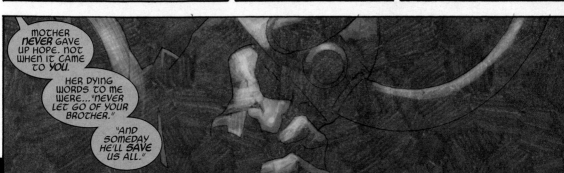

MOTHER NEVER GAVE UP HOPE. NOT WHEN IT CAME TO YOU.

HER DYING WORDS TO ME WERE..."NEVER LET GO OF YOUR BROTHER."

"AND SOMEDAY HE'LL SAVE US ALL."

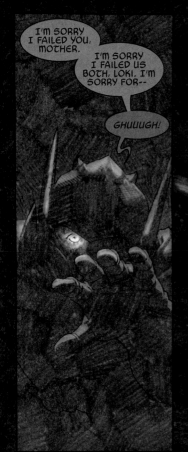

I'M SORRY I FAILED YOU, MOTHER.

I'M SORRY I FAILED US BOTH, LOKI. I'M SORRY FOR--

GHUUUGH!

THE UNIVERSE IS A DESICCATED HUSK.

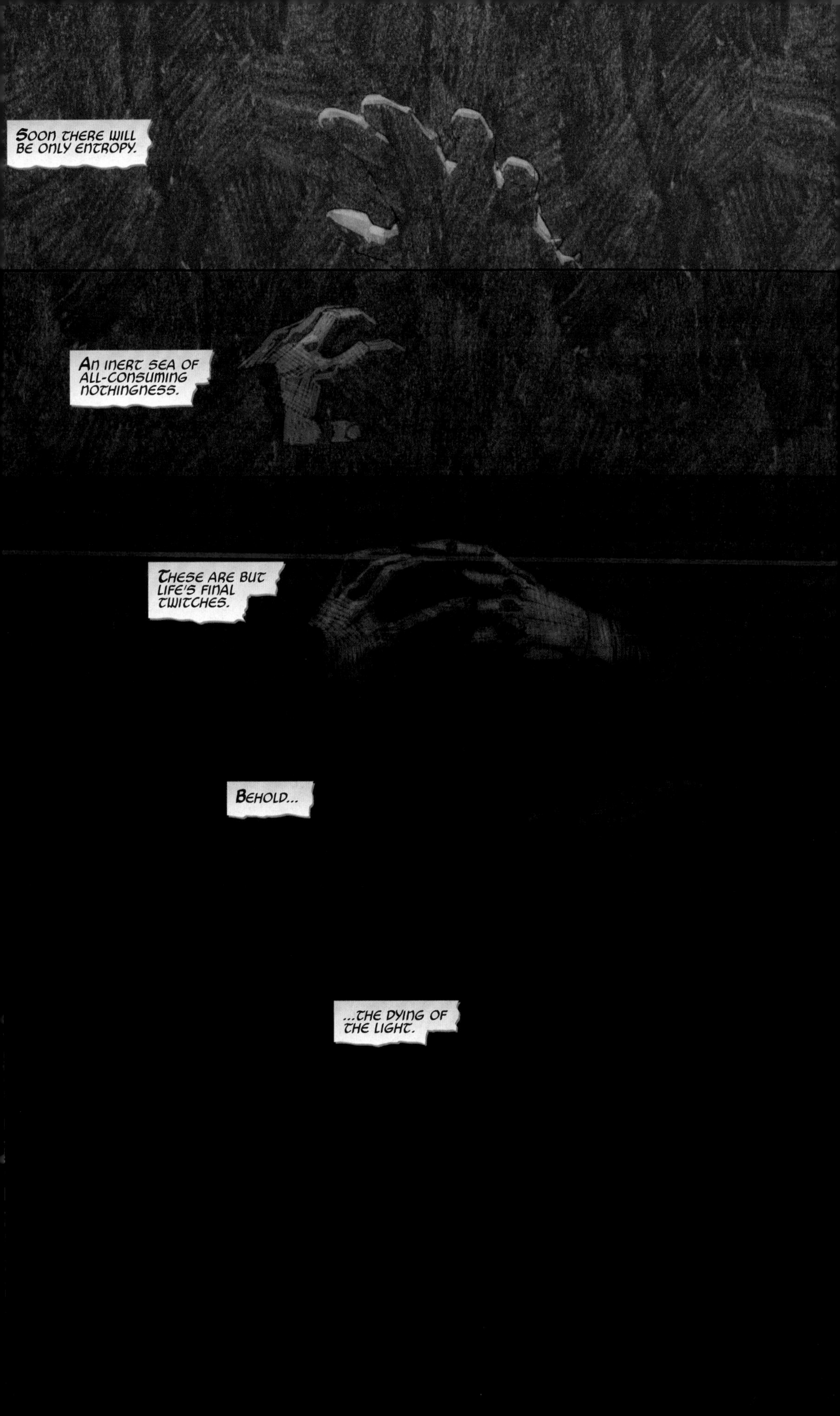
SOON THERE WILL BE ONLY ENTROPY.
AN INERT SEA OF ALL-CONSUMING NOTHINGNESS.
THESE ARE BUT LIFE'S FINAL TWITCHES.
BEHOLD...
...THE DYING OF THE LIGHT.

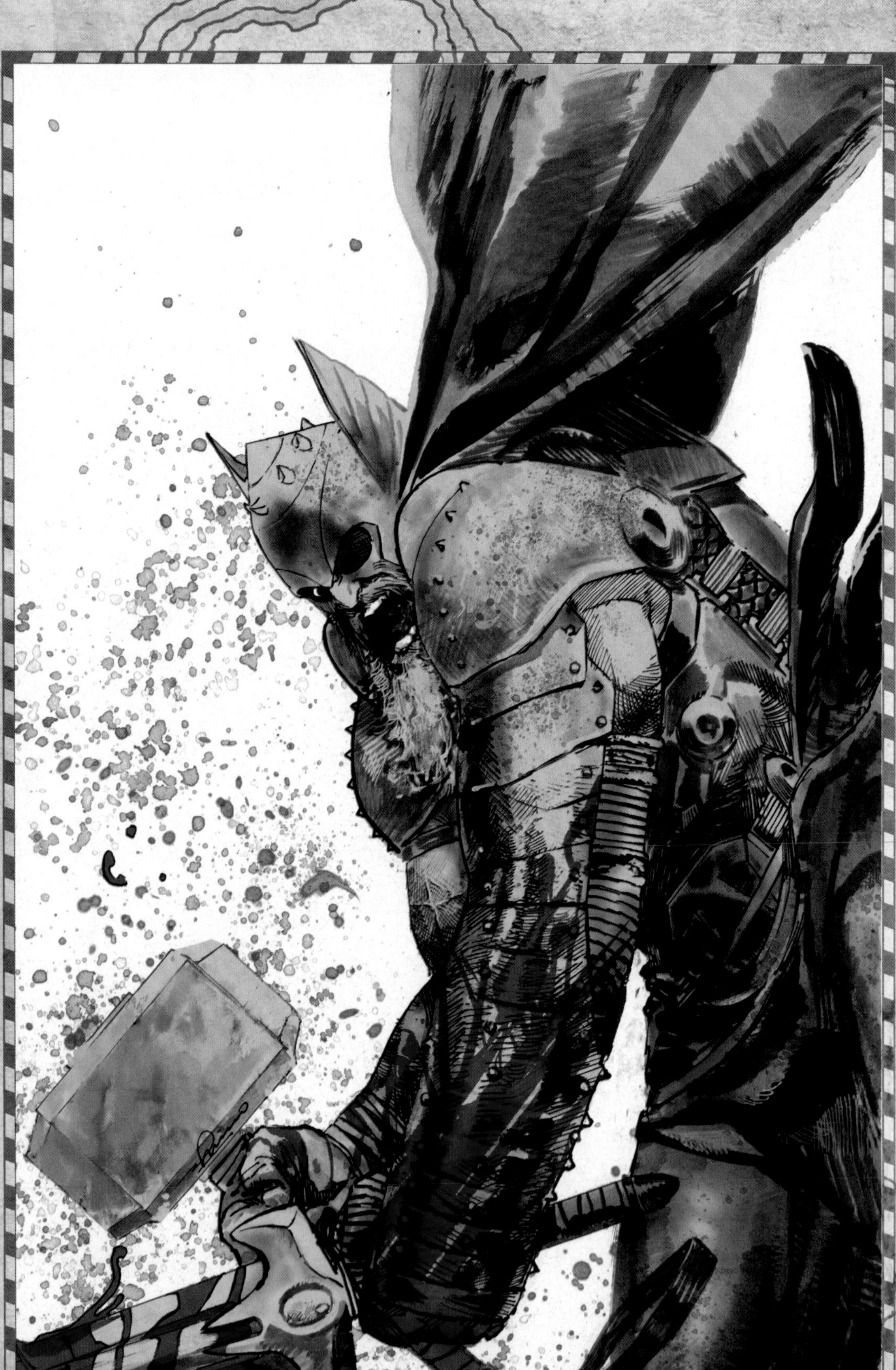

#1 VARIANT BY GERARDO ZAFFINO

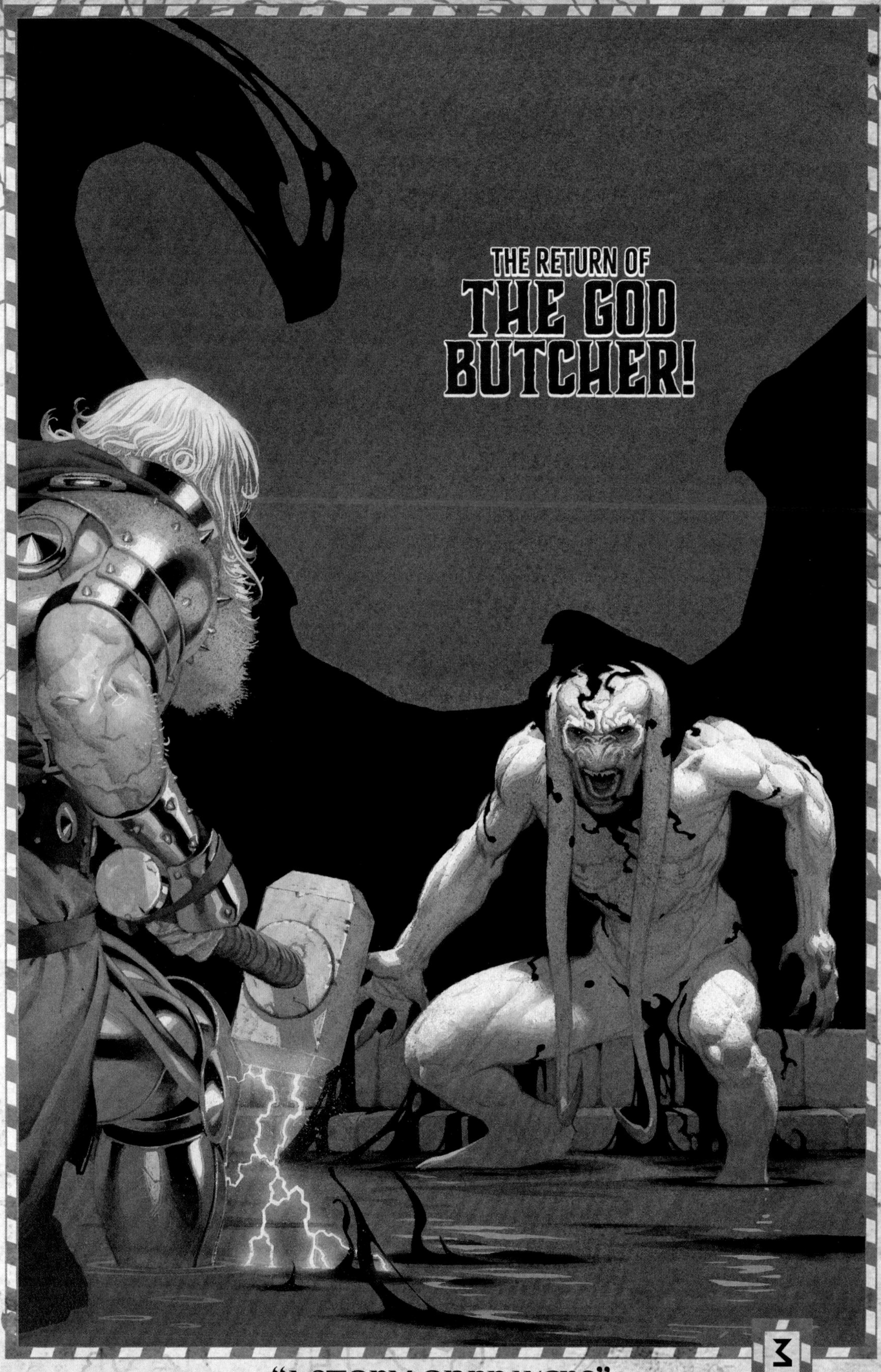
THE RETURN OF
THE GOD
BUTCHER!

3

"A STORM OF PRAYERS"

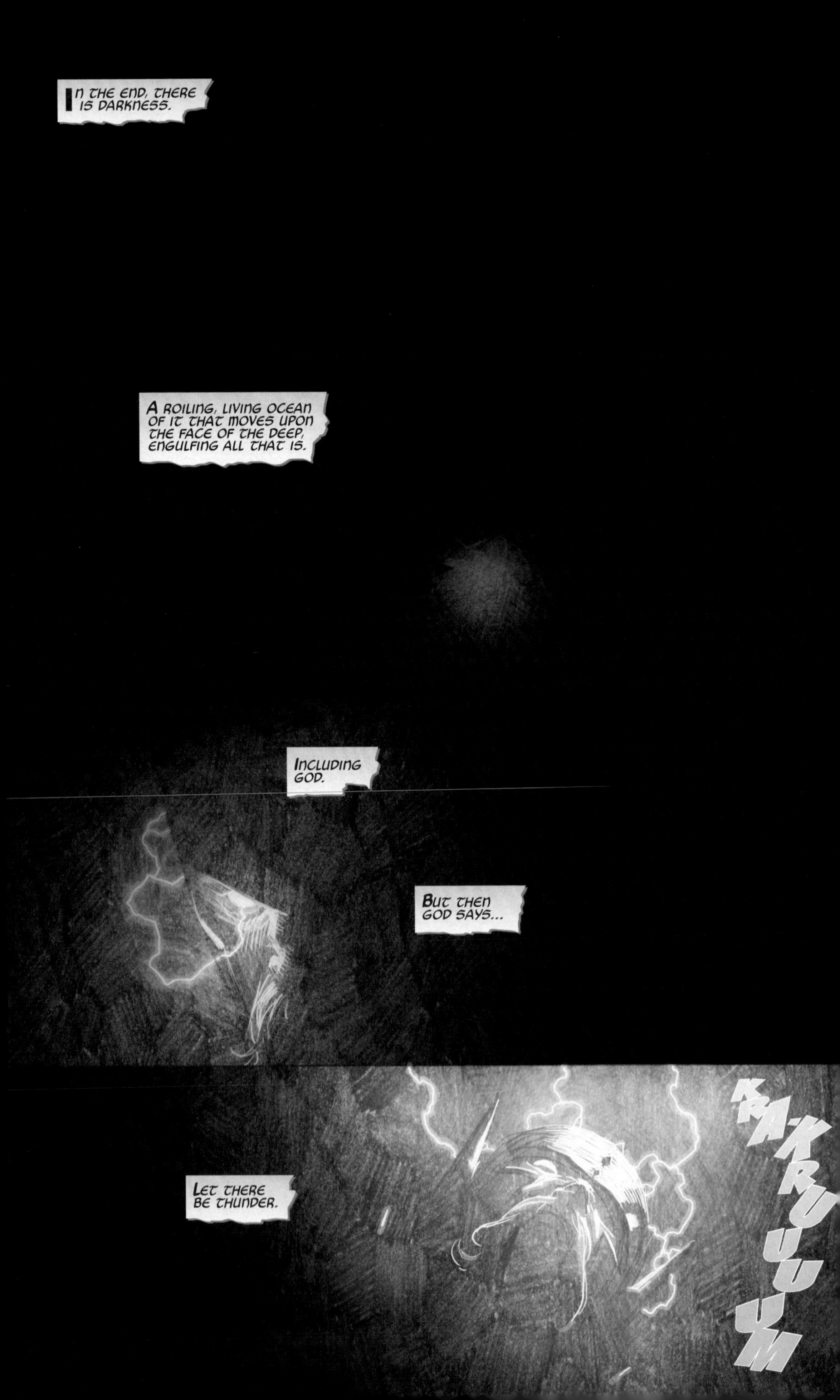
In the end, there is darkness.
A roiling, living ocean of it that moves upon the face of the deep, engulfing all that is.
Including God.
But then God says...
Let there be thunder.
KRA-KRUUUUM

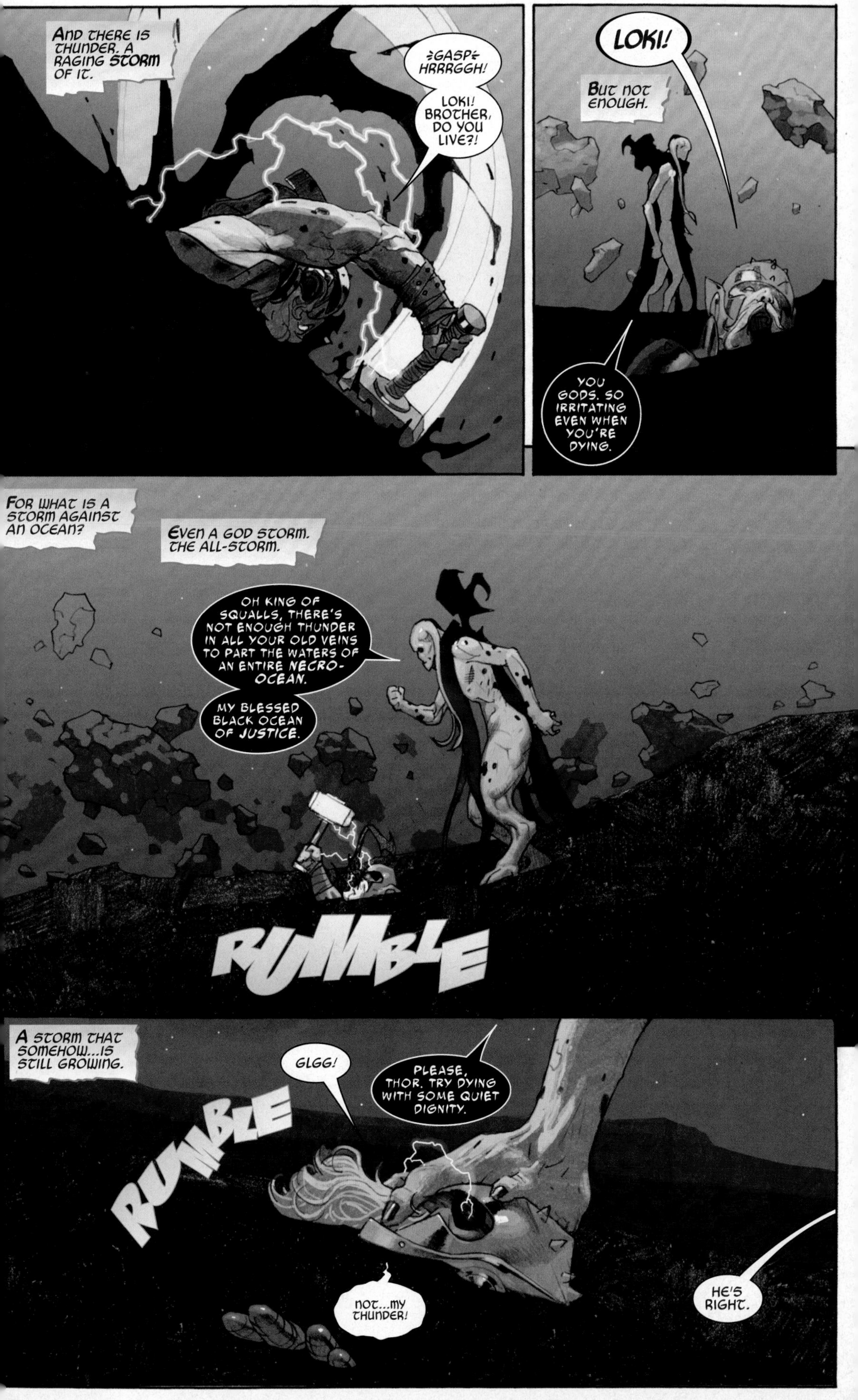

AND THERE IS THUNDER. A RAGING STORM OF IT.
≈GASP≈ HRRRGGH!
LOKI! BROTHER, DO YOU LIVE?!
LOKI!
BUT NOT ENOUGH.
YOU GODS. SO IRRITATING EVEN WHEN YOU'RE DYING.
FOR WHAT IS A STORM AGAINST AN OCEAN?
EVEN A GOD STORM. THE ALL-STORM.
OH KING OF SQUALLS, THERE'S NOT ENOUGH THUNDER IN ALL YOUR OLD VEINS TO PART THE WATERS OF AN ENTIRE NECRO-OCEAN.
MY BLESSED BLACK OCEAN OF JUSTICE.
RUMBLE
A STORM THAT SOMEHOW...IS STILL GROWING.
GLGG!
PLEASE, THOR. TRY DYING WITH SOME QUIET DIGNITY.
RUMBLE
NOT...MY THUNDER!
HE'S RIGHT.

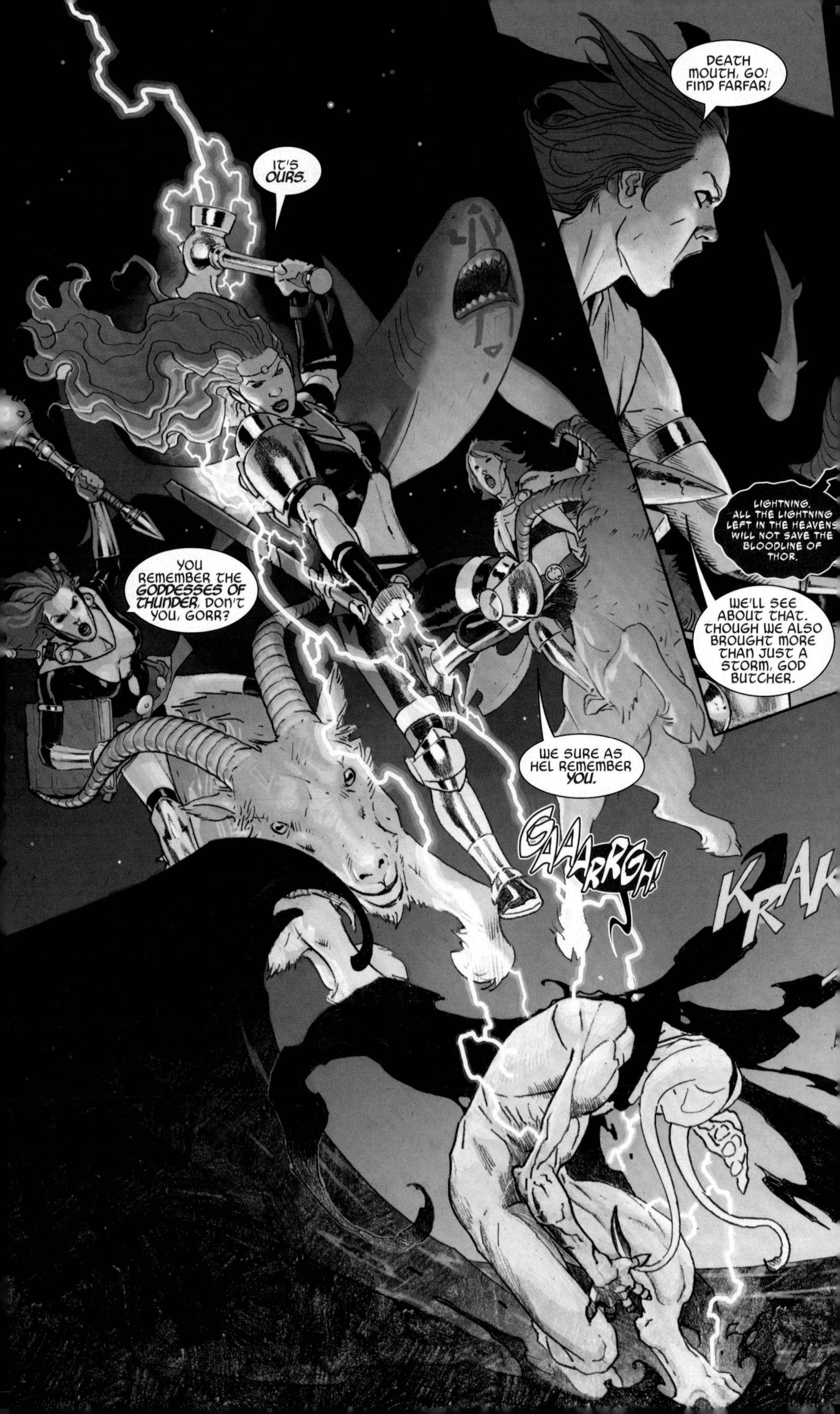
DEATH MOUTH, GO! FIND FARFAR!
IT'S OURS.
LIGHTNING. ALL THE LIGHTNING LEFT IN THE HEAVENS WILL NOT SAVE THE BLOODLINE OF THOR.
YOU REMEMBER THE GODDESSES OF THUNDER, DON'T YOU, GORR?
WE'LL SEE ABOUT THAT. THOUGH WE ALSO BROUGHT MORE THAN JUST A STORM, GOD BUTCHER.
WE SURE AS HEL REMEMBER YOU.
GAAARRGH!
KRAK

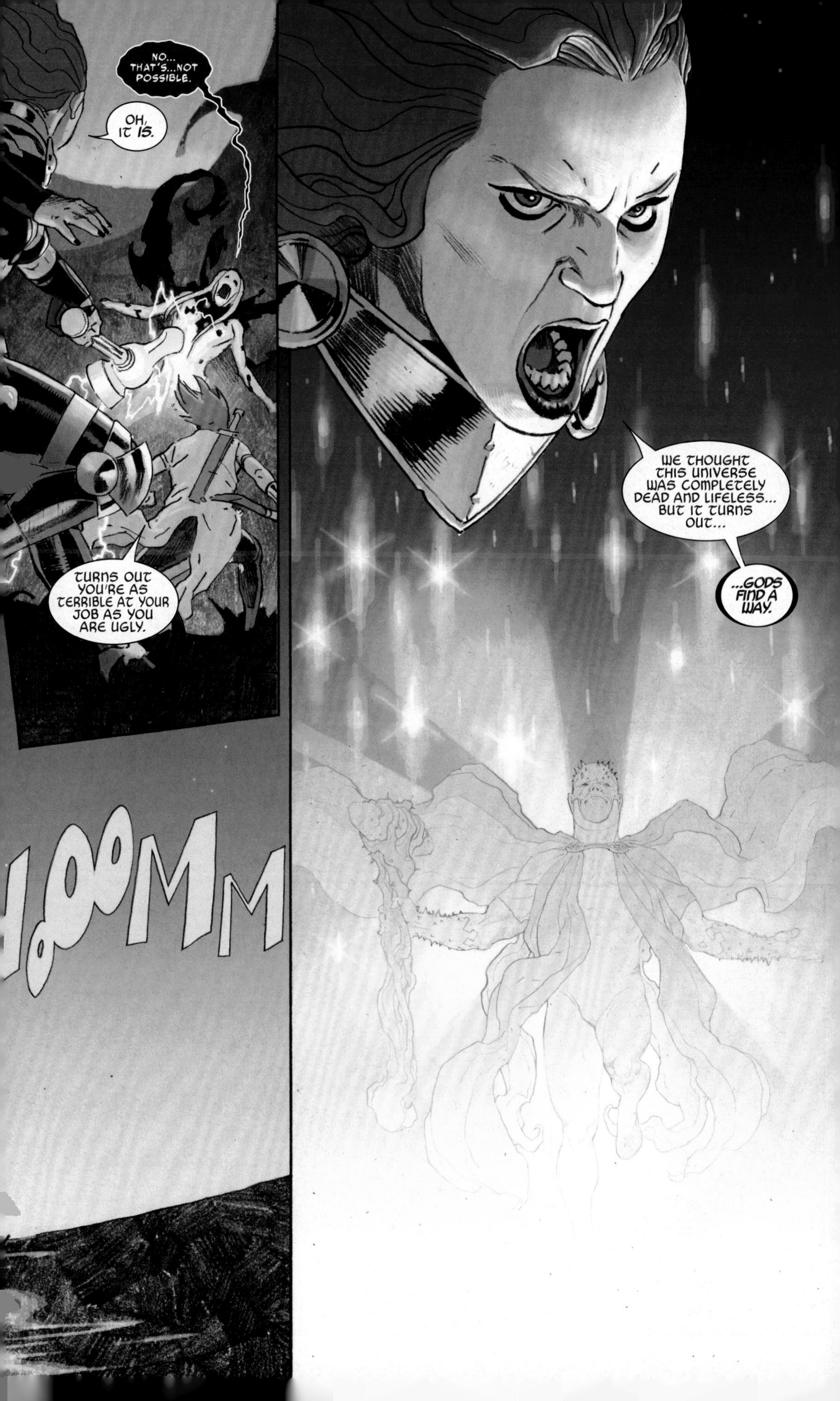

NO... THAT'S...NOT POSSIBLE.
OH, IT IS.
TURNS OUT YOU'RE AS TERRIBLE AT YOUR JOB AS YOU ARE UGLY.
WOOMM
WE THOUGHT THIS UNIVERSE WAS COMPLETELY DEAD AND LIFELESS... BUT IT TURNS OUT...
...GODS FIND A WAY.

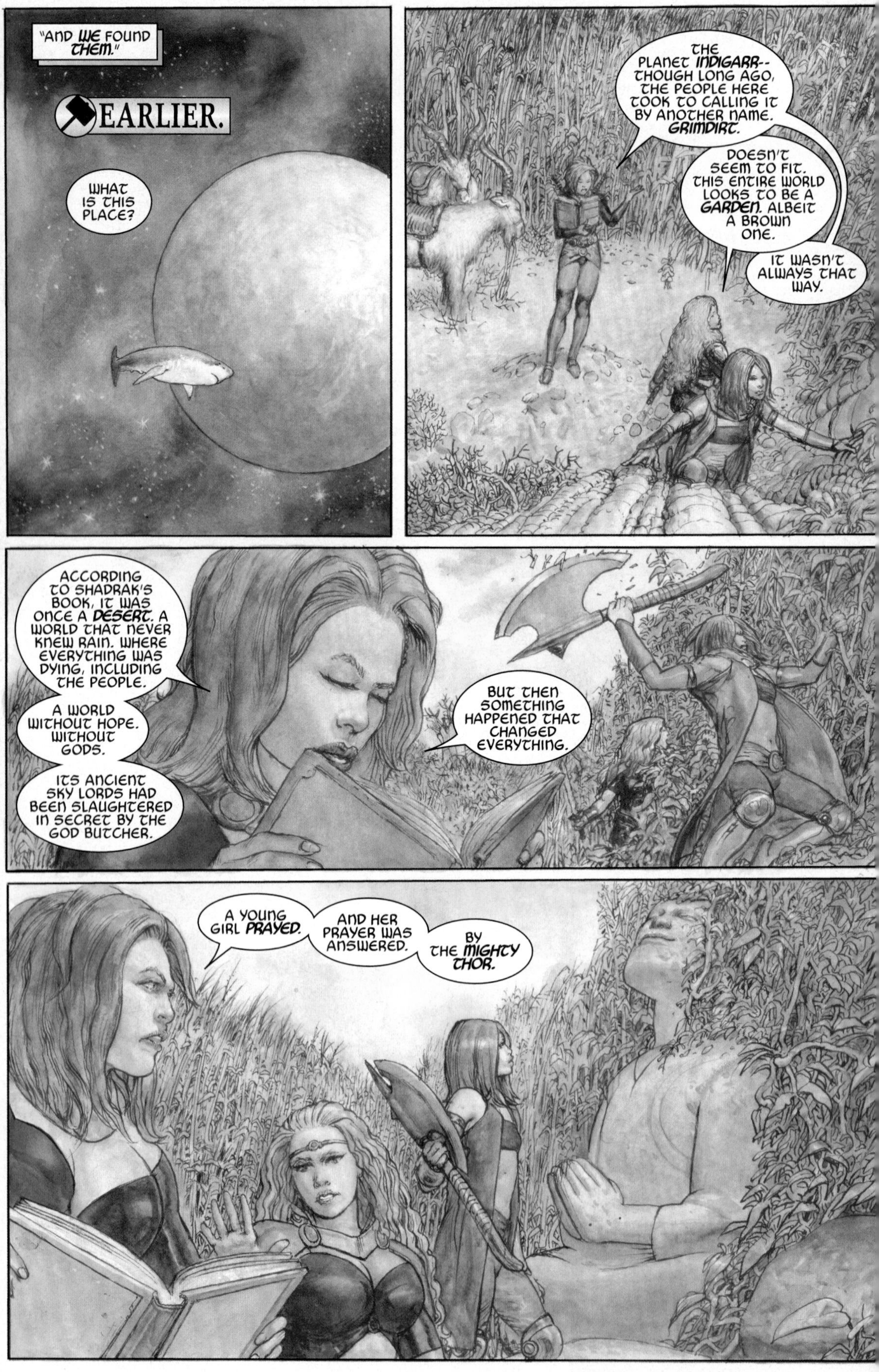
"AND WE FOUND THEM."
EARLIER.
WHAT IS THIS PLACE?
THE PLANET INDIGARR-- THOUGH LONG AGO, THE PEOPLE HERE TOOK TO CALLING IT BY ANOTHER NAME. GRIMDIRT.
DOESN'T SEEM TO FIT. THIS ENTIRE WORLD LOOKS TO BE A GARDEN. ALBEIT A BROWN ONE.
IT WASN'T ALWAYS THAT WAY.
ACCORDING TO SHADRAK'S BOOK, IT WAS ONCE A DESERT. A WORLD THAT NEVER KNEW RAIN. WHERE EVERYTHING WAS DYING, INCLUDING THE PEOPLE.
A WORLD WITHOUT HOPE. WITHOUT GODS.
ITS ANCIENT SKY LORDS HAD BEEN SLAUGHTERED IN SECRET BY THE GOD BUTCHER.
BUT THEN SOMETHING HAPPENED THAT CHANGED EVERYTHING.
A YOUNG GIRL PRAYED.
AND HER PRAYER WAS ANSWERED.
BY THE MIGHTY THOR.

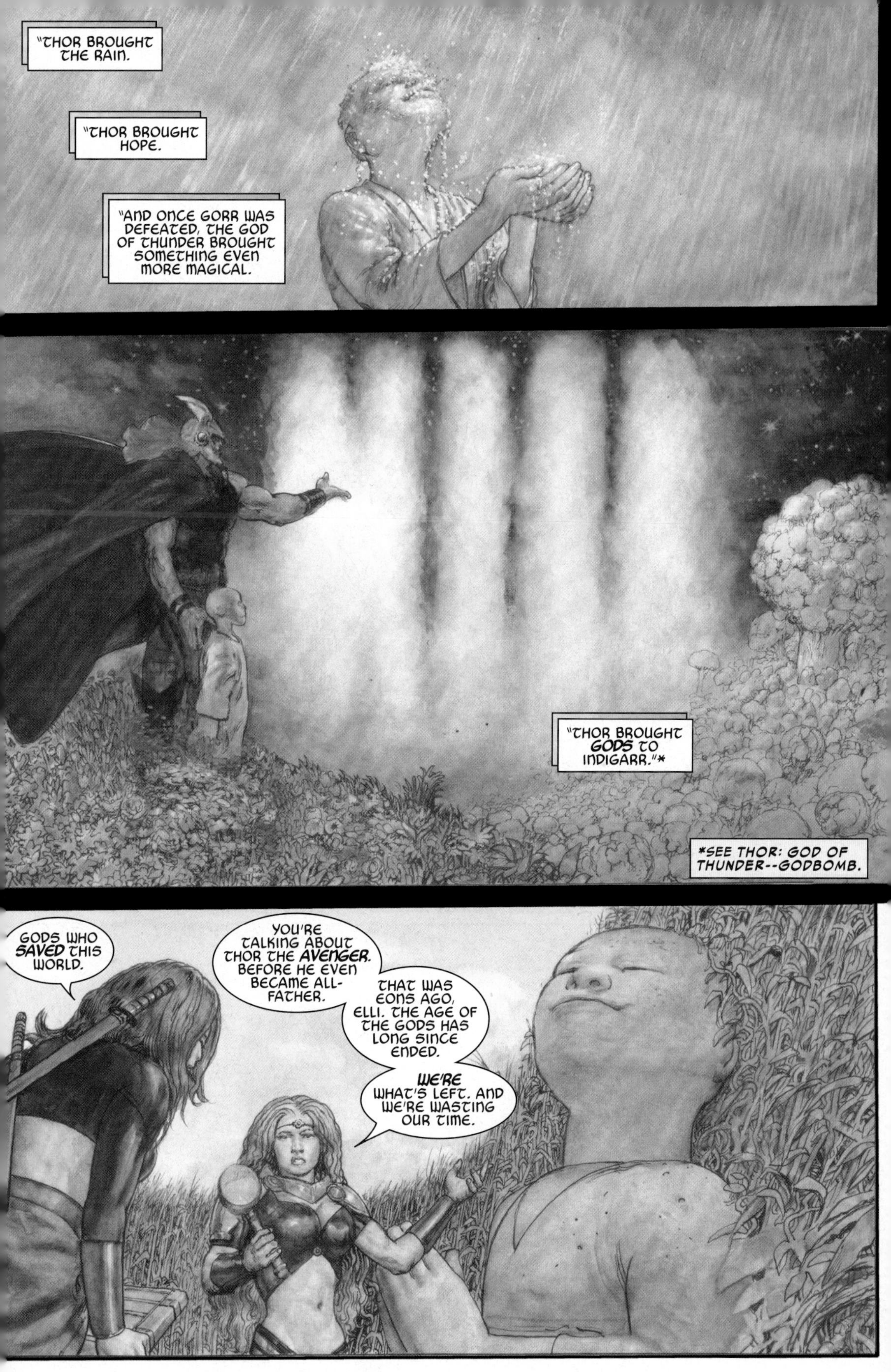
"THOR BROUGHT THE RAIN.
"THOR BROUGHT HOPE.
"AND ONCE GORR WAS DEFEATED, THE GOD OF THUNDER BROUGHT SOMETHING EVEN MORE MAGICAL.
"THOR BROUGHT GODS TO INDIGARR."*
*SEE THOR: GOD OF THUNDER--GODBOMB.
GODS WHO SAVED THIS WORLD.
YOU'RE TALKING ABOUT THOR THE AVENGER. BEFORE HE EVEN BECAME ALL-FATHER.
THAT WAS EONS AGO, ELLI. THE AGE OF THE GODS HAS LONG SINCE ENDED.
WE'RE WHAT'S LEFT. AND WE'RE WASTING OUR TIME.

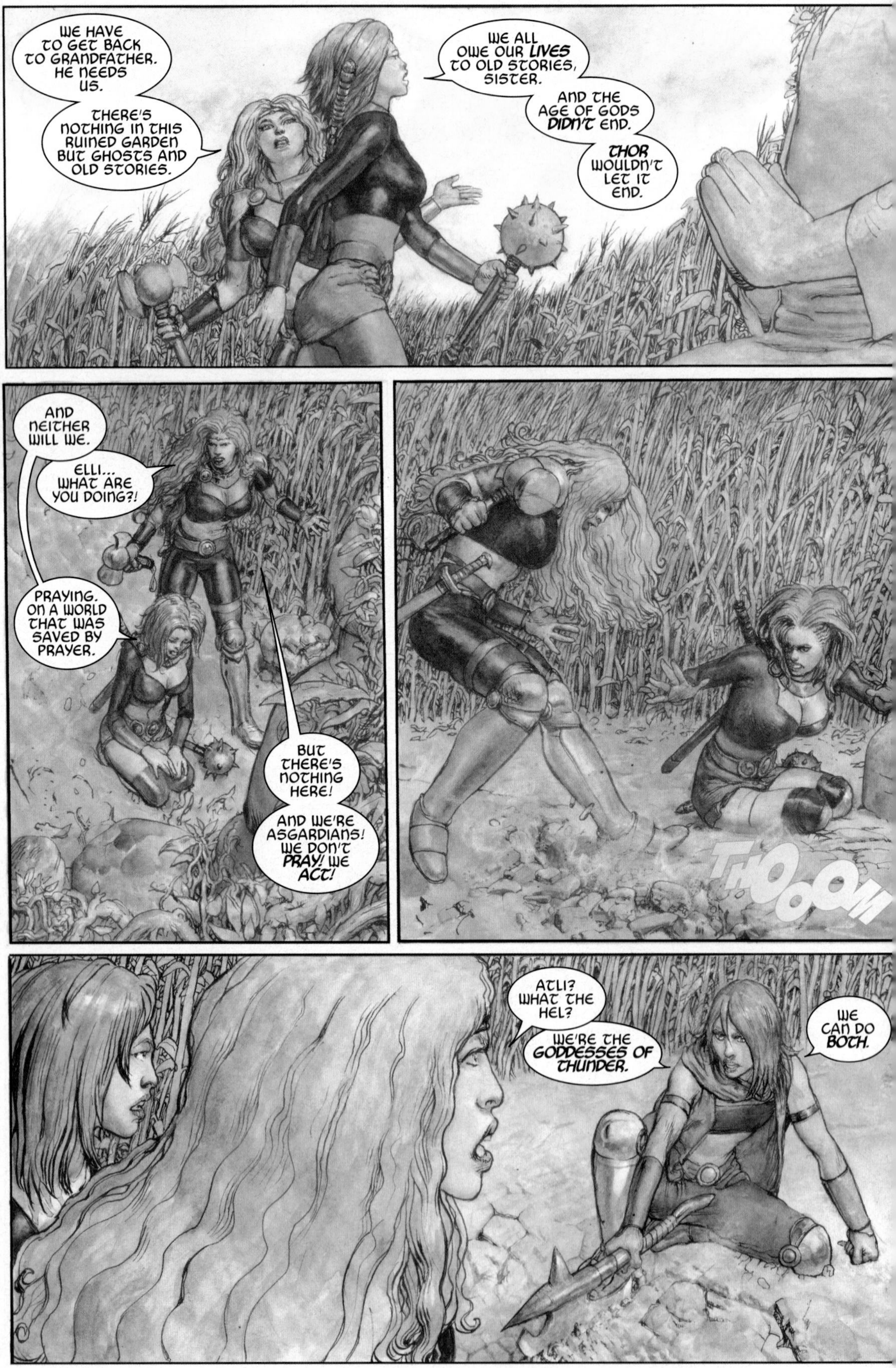
WE HAVE TO GET BACK TO GRANDFATHER. HE NEEDS US.
THERE'S NOTHING IN THIS RUINED GARDEN BUT GHOSTS AND OLD STORIES.
WE ALL OWE OUR LIVES TO OLD STORIES, SISTER.
AND THE AGE OF GODS DIDN'T END.
THOR WOULDN'T LET IT END.
AND NEITHER WILL WE.
ELLI... WHAT ARE YOU DOING?!
PRAYING. ON A WORLD THAT WAS SAVED BY PRAYER.
BUT THERE'S NOTHING HERE!
AND WE'RE ASGARDIANS! WE DON'T PRAY! WE ACT!
THOOOOM
ATLI? WHAT THE HEL?
WE'RE THE GODDESSES OF THUNDER.
WE CAN DO BOTH.

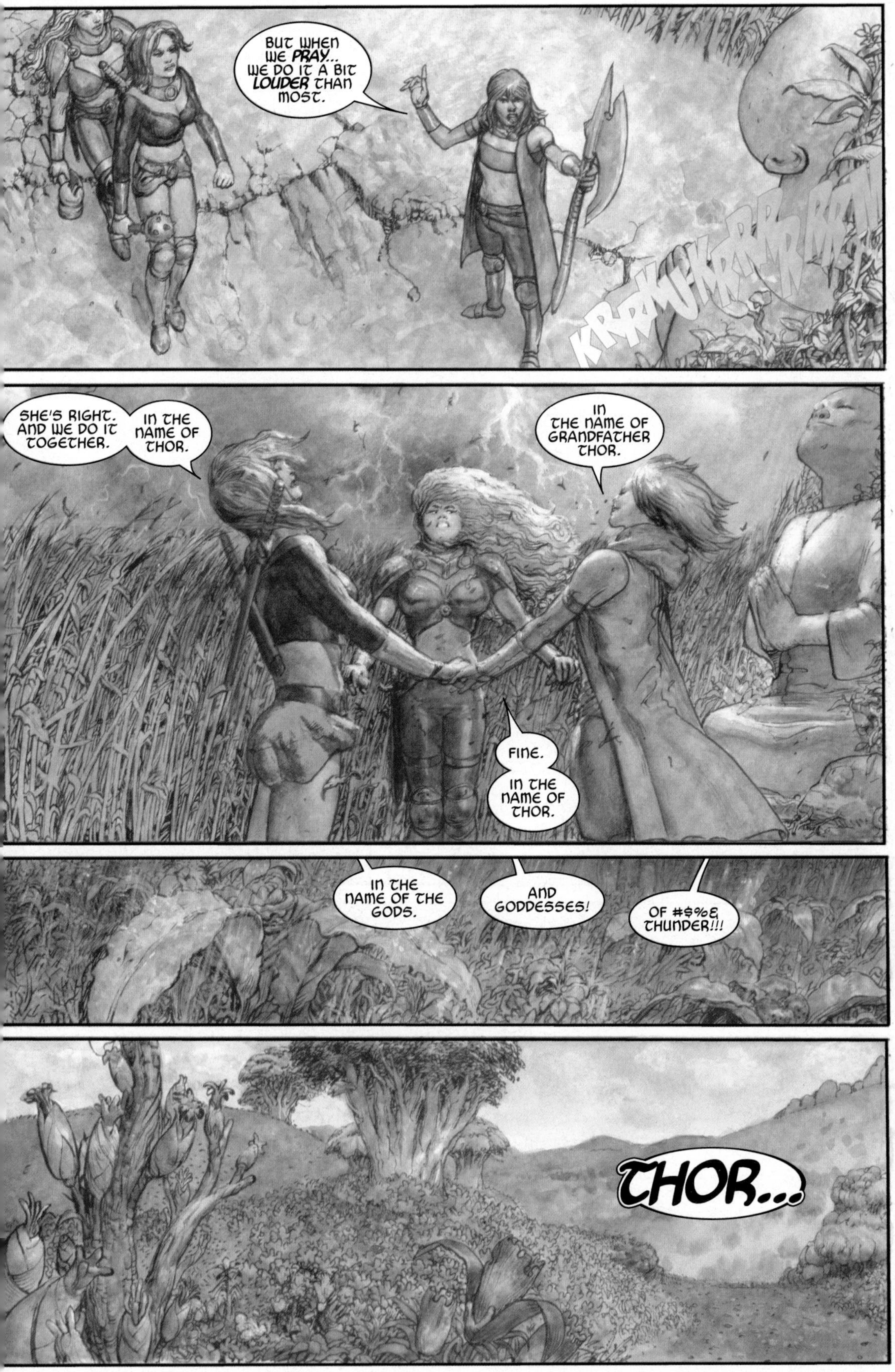

BUT WHEN WE PRAY... WE DO IT A BIT LOUDER THAN MOST.
KRRKKKRRRRRRRRRR
SHE'S RIGHT. AND WE DO IT TOGETHER.
IN THE NAME OF THOR.
IN THE NAME OF GRANDFATHER THOR.
FINE.
IN THE NAME OF THOR.
IN THE NAME OF THE GODS.
AND GODDESSES!
OF #$%& THUNDER!!!
THOR...

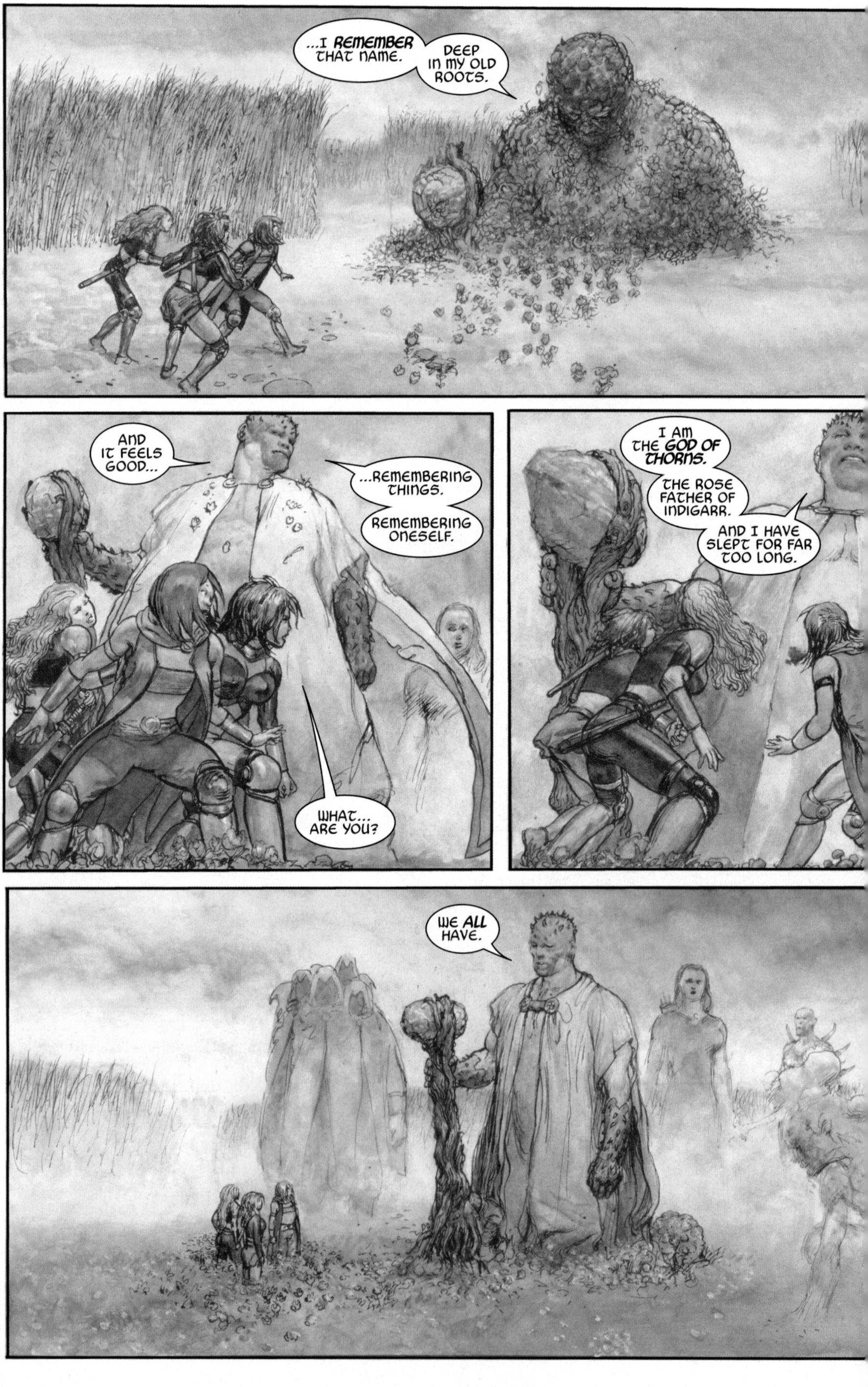
...I REMEMBER THAT NAME.
DEEP IN MY OLD ROOTS.
AND IT FEELS GOOD...
...REMEMBERING THINGS.
REMEMBERING ONESELF.
WHAT... ARE YOU?
I AM THE GOD OF THORNS.
THE ROSE FATHER OF INDIGARR.
AND I HAVE SLEPT FOR FAR TOO LONG.
WE ALL HAVE.

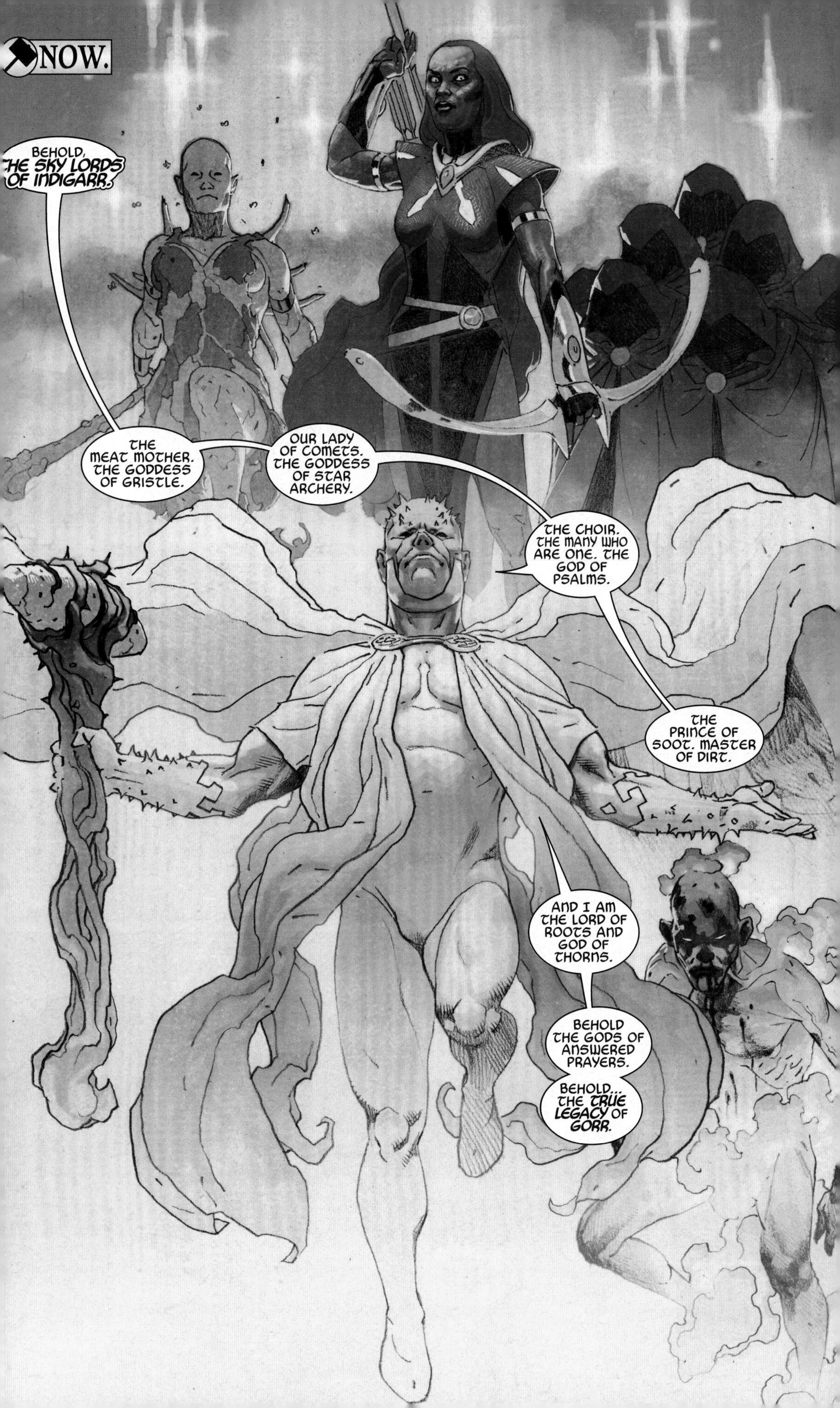
NOW.
BEHOLD, THE SKY LORDS OF INDIGARR.
THE MEAT MOTHER. THE GODDESS OF GRISTLE.
OUR LADY OF COMETS. THE GODDESS OF STAR ARCHERY.
THE CHOIR. THE MANY WHO ARE ONE. THE GOD OF PSALMS.
THE PRINCE OF SOOT. MASTER OF DIRT.
AND I AM THE LORD OF ROOTS AND GOD OF THORNS.
BEHOLD THE GODS OF ANSWERED PRAYERS.
BEHOLD... THE TRUE LEGACY OF GORR.

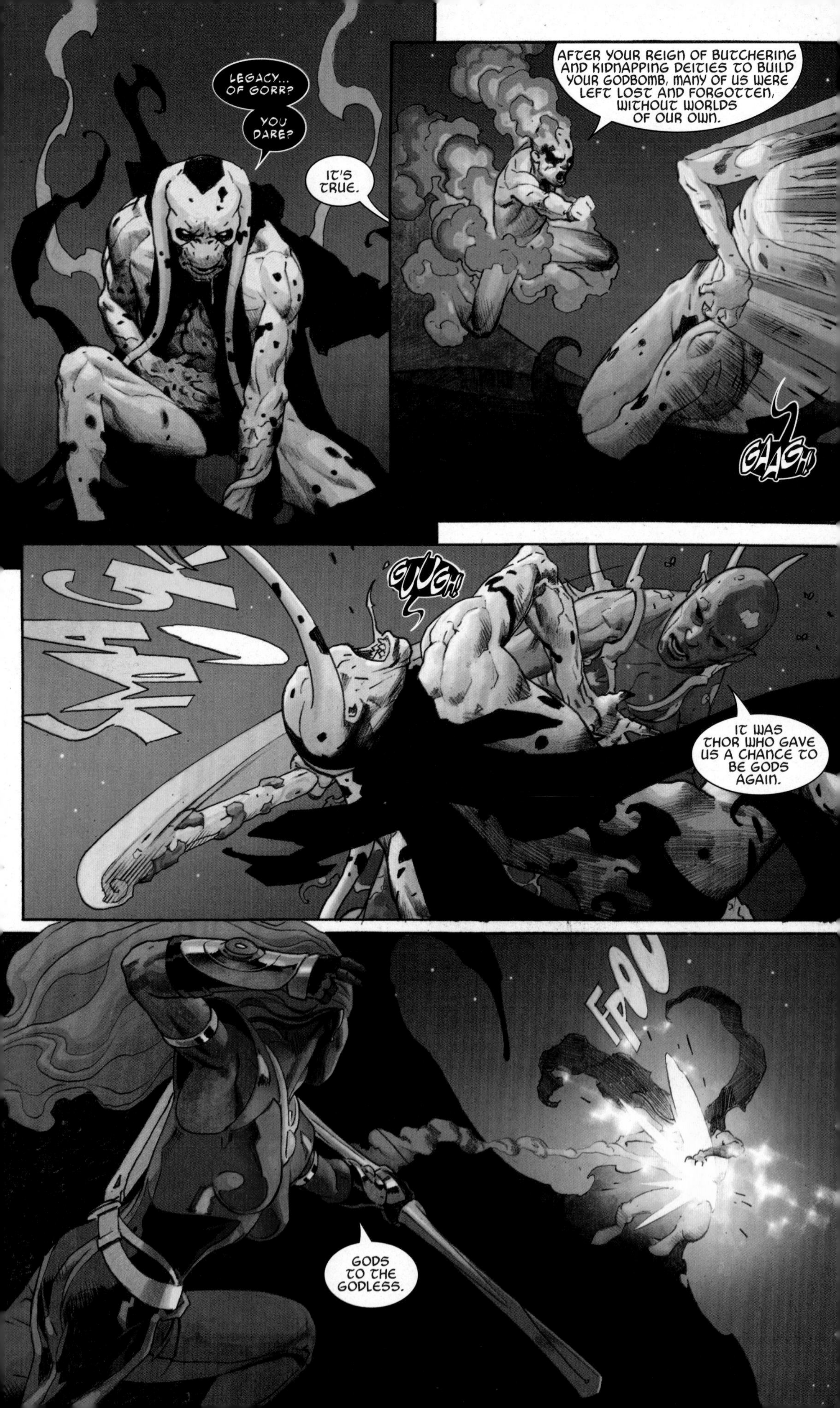
LEGACY... OF GORR?
YOU DARE?
IT'S TRUE.
AFTER YOUR REIGN OF BUTCHERING AND KIDNAPPING DEITIES TO BUILD YOUR GODBOMB, MANY OF US WERE LEFT LOST AND FORGOTTEN, WITHOUT WORLDS OF OUR OWN.
GAAGH!
GUUGH!
IT WAS THOR WHO GAVE US A CHANCE TO BE GODS AGAIN.
GODS TO THE GODLESS.

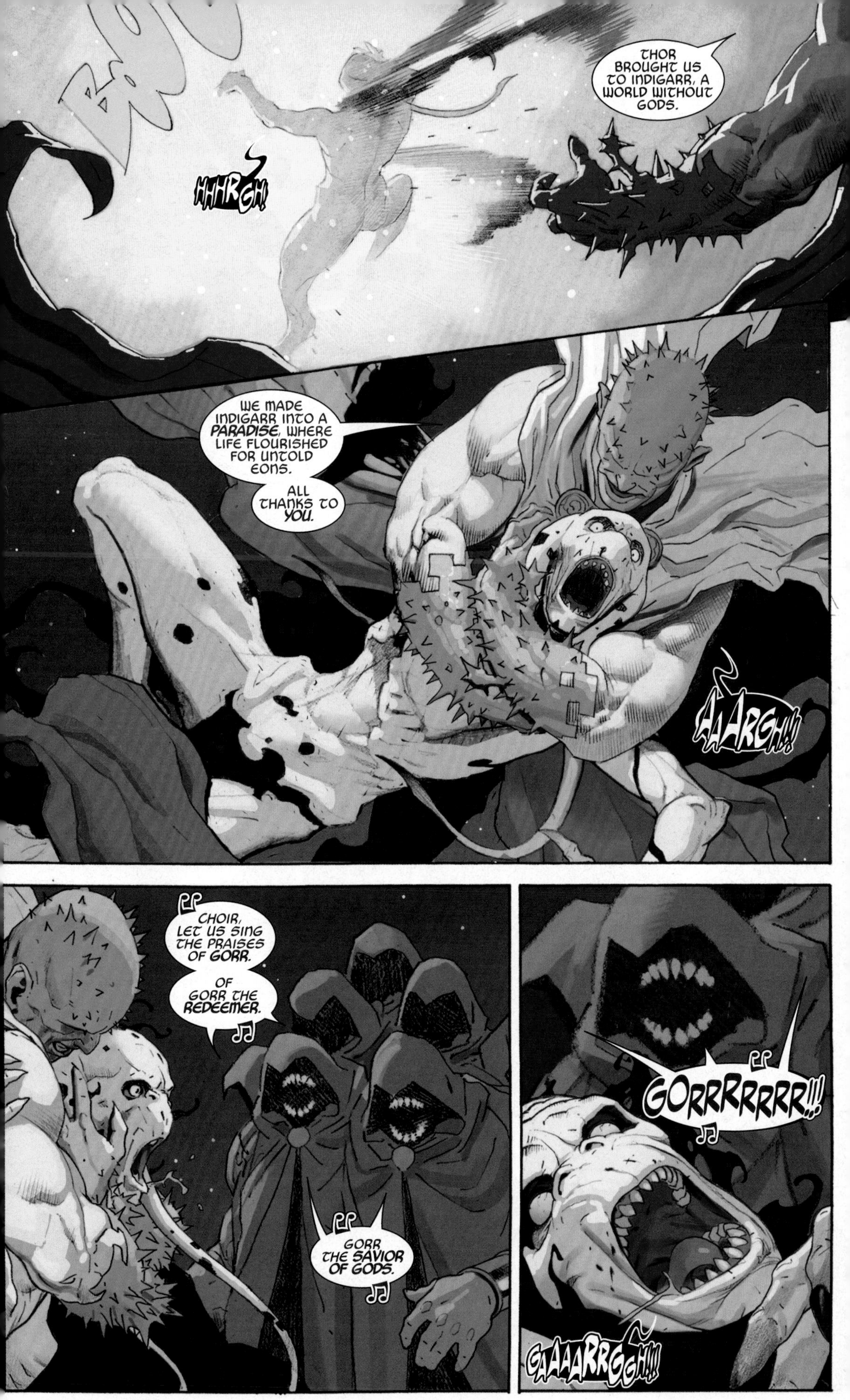
HHHRGH!
THOR BROUGHT US TO INDIGARR, A WORLD WITHOUT GODS.
WE MADE INDIGARR INTO A *PARADISE*, WHERE LIFE FLOURISHED FOR UNTOLD EONS.
ALL THANKS TO *YOU*.
AAARGH!!
CHOIR, LET US SING THE PRAISES OF **GORR**.
OF GORR THE **REDEEMER**.
GORR THE **SAVIOR** OF GODS.
GORRRRRRR!!!
GAAAARRGGH!!!

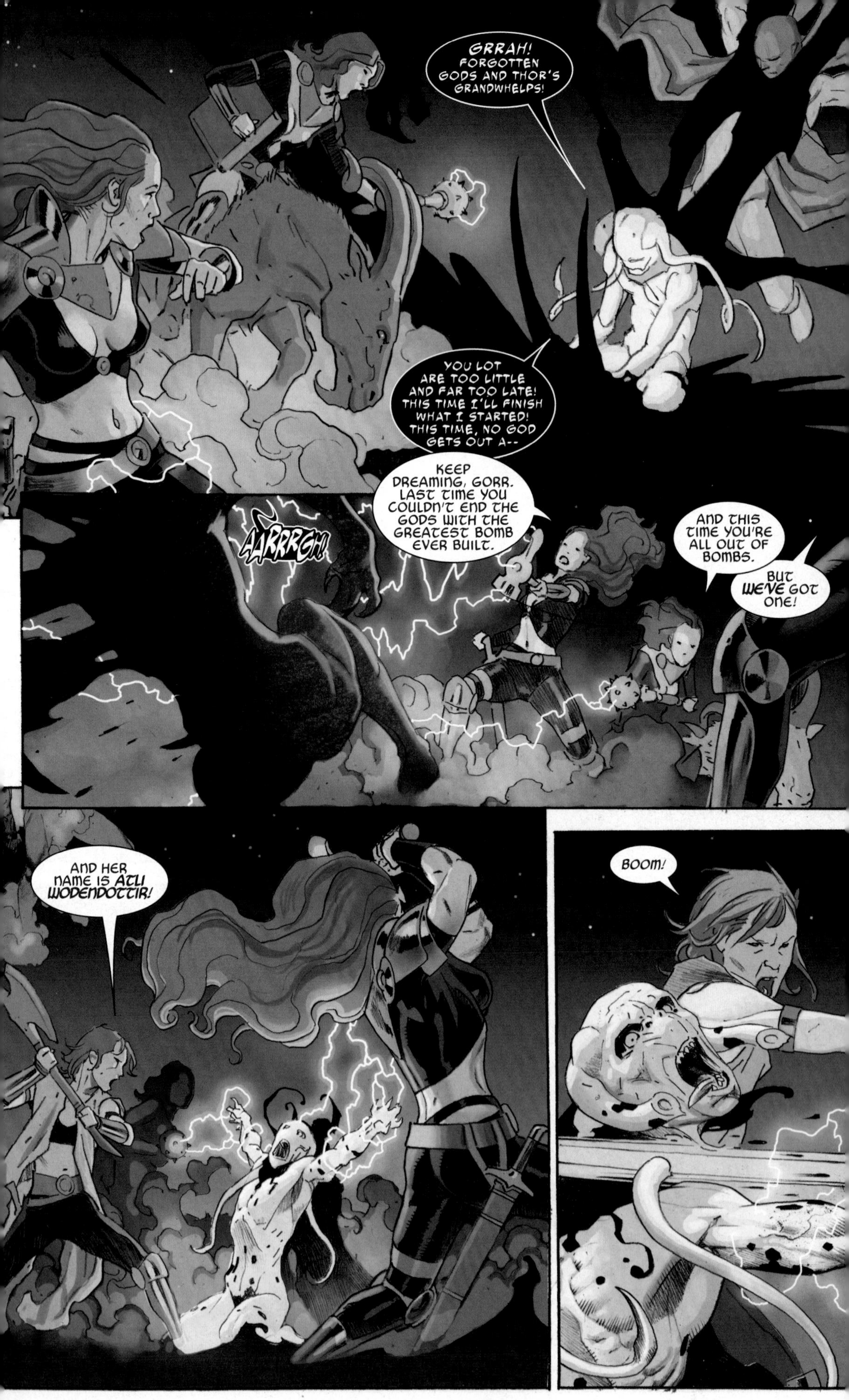

GRRAH! FORGOTTEN GODS AND THOR'S GRANDWHELPS!
YOU LOT ARE TOO LITTLE AND FAR TOO LATE! THIS TIME I'LL FINISH WHAT I STARTED! THIS TIME, NO GOD GETS OUT A--
AARRRGH!
KEEP DREAMING, GORR. LAST TIME YOU COULDN'T END THE GODS WITH THE GREATEST BOMB EVER BUILT.
AND THIS TIME YOU'RE ALL OUT OF BOMBS.
BUT WE'VE GOT ONE!
AND HER NAME IS ATLI WODENDOTTIR!
BOOM!

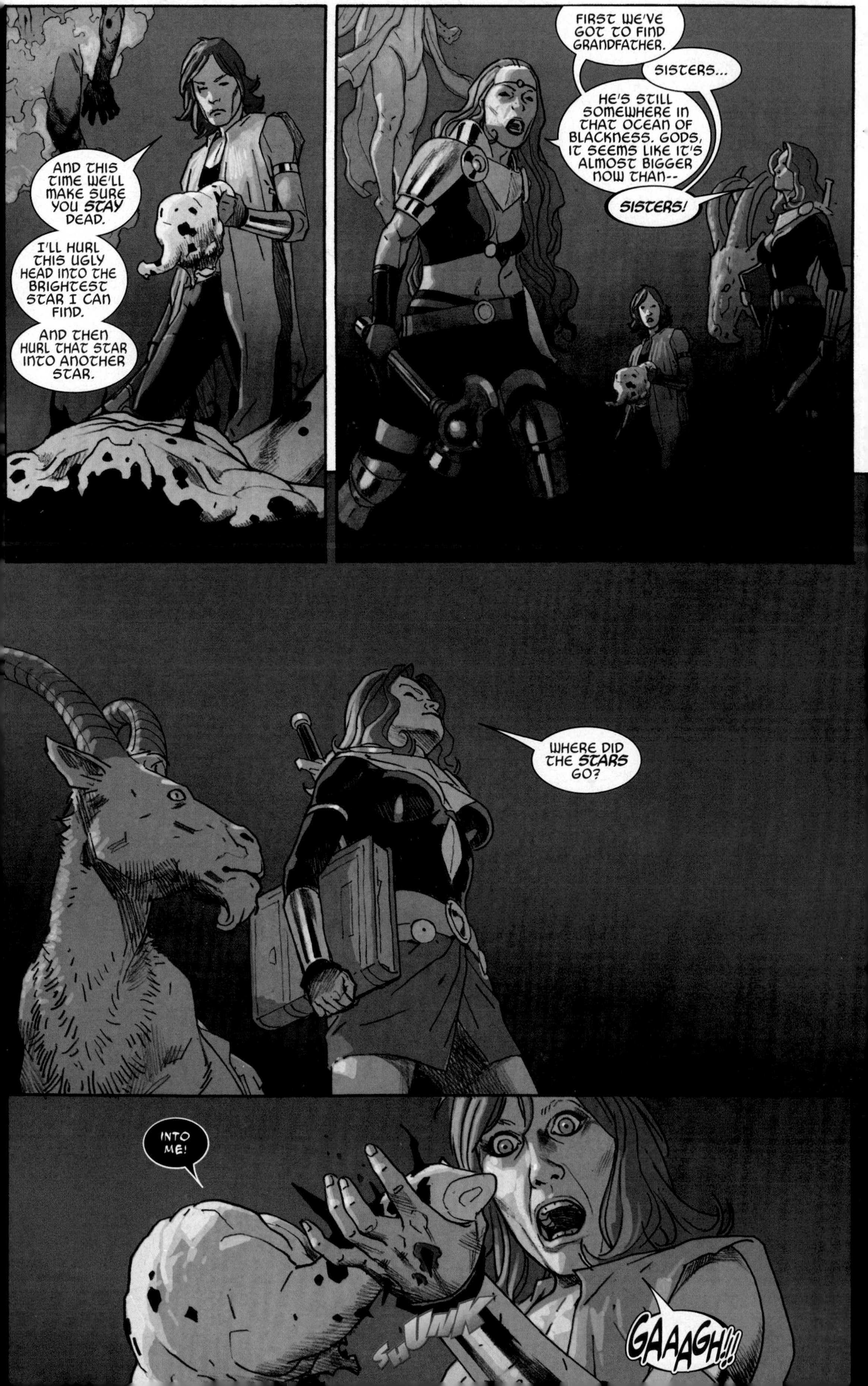
AND THIS TIME WE'LL MAKE SURE YOU STAY DEAD.
I'LL HURL THIS UGLY HEAD INTO THE BRIGHTEST STAR I CAN FIND.
AND THEN HURL THAT STAR INTO ANOTHER STAR.
FIRST WE'VE GOT TO FIND GRANDFATHER.
SISTERS...
HE'S STILL SOMEWHERE IN THAT OCEAN OF BLACKNESS. GODS, IT SEEMS LIKE IT'S ALMOST BIGGER NOW THAN--
SISTERS!
WHERE DID THE STARS GO?
INTO ME!
SHUNK
GAAAGH!!!

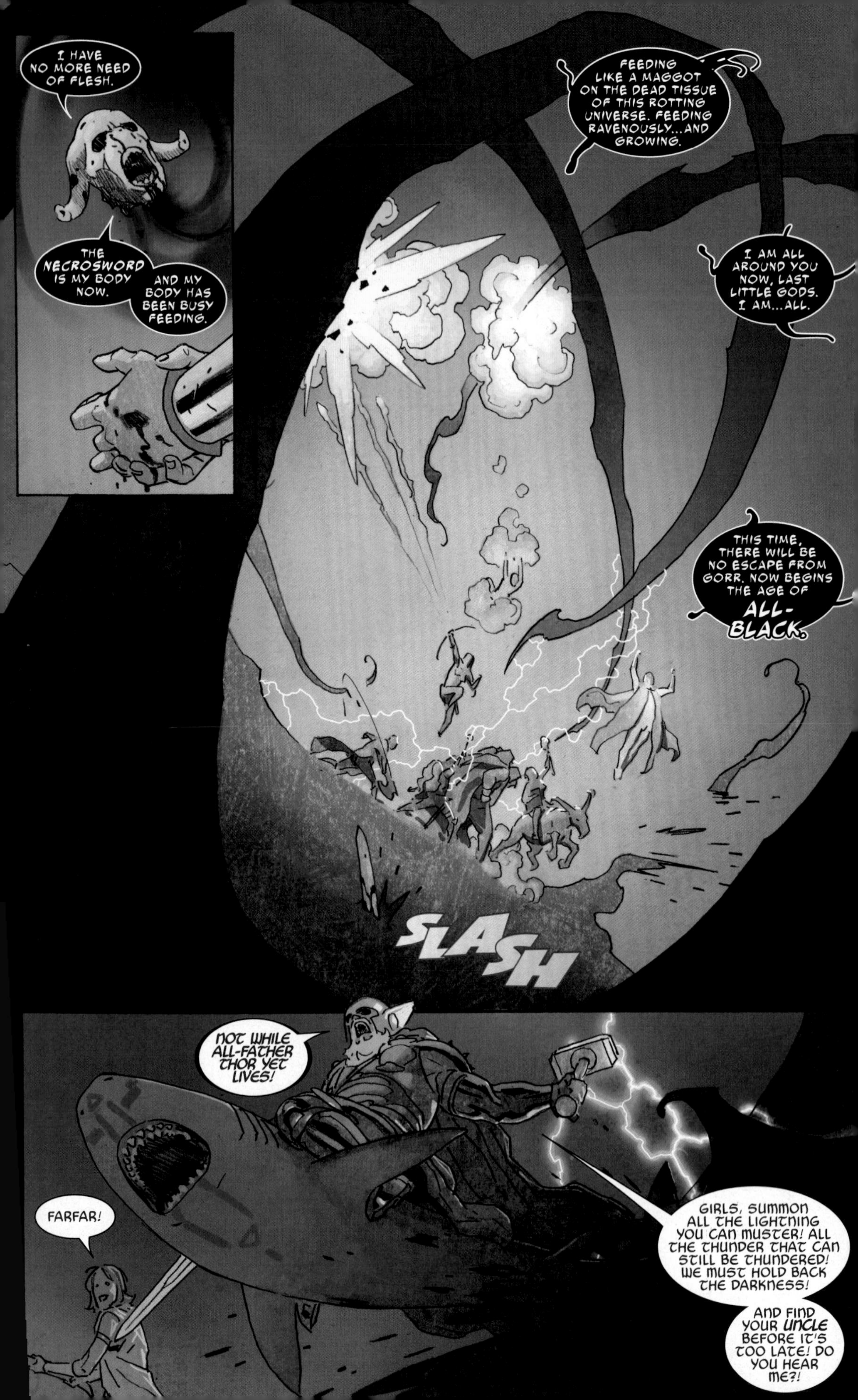
I HAVE NO MORE NEED OF FLESH.
THE NECROSWORD IS MY BODY NOW.
AND MY BODY HAS BEEN BUSY FEEDING.
FEEDING LIKE A MAGGOT ON THE DEAD TISSUE OF THIS ROTTING UNIVERSE. FEEDING RAVENOUSLY...AND GROWING.
I AM ALL AROUND YOU NOW, LAST LITTLE GODS. I AM...ALL.
THIS TIME, THERE WILL BE NO ESCAPE FROM GORR. NOW BEGINS THE AGE OF ALL-BLACK.
SLASH
NOT WHILE ALL-FATHER THOR YET LIVES!
FARFAR!
GIRLS, SUMMON ALL THE LIGHTNING YOU CAN MUSTER! ALL THE THUNDER THAT CAN STILL BE THUNDERED! WE MUST HOLD BACK THE DARKNESS!
AND FIND YOUR UNCLE BEFORE IT'S TOO LATE! DO YOU HEAR ME?!

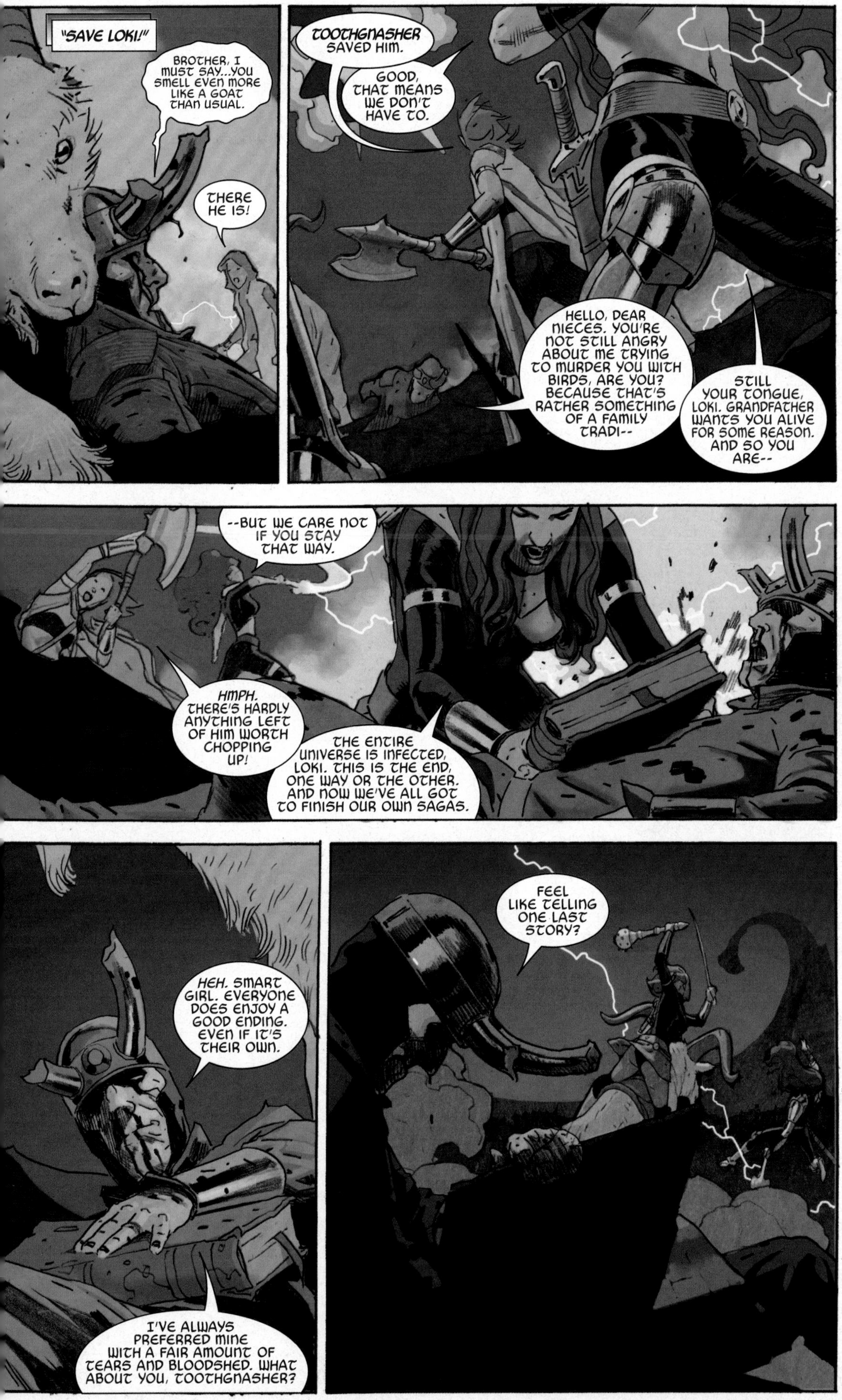
"SAVE LOKI!"
BROTHER, I MUST SAY...YOU SMELL EVEN MORE LIKE A GOAT THAN USUAL.
THERE HE IS!
TOOTHGNASHER SAVED HIM.
GOOD, THAT MEANS WE DON'T HAVE TO.
HELLO, DEAR NIECES. YOU'RE NOT STILL ANGRY ABOUT ME TRYING TO MURDER YOU WITH BIRDS, ARE YOU? BECAUSE THAT'S RATHER SOMETHING OF A FAMILY TRADI--
STILL YOUR TONGUE, LOKI. GRANDFATHER WANTS YOU ALIVE FOR SOME REASON. AND SO YOU ARE--
--BUT WE CARE NOT IF YOU STAY THAT WAY.
HMPH. THERE'S HARDLY ANYTHING LEFT OF HIM WORTH CHOPPING UP!
THE ENTIRE UNIVERSE IS INFECTED, LOKI. THIS IS THE END, ONE WAY OR THE OTHER. AND NOW WE'VE ALL GOT TO FINISH OUR OWN SAGAS.
HEH. SMART GIRL. EVERYONE DOES ENJOY A GOOD ENDING. EVEN IF IT'S THEIR OWN.
I'VE ALWAYS PREFERRED MINE WITH A FAIR AMOUNT OF TEARS AND BLOODSHED. WHAT ABOUT YOU, TOOTHGNASHER?
FEEL LIKE TELLING ONE LAST STORY?

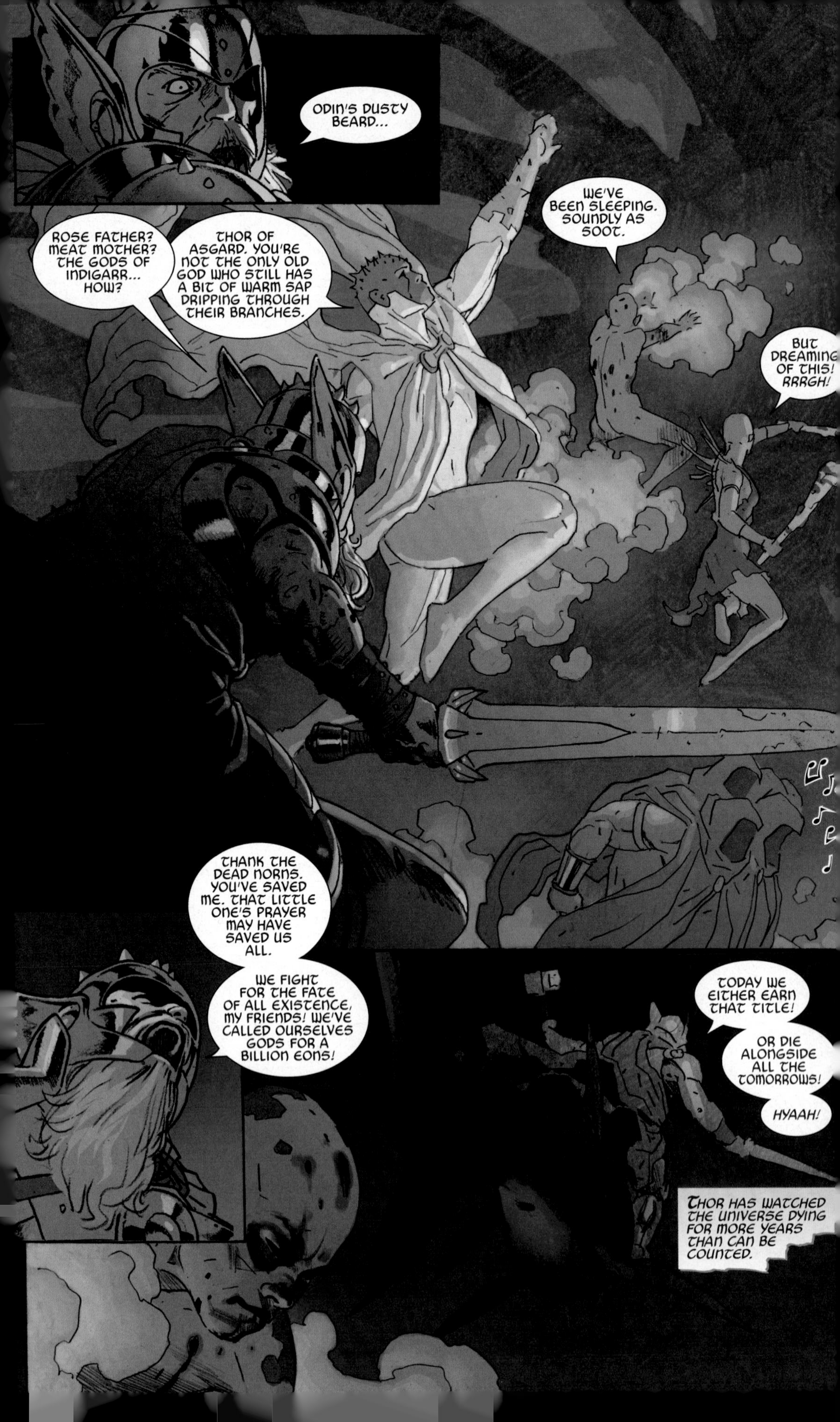
ODIN'S DUSTY BEARD...
ROSE FATHER? MEAT MOTHER? THE GODS OF INDIGARR... HOW?
THOR OF ASGARD. YOU'RE NOT THE ONLY OLD GOD WHO STILL HAS A BIT OF WARM SAP DRIPPING THROUGH THEIR BRANCHES.
WE'VE BEEN SLEEPING. SOUNDLY AS SOOT.
BUT DREAMING OF THIS! RRRGH!
THANK THE DEAD NORNS. YOU'VE SAVED ME. THAT LITTLE ONE'S PRAYER MAY HAVE SAVED US ALL.
WE FIGHT FOR THE FATE OF ALL EXISTENCE, MY FRIENDS! WE'VE CALLED OURSELVES GODS FOR A BILLION EONS!
TODAY WE EITHER EARN THAT TITLE!
OR DIE ALONGSIDE ALL THE TOMORROWS!
HYAAH!
THOR HAS WATCHED THE UNIVERSE DYING FOR MORE YEARS THAN CAN BE COUNTED.

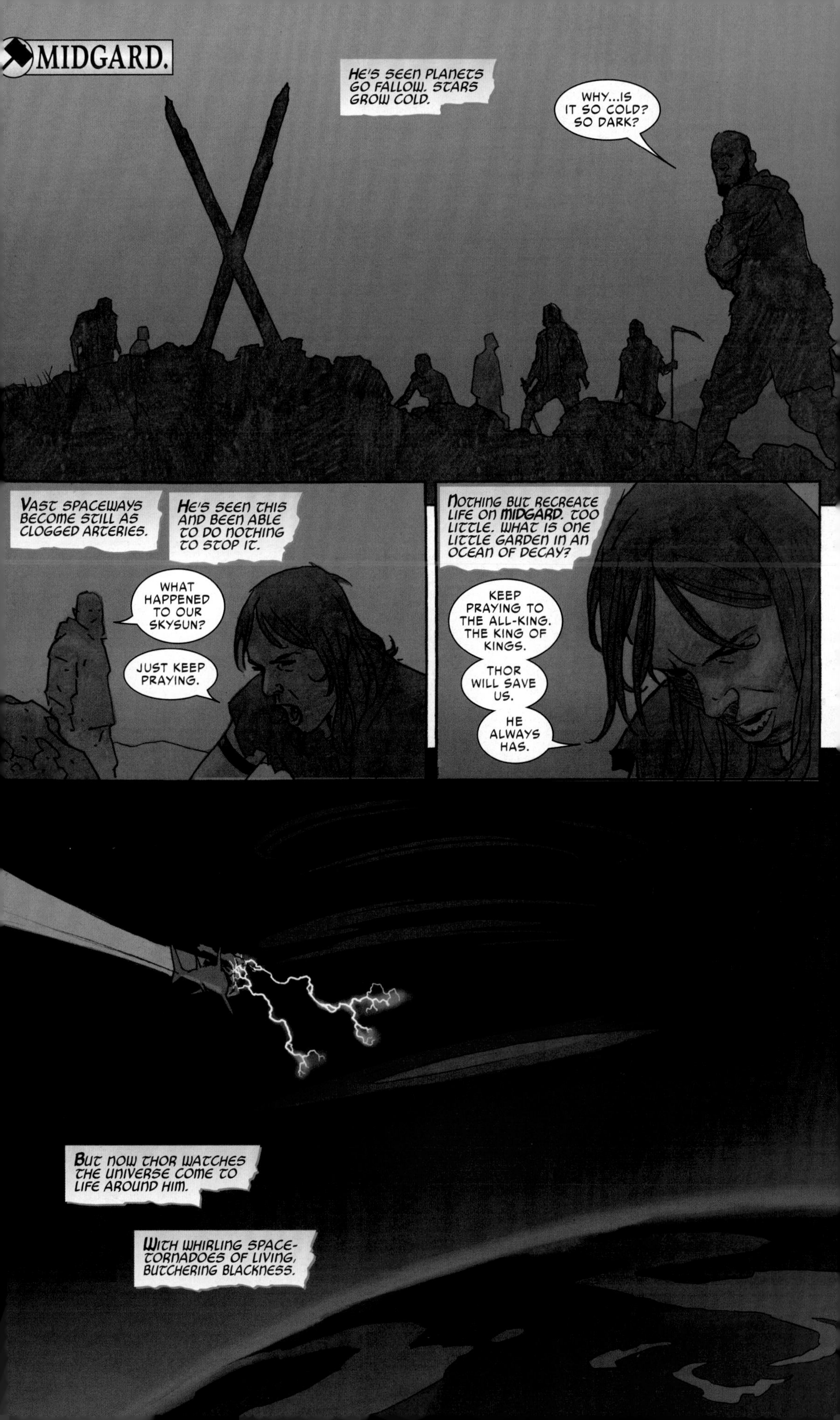
MIDGARD.
HE'S SEEN PLANETS GO FALLOW. STARS GROW COLD.
WHY...IS IT SO COLD? SO DARK?
VAST SPACEWAYS BECOME STILL AS CLOGGED ARTERIES.
HE'S SEEN THIS AND BEEN ABLE TO DO NOTHING TO STOP IT.
WHAT HAPPENED TO OUR SKYSUN?
JUST KEEP PRAYING.
NOTHING BUT RECREATE LIFE ON MIDGARD. TOO LITTLE. WHAT IS ONE LITTLE GARDEN IN AN OCEAN OF DECAY?
KEEP PRAYING TO THE ALL-KING. THE KING OF KINGS.
THOR WILL SAVE US.
HE ALWAYS HAS.
BUT NOW THOR WATCHES THE UNIVERSE COME TO LIFE AROUND HIM.
WITH WHIRLING SPACE-TORNADOES OF LIVING, BUTCHERING BLACKNESS.

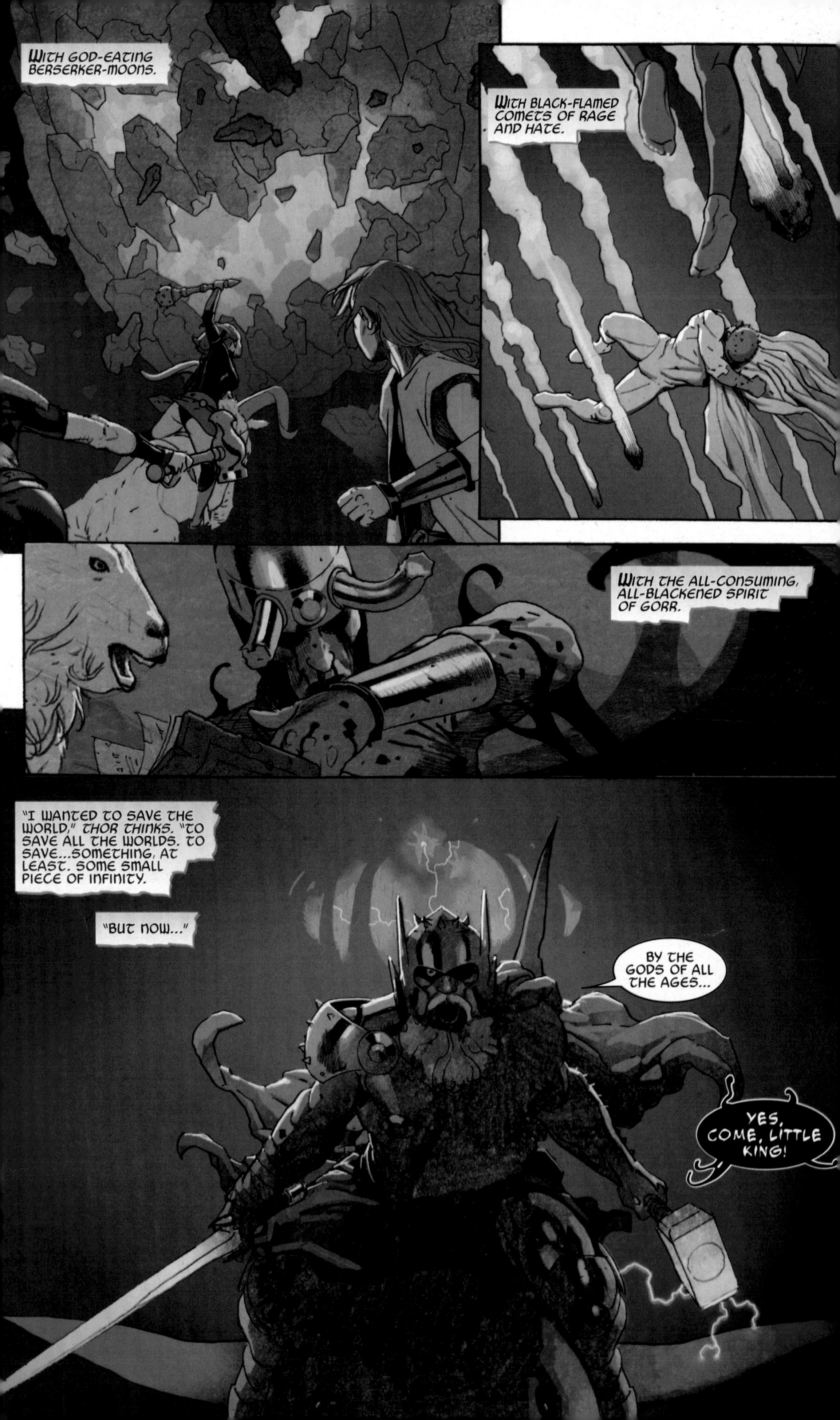

WITH GOD-EATING BERSERKER-MOONS.
WITH BLACK-FLAMED COMETS OF RAGE AND HATE.
WITH THE ALL-CONSUMING, ALL-BLACKENED SPIRIT OF GORR.
"I WANTED TO SAVE THE WORLD," THOR THINKS. "TO SAVE ALL THE WORLDS. TO SAVE...SOMETHING, AT LEAST. SOME SMALL PIECE OF INFINITY.
"BUT NOW..."
BY THE GODS OF ALL THE AGES...
YES, COME, LITTLE KING!

"...NOW I HAVE TO KILL IT," THINKS THE LAST KING OF THE GODS.
"I HAVE TO KILL IT ALL."
WELCOME TO ALL-BLACK THE NECRO-VERSE!

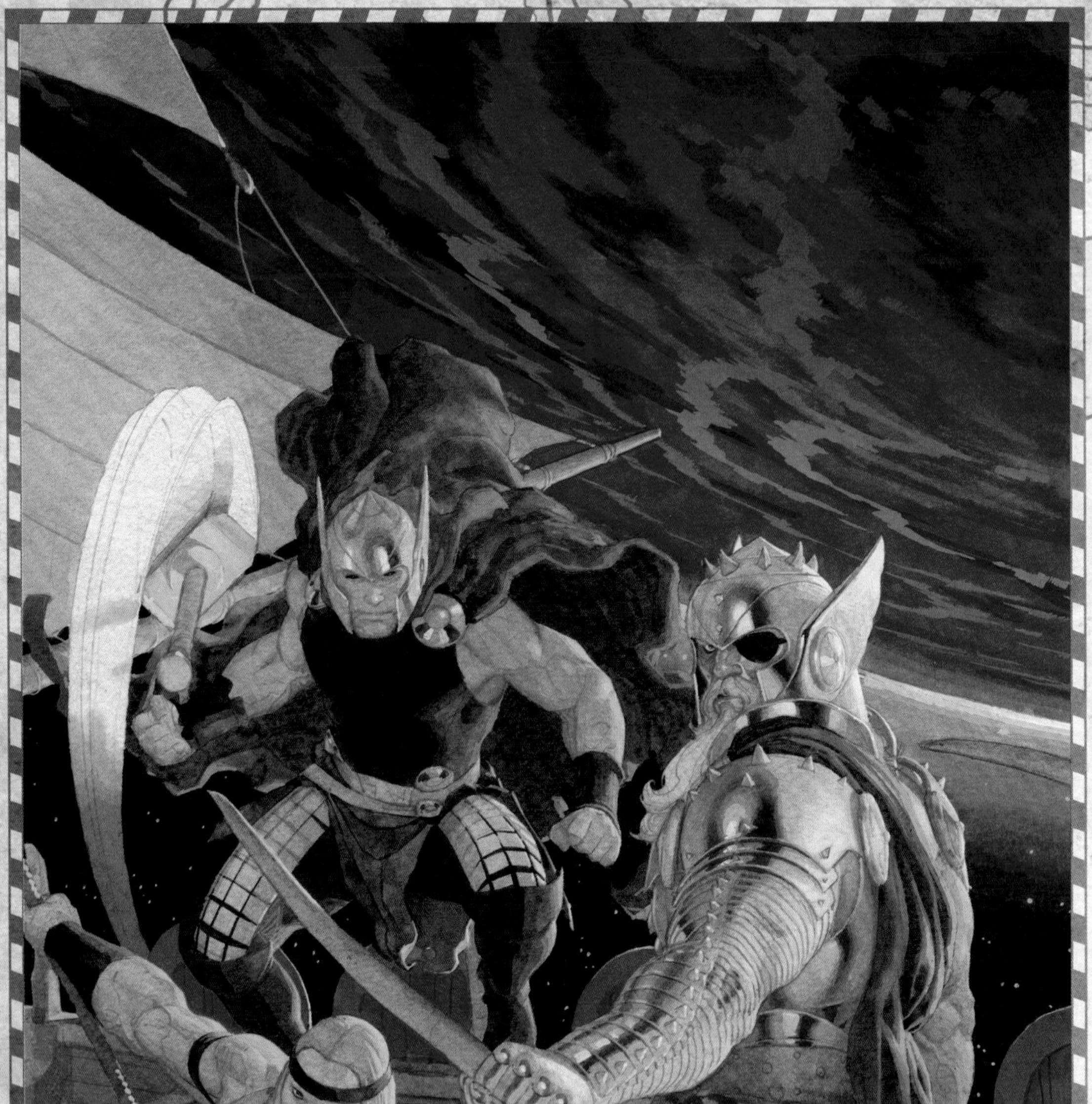

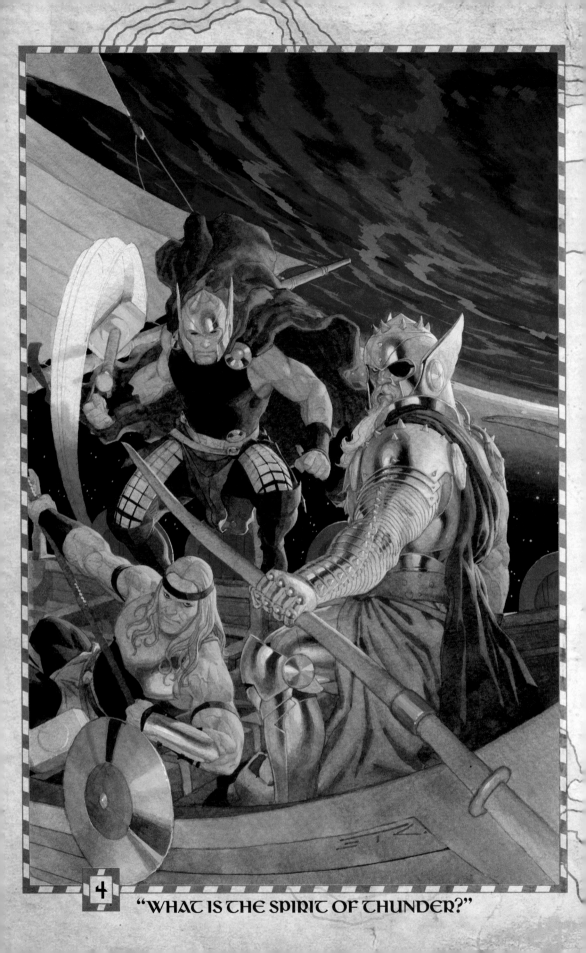

4

"WHAT IS THE SPIRIT OF THUNDER?"

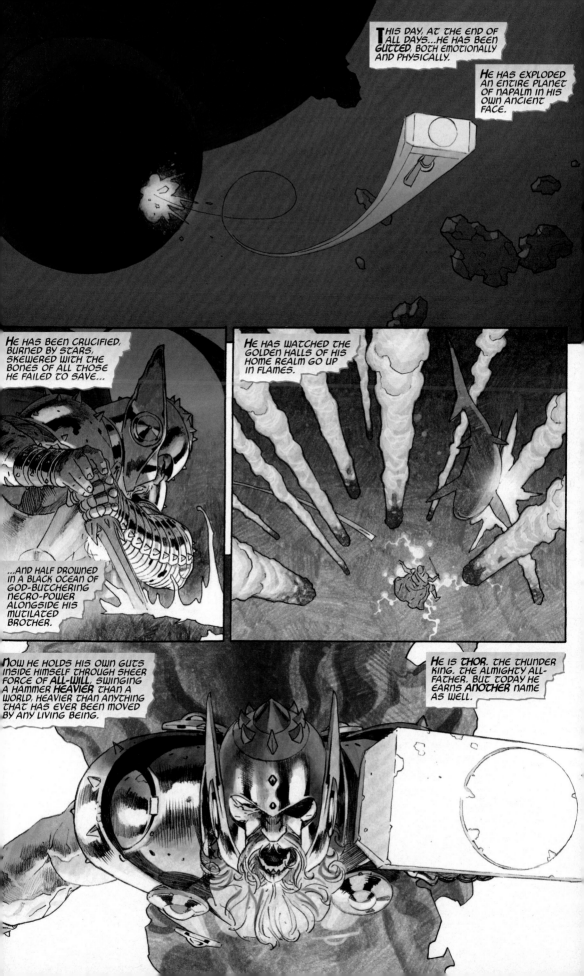

THIS DAY, AT THE END OF ALL DAYS...HE HAS BEEN **GUTTED**, BOTH EMOTIONALLY AND PHYSICALLY.

HE HAS EXPLODED AN ENTIRE PLANET OF NAPALM IN HIS OWN ANCIENT FACE.

HE HAS BEEN CRUCIFIED, BURNED BY STARS, SKEWERED WITH THE BONES OF ALL THOSE HE FAILED TO SAVE...

HE HAS WATCHED THE GOLDEN HALLS OF HIS HOME REALM GO UP IN FLAMES.

...AND HALF DROWNED IN A BLACK OCEAN OF GOD-BUTCHERING NECRO-POWER ALONGSIDE HIS MUTILATED BROTHER.

NOW HE HOLDS HIS OWN GUTS INSIDE HIMSELF THROUGH SHEER FORCE OF **ALL-WILL**, SWINGING A HAMMER **HEAVIER** THAN A WORLD, HEAVIER THAN ANYTHING THAT HAS EVER BEEN MOVED BY ANY LIVING BEING.

HE IS **THOR**. THE THUNDER KING. THE ALMIGHTY ALL-FATHER. BUT TODAY HE EARNS **ANOTHER** NAME AS WELL.

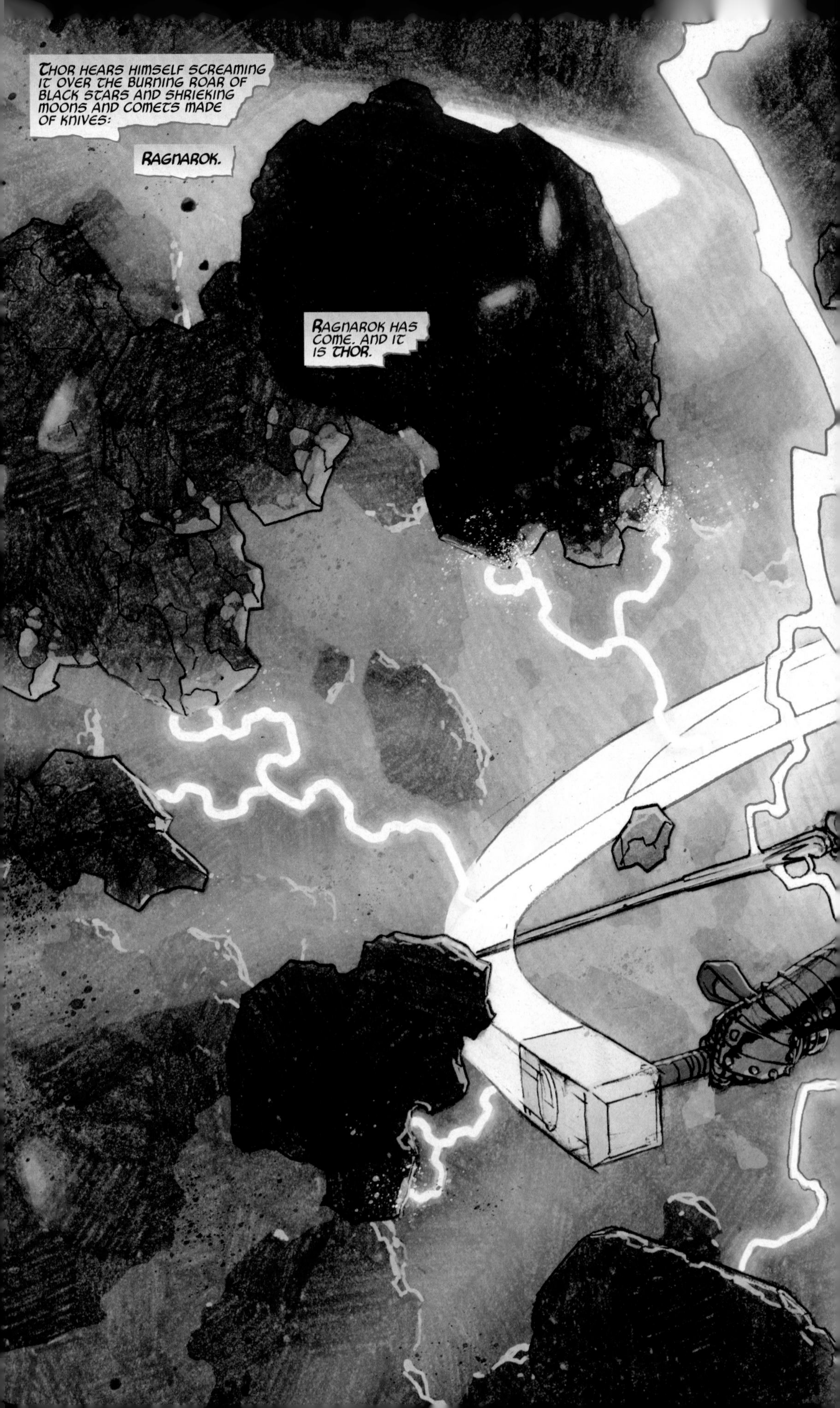
THOR HEARS HIMSELF SCREAMING IT OVER THE BURNING ROAR OF BLACK STARS AND SHRIEKING MOONS AND COMETS MADE OF KNIVES:
RAGNAROK.
RAGNAROK HAS COME. AND IT IS THOR.

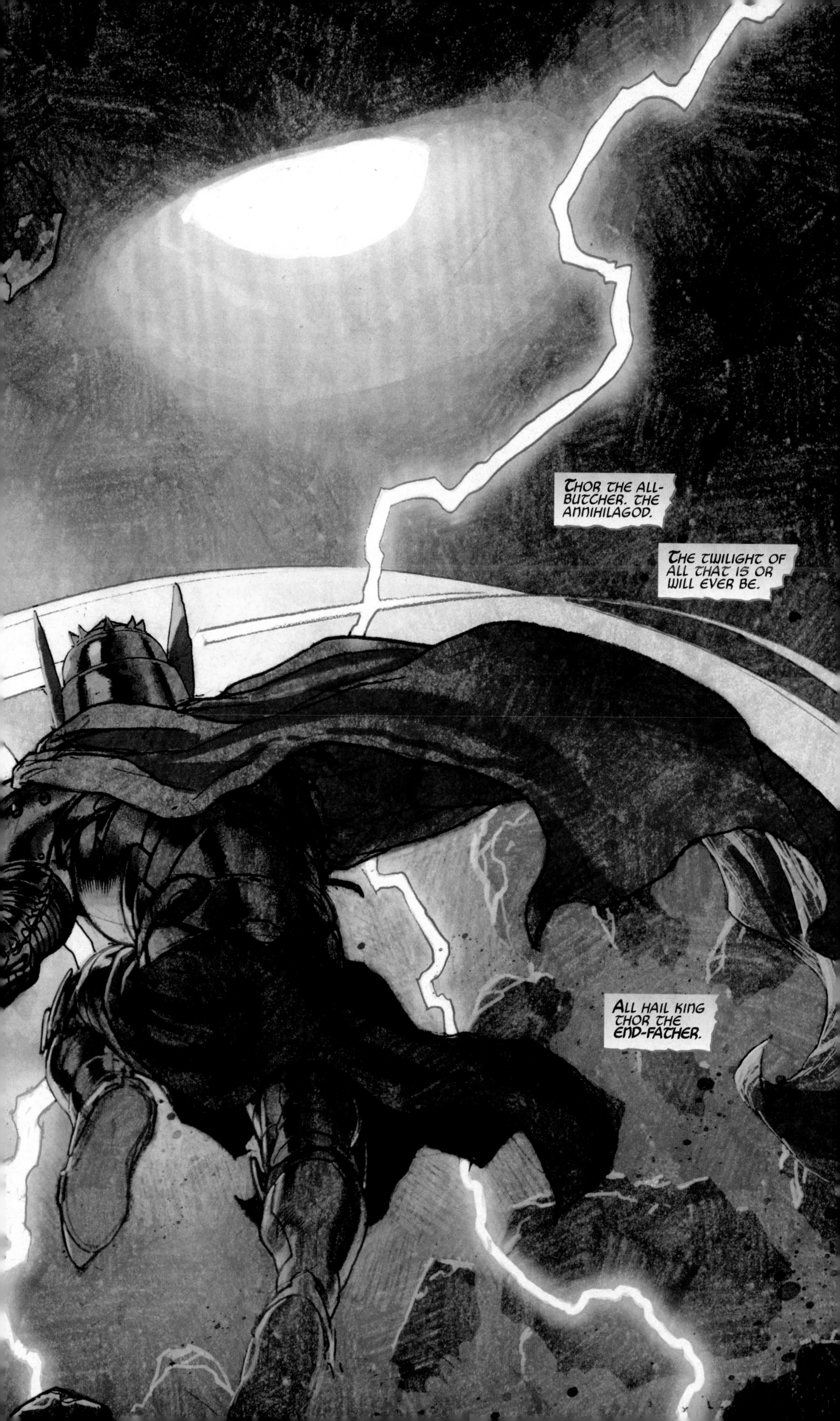
THOR THE ALL-BUTCHER. THE ANNIHILAGOD.
THE TWILIGHT OF ALL THAT IS OR WILL EVER BE.
ALL HAIL KING THOR THE END-FATHER.

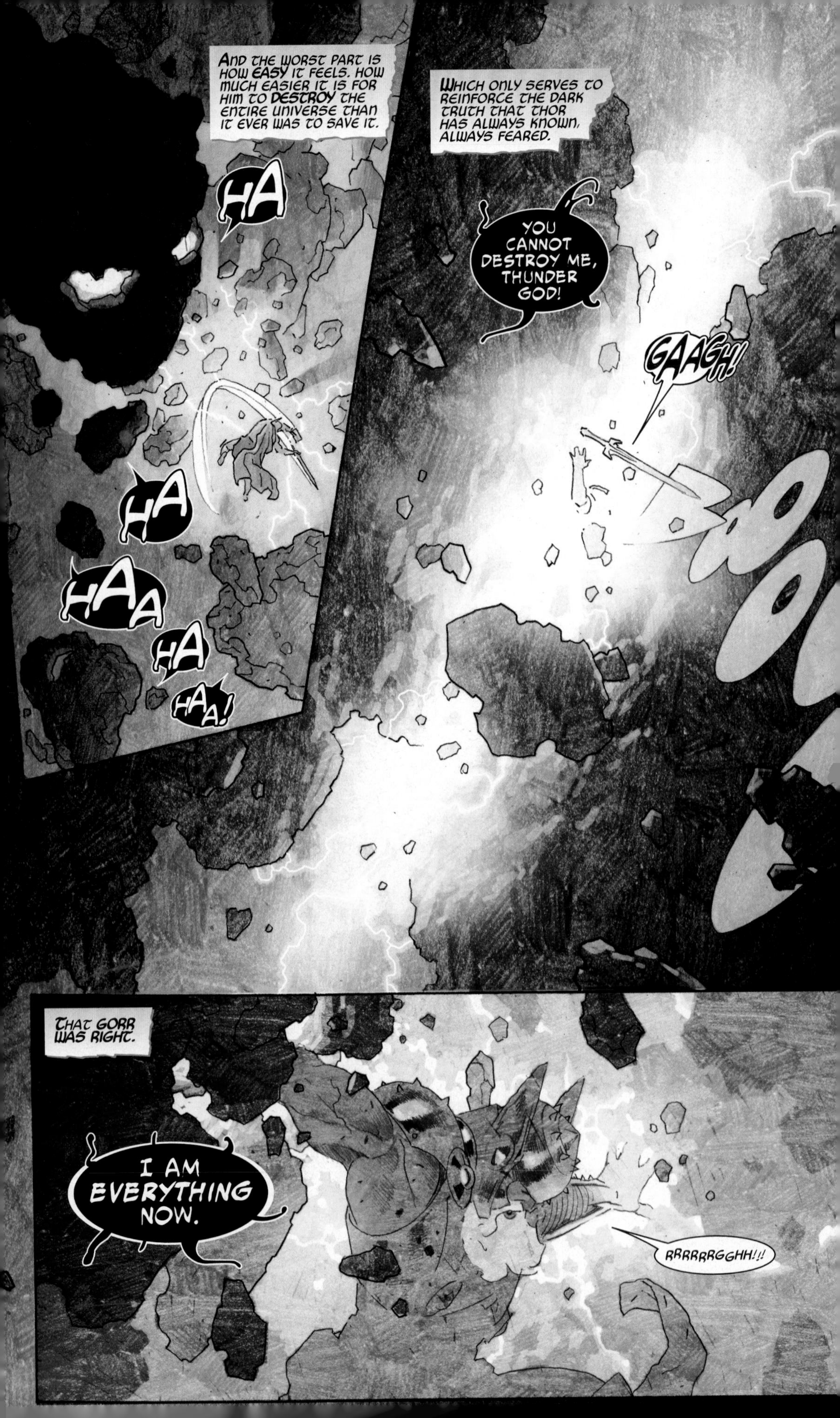
And the worst part is how EASY it feels. How much easier it is for him to DESTROY the entire universe than it ever was to save it.
HA
HA
HAA
HA
HAA!
Which only serves to reinforce the dark truth that Thor has always known, always feared.
YOU CANNOT DESTROY ME, THUNDER GOD!
GAAGH!
That Gorr was right.
I AM EVERYTHING NOW.
RRRRRRGGHH!!!

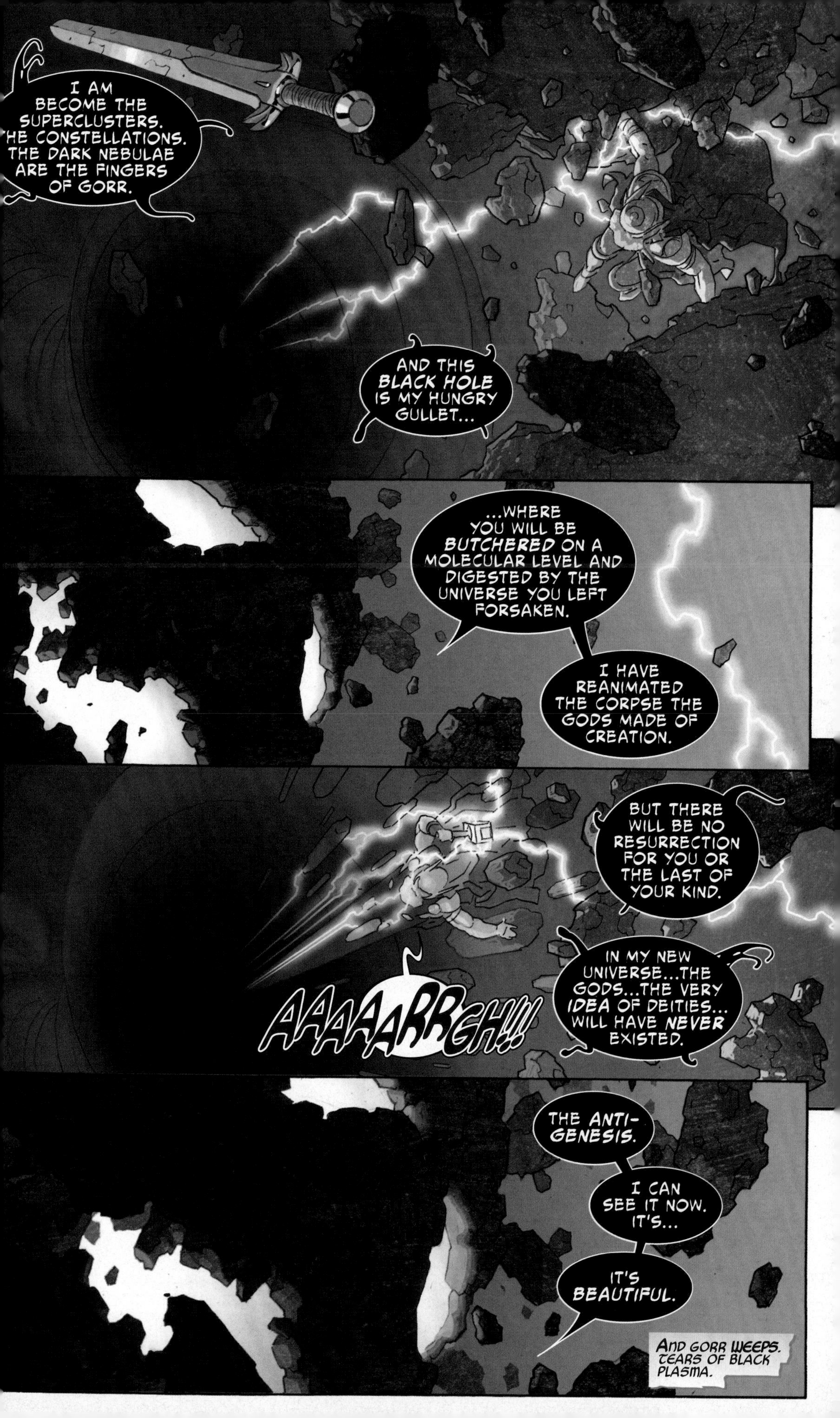

I AM BECOME THE SUPERCLUSTERS. THE CONSTELLATIONS. THE DARK NEBULAE ARE THE FINGERS OF GORR.
AND THIS BLACK HOLE IS MY HUNGRY GULLET...
...WHERE YOU WILL BE BUTCHERED ON A MOLECULAR LEVEL AND DIGESTED BY THE UNIVERSE YOU LEFT FORSAKEN.
I HAVE REANIMATED THE CORPSE THE GODS MADE OF CREATION.
BUT THERE WILL BE NO RESURRECTION FOR YOU OR THE LAST OF YOUR KIND.
AAAAARRGH!!
IN MY NEW UNIVERSE...THE GODS...THE VERY IDEA OF DEITIES... WILL HAVE NEVER EXISTED.
THE ANTI-GENESIS.
I CAN SEE IT NOW. IT'S...
IT'S BEAUTIFUL.
AND GORR WEEPS. TEARS OF BLACK PLASMA.

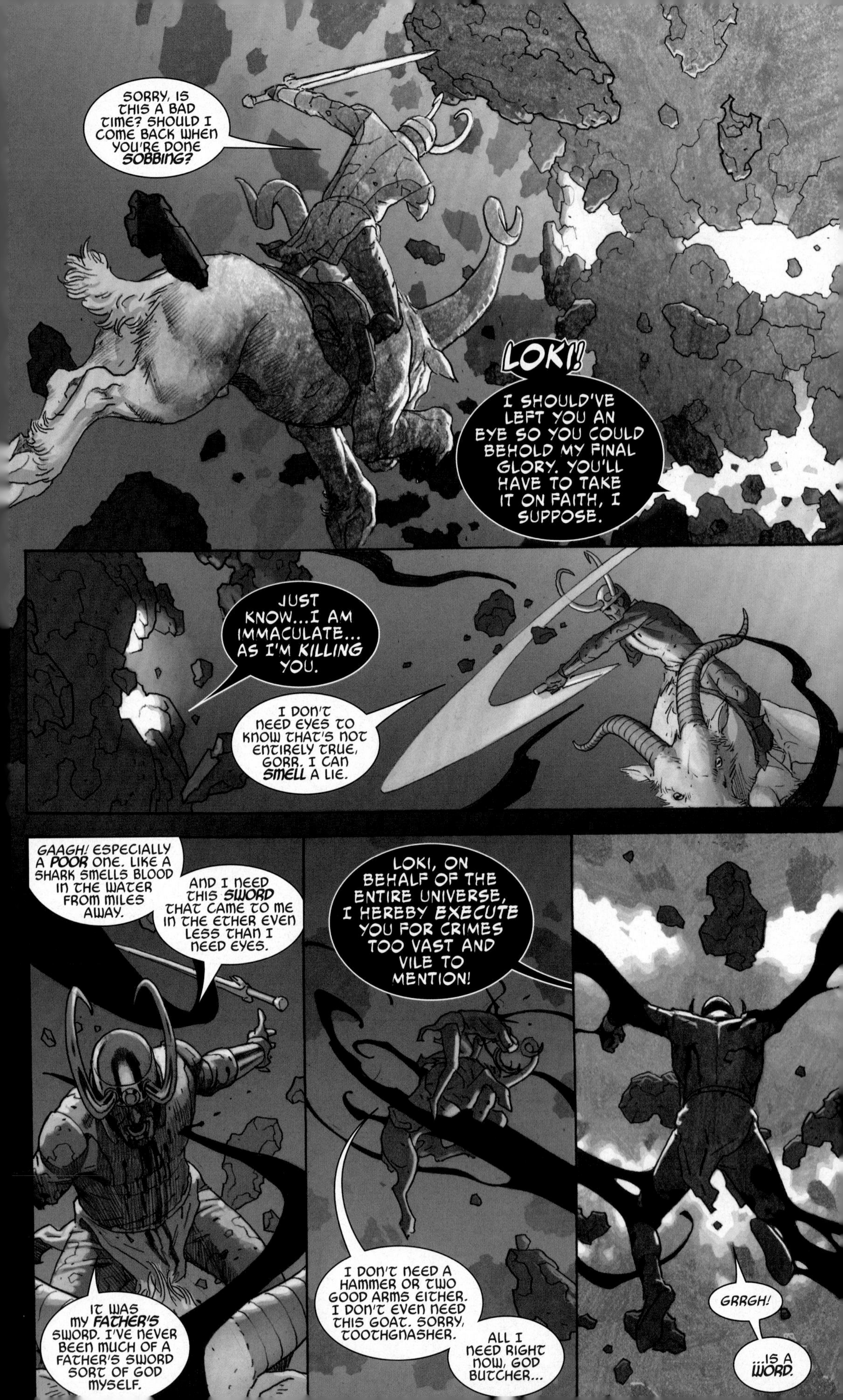

SORRY, IS THIS A BAD TIME? SHOULD I COME BACK WHEN YOU'RE DONE SOBBING?
LOKI!
I SHOULD'VE LEFT YOU AN EYE SO YOU COULD BEHOLD MY FINAL GLORY. YOU'LL HAVE TO TAKE IT ON FAITH, I SUPPOSE.
JUST KNOW...I AM IMMACULATE... AS I'M KILLING YOU.
I DON'T NEED EYES TO KNOW THAT'S NOT ENTIRELY TRUE, GORR. I CAN SMELL A LIE.
GAAGH! ESPECIALLY A POOR ONE. LIKE A SHARK SMELLS BLOOD IN THE WATER FROM MILES AWAY.
AND I NEED THIS SWORD THAT CAME TO ME IN THE ETHER EVEN LESS THAN I NEED EYES.
IT WAS MY FATHER'S SWORD. I'VE NEVER BEEN MUCH OF A FATHER'S SWORD SORT OF GOD MYSELF.
LOKI, ON BEHALF OF THE ENTIRE UNIVERSE, I HEREBY EXECUTE YOU FOR CRIMES TOO VAST AND VILE TO MENTION!
I DON'T NEED A HAMMER OR TWO GOOD ARMS EITHER. I DON'T EVEN NEED THIS GOAT. SORRY, TOOTHGNASHER.
ALL I NEED RIGHT NOW, GOD BUTCHER...
GRRGH!
...IS A WORD.

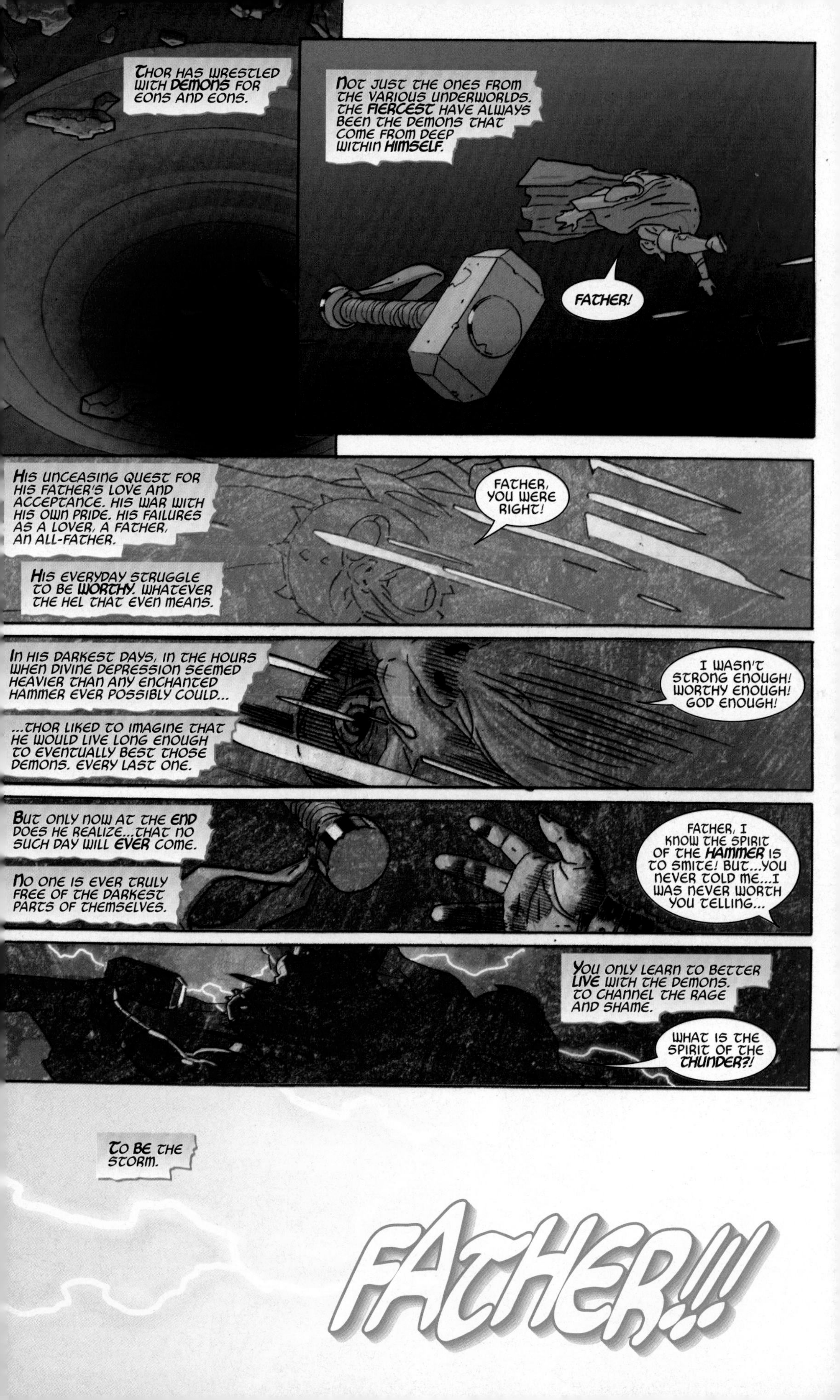

THOR HAS WRESTLED WITH DEMONS FOR EONS AND EONS.
NOT JUST THE ONES FROM THE VARIOUS UNDERWORLDS. THE FIERCEST HAVE ALWAYS BEEN THE DEMONS THAT COME FROM DEEP WITHIN HIMSELF.
FATHER!
HIS UNCEASING QUEST FOR HIS FATHER'S LOVE AND ACCEPTANCE. HIS WAR WITH HIS OWN PRIDE. HIS FAILURES AS A LOVER, A FATHER, AN ALL-FATHER.
HIS EVERYDAY STRUGGLE TO BE WORTHY. WHATEVER THE HEL THAT EVEN MEANS.
FATHER, YOU WERE RIGHT!
IN HIS DARKEST DAYS, IN THE HOURS WHEN DIVINE DEPRESSION SEEMED HEAVIER THAN ANY ENCHANTED HAMMER EVER POSSIBLY COULD...
...THOR LIKED TO IMAGINE THAT HE WOULD LIVE LONG ENOUGH TO EVENTUALLY BEST THOSE DEMONS. EVERY LAST ONE.
I WASN'T STRONG ENOUGH! WORTHY ENOUGH! GOD ENOUGH!
BUT ONLY NOW AT THE END DOES HE REALIZE...THAT NO SUCH DAY WILL EVER COME.
NO ONE IS EVER TRULY FREE OF THE DARKEST PARTS OF THEMSELVES.
FATHER, I KNOW THE SPIRIT OF THE HAMMER IS TO SMITE! BUT...YOU NEVER TOLD ME...I WAS NEVER WORTH YOU TELLING...
YOU ONLY LEARN TO BETTER LIVE WITH THE DEMONS. TO CHANNEL THE RAGE AND SHAME.
WHAT IS THE SPIRIT OF THE THUNDER?!
TO BE THE STORM.
FATHER!!

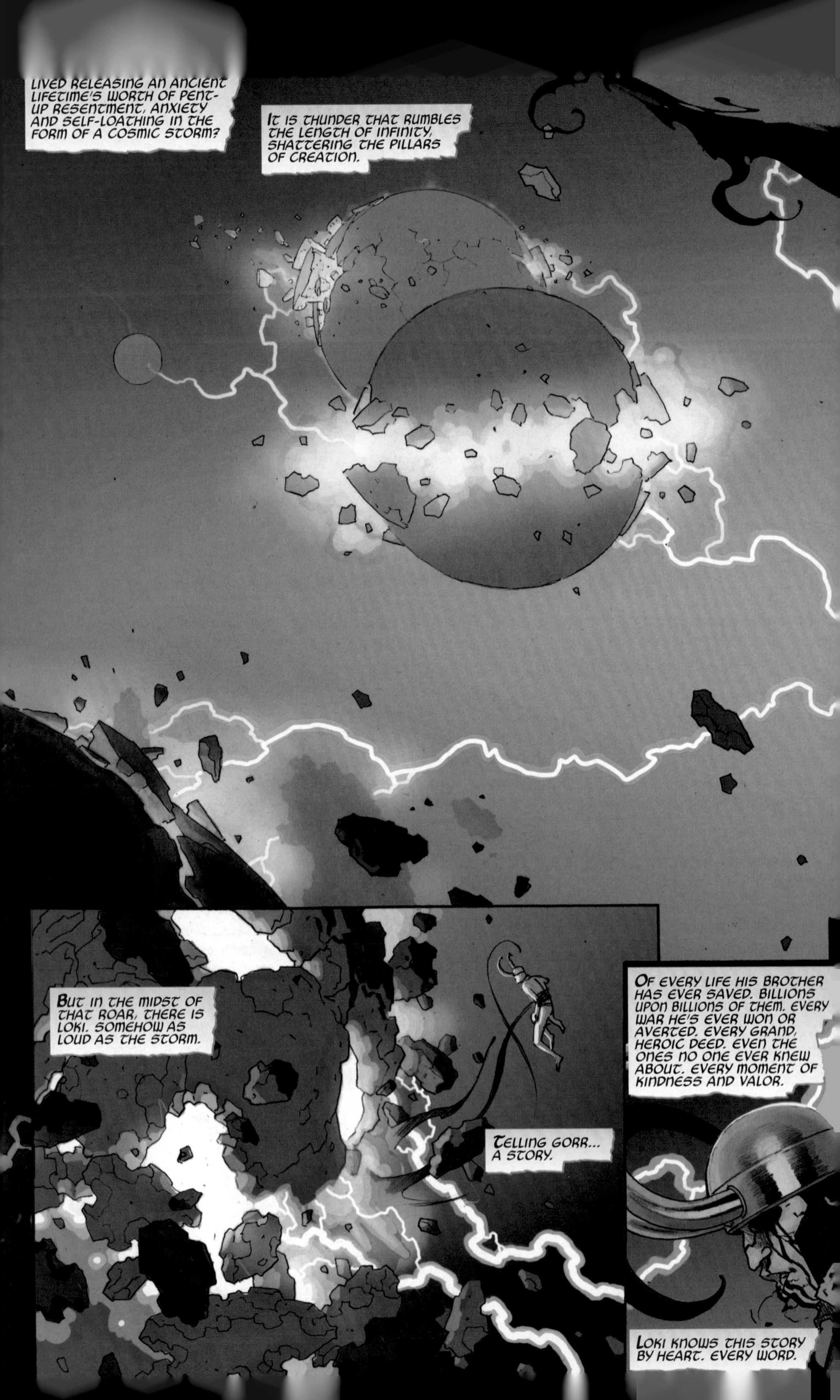

LIVED RELEASING AN ANCIENT LIFETIME'S WORTH OF PENT-UP RESENTMENT, ANXIETY AND SELF-LOATHING IN THE FORM OF A COSMIC STORM?
IT IS THUNDER THAT RUMBLES THE LENGTH OF INFINITY, SHATTERING THE PILLARS OF CREATION.
BUT IN THE MIDST OF THAT ROAR, THERE IS LOKI. SOMEHOW AS LOUD AS THE STORM.
TELLING GORR... A STORY.
OF EVERY LIFE HIS BROTHER HAS EVER SAVED. BILLIONS UPON BILLIONS OF THEM. EVERY WAR HE'S EVER WON OR AVERTED. EVERY GRAND, HEROIC DEED. EVEN THE ONES NO ONE EVER KNEW ABOUT. EVERY MOMENT OF KINDNESS AND VALOR.
LOKI KNOWS THIS STORY BY HEART. EVERY WORD.

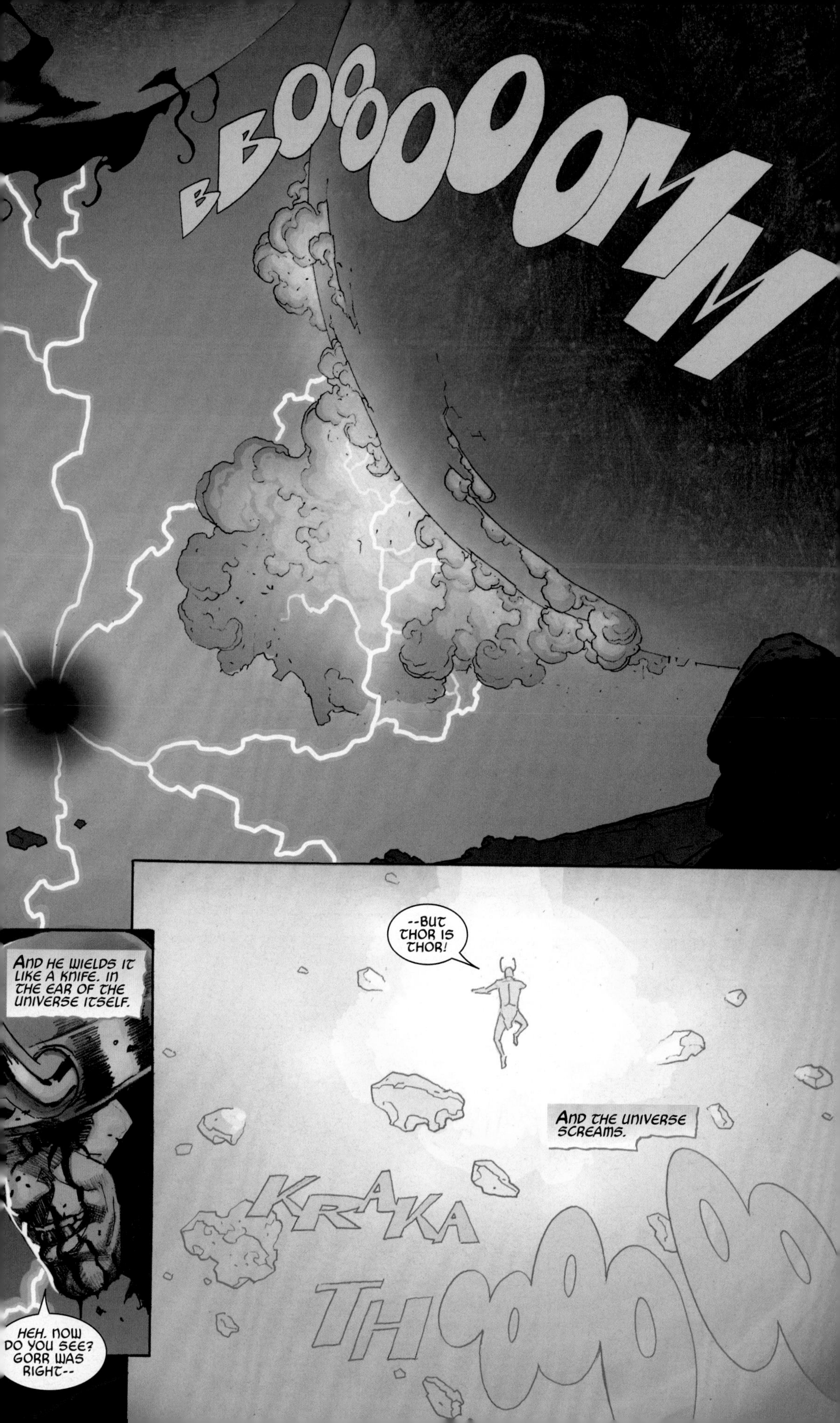
BBOOOOOMM
And he wields it like a knife. In the ear of the universe itself.
Heh. Now do you see? Gorr was right--
--But Thor is Thor!
And the universe screams.
KRAKA THOOOOOM

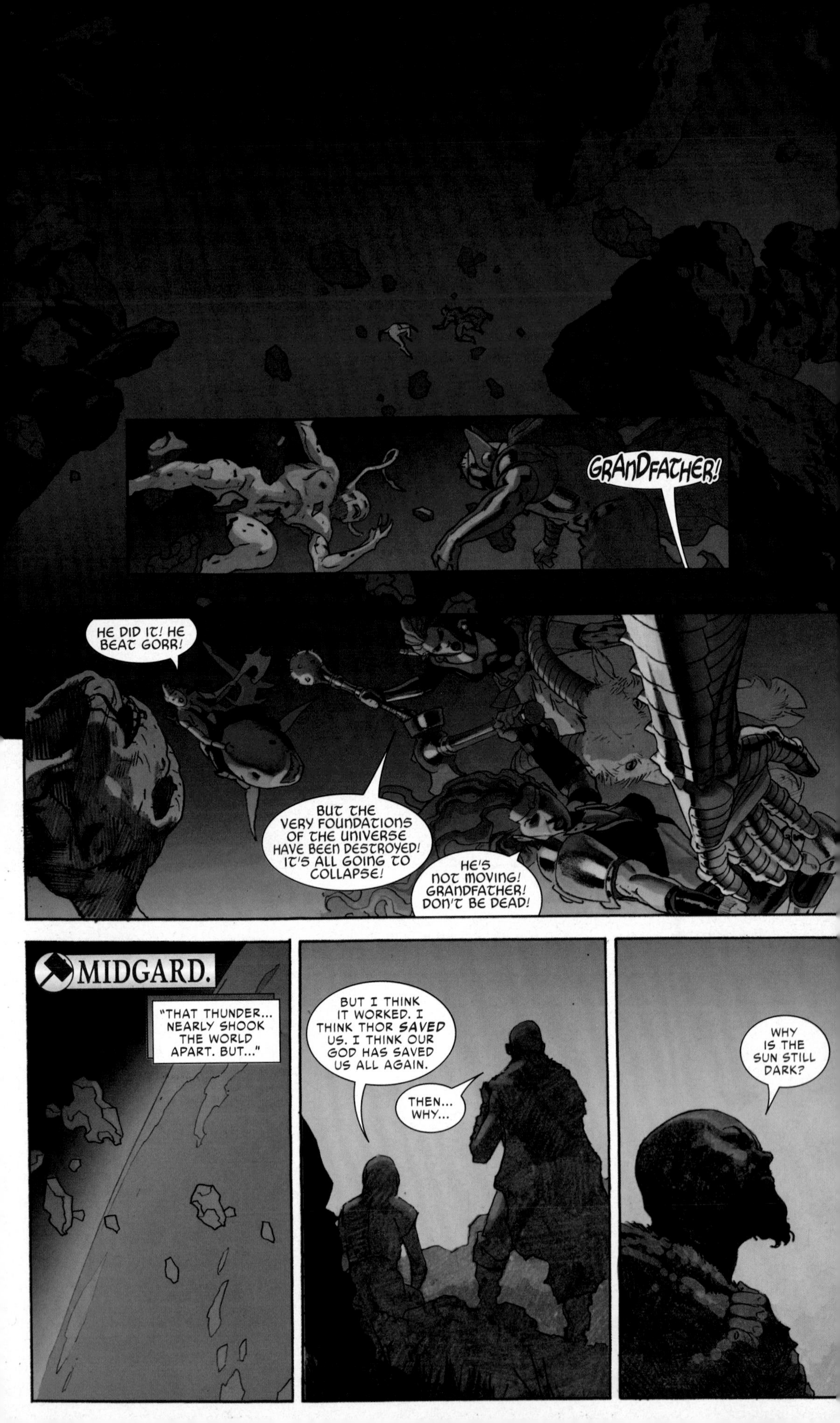
GRANDFATHER!
HE DID IT! HE BEAT GORR!
BUT THE VERY FOUNDATIONS OF THE UNIVERSE HAVE BEEN DESTROYED! IT'S ALL GOING TO COLLAPSE!
HE'S NOT MOVING! GRANDFATHER! DON'T BE DEAD!
MIDGARD.
"THAT THUNDER... NEARLY SHOOK THE WORLD APART. BUT..."
BUT I THINK IT WORKED. I THINK THOR *SAVED* US. I THINK OUR GOD HAS SAVED US ALL AGAIN.
THEN... WHY...
WHY IS THE SUN STILL DARK?

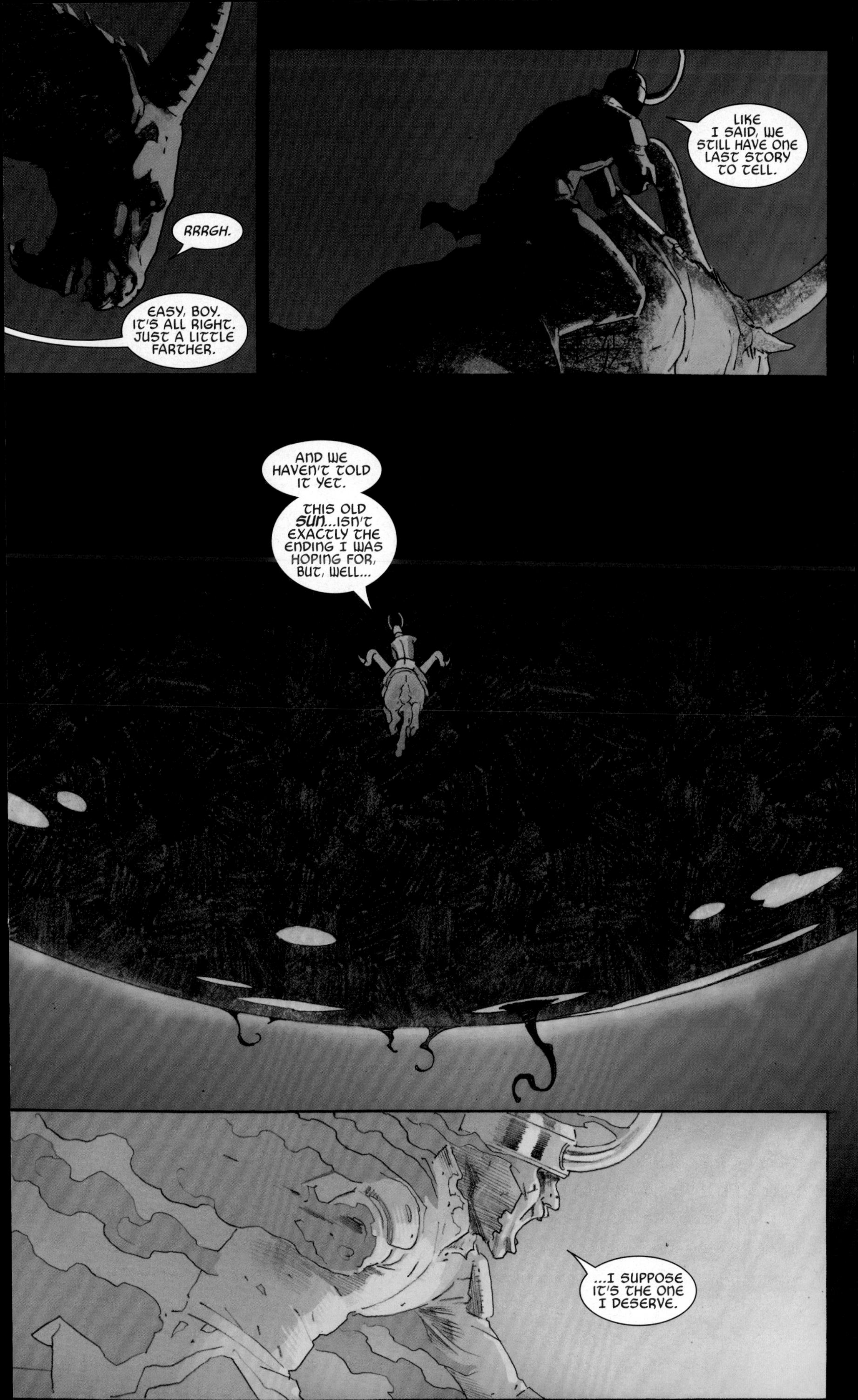
RRRGH.
EASY, BOY. IT'S ALL RIGHT. JUST A LITTLE FARTHER.
LIKE I SAID, WE STILL HAVE ONE LAST STORY TO TELL.
AND WE HAVEN'T TOLD IT YET.
THIS OLD SUN...ISN'T EXACTLY THE ENDING I WAS HOPING FOR, BUT, WELL...
...I SUPPOSE IT'S THE ONE I DESERVE.

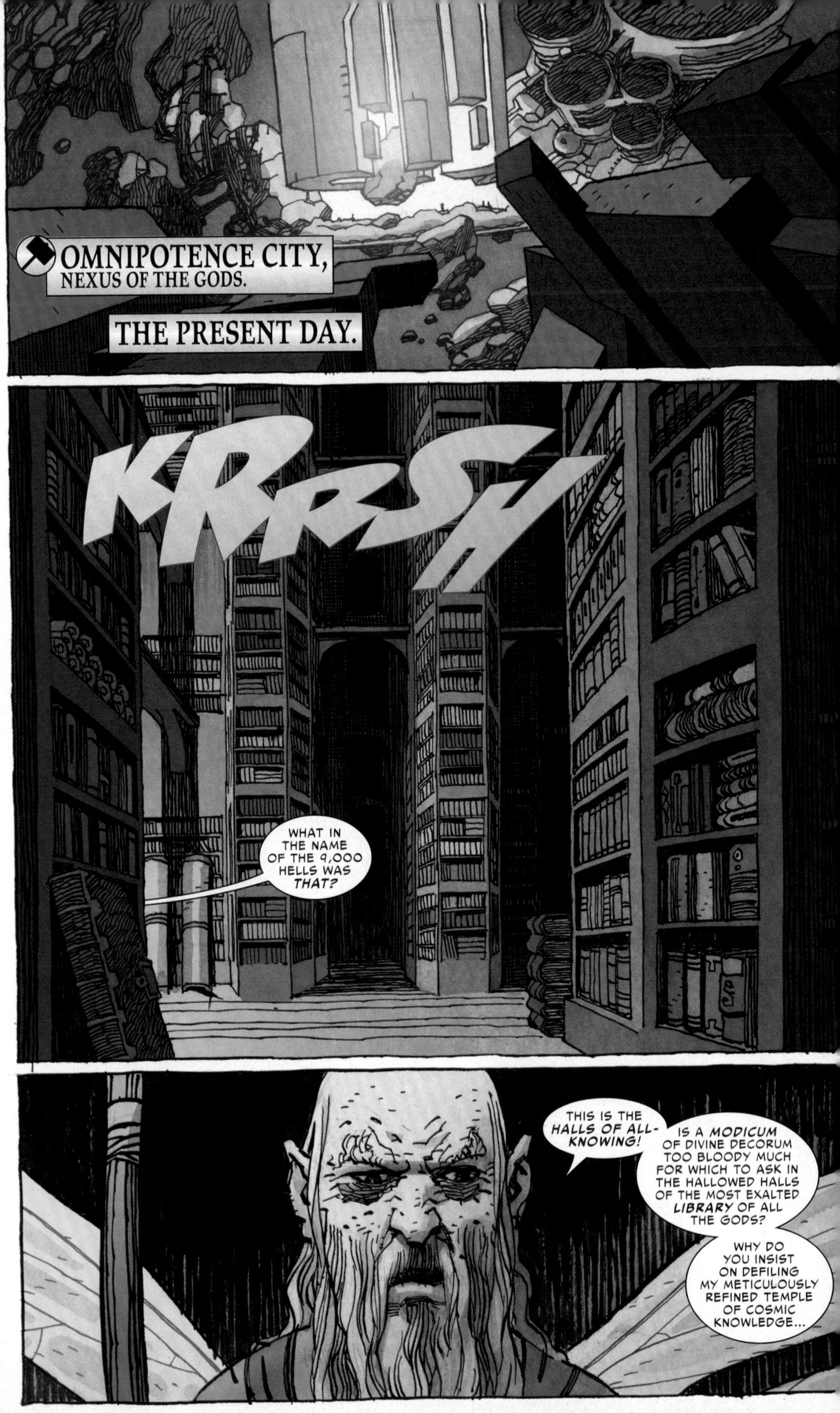
OMNIPOTENCE CITY,
NEXUS OF THE GODS.
THE PRESENT DAY.
KRRSH
WHAT IN THE NAME OF THE 9,000 HELLS WAS *THAT?*
THIS IS THE *HALLS OF ALL-KNOWING!*
IS A *MODICUM* OF DIVINE DECORUM TOO BLOODY MUCH FOR WHICH TO ASK IN THE HALLOWED HALLS OF THE MOST EXALTED *LIBRARY* OF ALL THE GODS?
WHY DO YOU INSIST ON DEFILING MY METICULOUSLY REFINED TEMPLE OF COSMIC KNOWLEDGE...

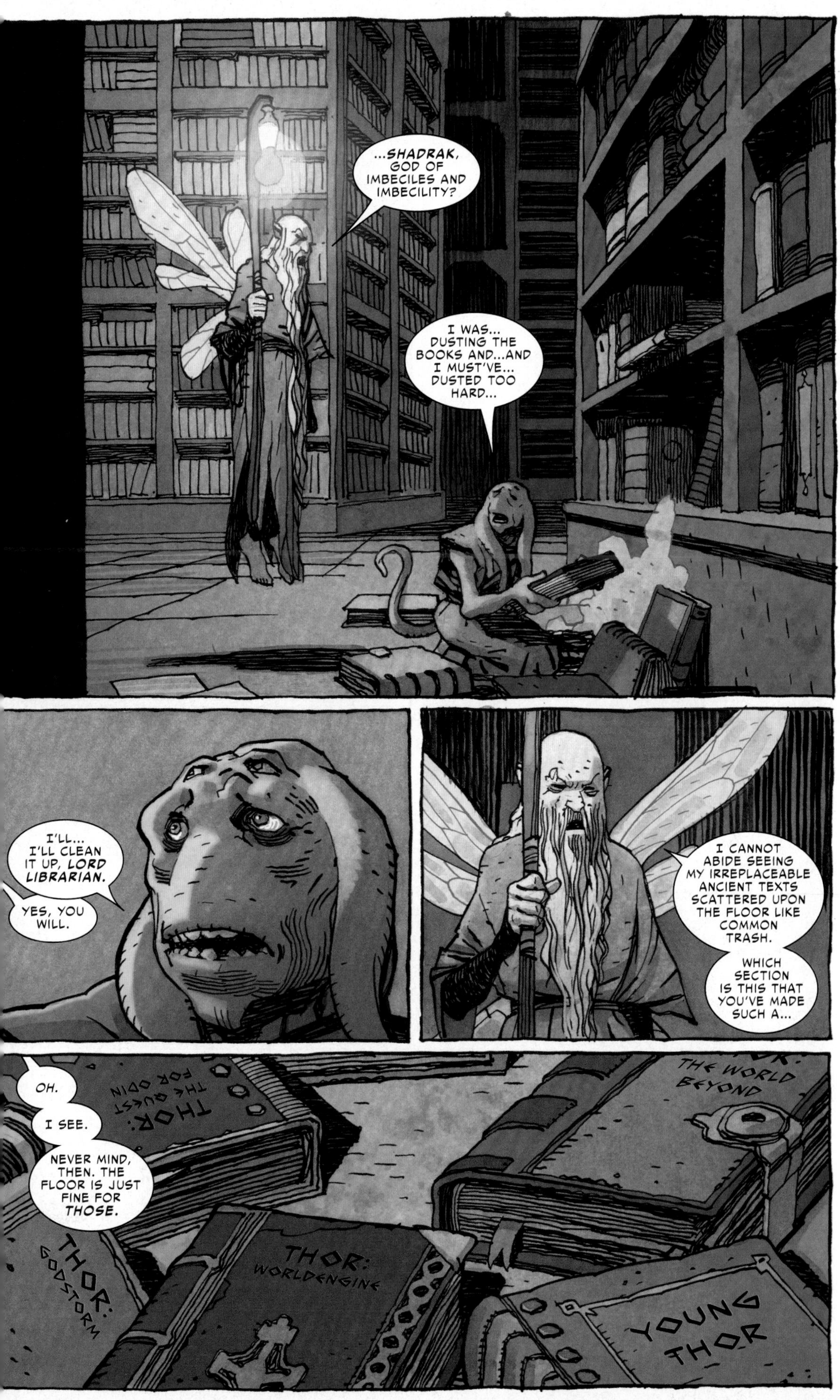
...SHADRAK, GOD OF IMBECILES AND IMBECILITY?
I WAS... DUSTING THE BOOKS AND...AND I MUST'VE... DUSTED TOO HARD...
I'LL... I'LL CLEAN IT UP, LORD LIBRARIAN.
YES, YOU WILL.
I CANNOT ABIDE SEEING MY IRREPLACEABLE ANCIENT TEXTS SCATTERED UPON THE FLOOR LIKE COMMON TRASH.
WHICH SECTION IS THIS THAT YOU'VE MADE SUCH A...
OH.
I SEE.
NEVER MIND, THEN. THE FLOOR IS JUST FINE FOR THOSE.
THOR: THE QUEST FOR ODIN
THE WORLD BEYOND
THOR: GODSTORM
THOR: WORLDENGINE
YOUNG THOR

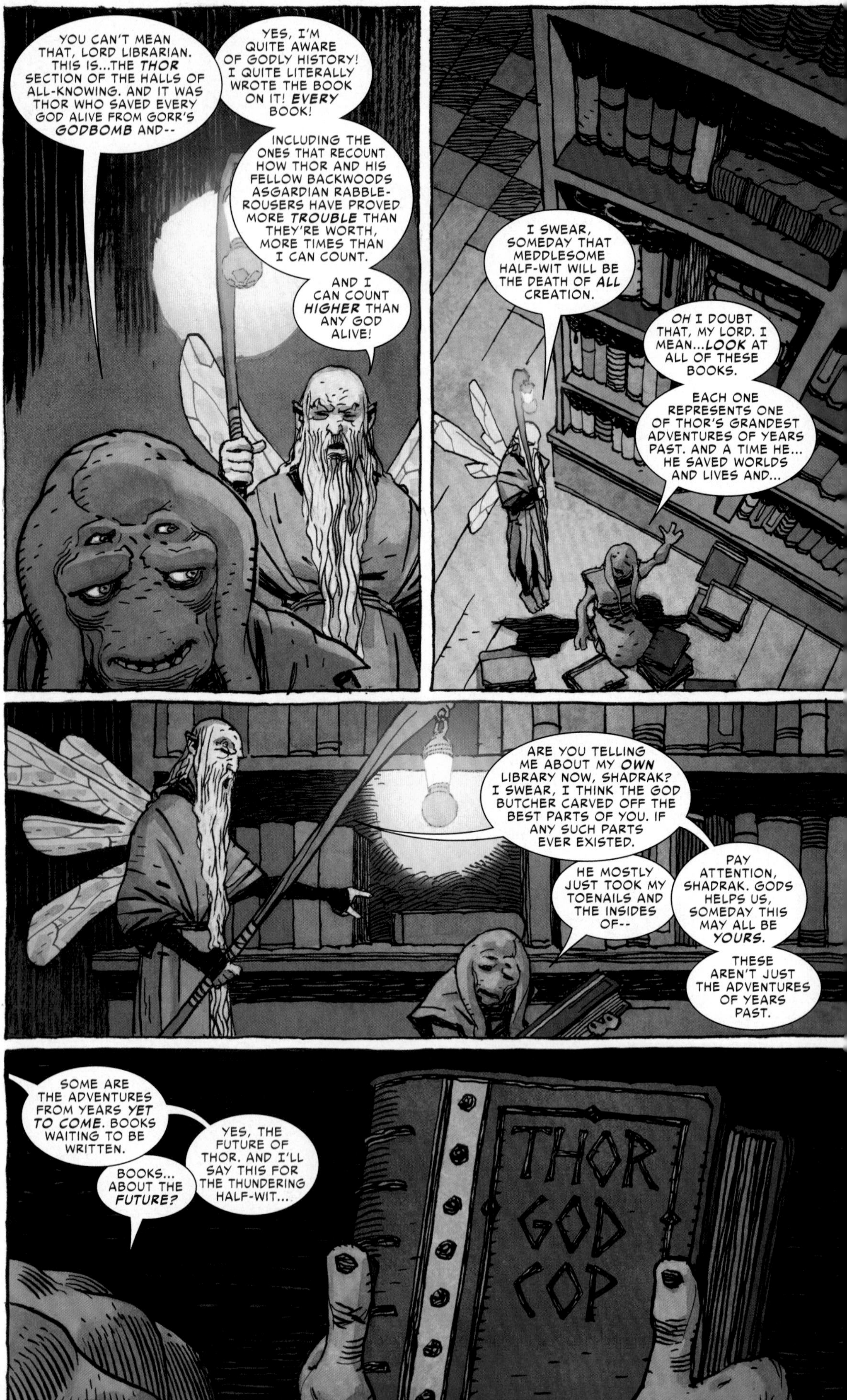
YOU CAN'T MEAN THAT, LORD LIBRARIAN. THIS IS...THE THOR SECTION OF THE HALLS OF ALL-KNOWING. AND IT WAS THOR WHO SAVED EVERY GOD ALIVE FROM GORR'S GODBOMB AND--
YES, I'M QUITE AWARE OF GODLY HISTORY! I QUITE LITERALLY WROTE THE BOOK ON IT! EVERY BOOK!
INCLUDING THE ONES THAT RECOUNT HOW THOR AND HIS FELLOW BACKWOODS ASGARDIAN RABBLE-ROUSERS HAVE PROVED MORE TROUBLE THAN THEY'RE WORTH, MORE TIMES THAN I CAN COUNT.
AND I CAN COUNT HIGHER THAN ANY GOD ALIVE!
I SWEAR, SOMEDAY THAT MEDDLESOME HALF-WIT WILL BE THE DEATH OF ALL CREATION.
OH I DOUBT THAT, MY LORD. I MEAN...LOOK AT ALL OF THESE BOOKS.
EACH ONE REPRESENTS ONE OF THOR'S GRANDEST ADVENTURES OF YEARS PAST. AND A TIME HE... HE SAVED WORLDS AND LIVES AND...
ARE YOU TELLING ME ABOUT MY OWN LIBRARY NOW, SHADRAK? I SWEAR, I THINK THE GOD BUTCHER CARVED OFF THE BEST PARTS OF YOU. IF ANY SUCH PARTS EVER EXISTED.
HE MOSTLY JUST TOOK MY TOENAILS AND THE INSIDES OF--
PAY ATTENTION, SHADRAK. GODS HELPS US, SOMEDAY THIS MAY ALL BE YOURS.
THESE AREN'T JUST THE ADVENTURES OF YEARS PAST.
SOME ARE THE ADVENTURES FROM YEARS YET TO COME. BOOKS WAITING TO BE WRITTEN.
BOOKS... ABOUT THE FUTURE?
YES, THE FUTURE OF THOR. AND I'LL SAY THIS FOR THE THUNDERING HALF-WIT...
THOR GOD COP

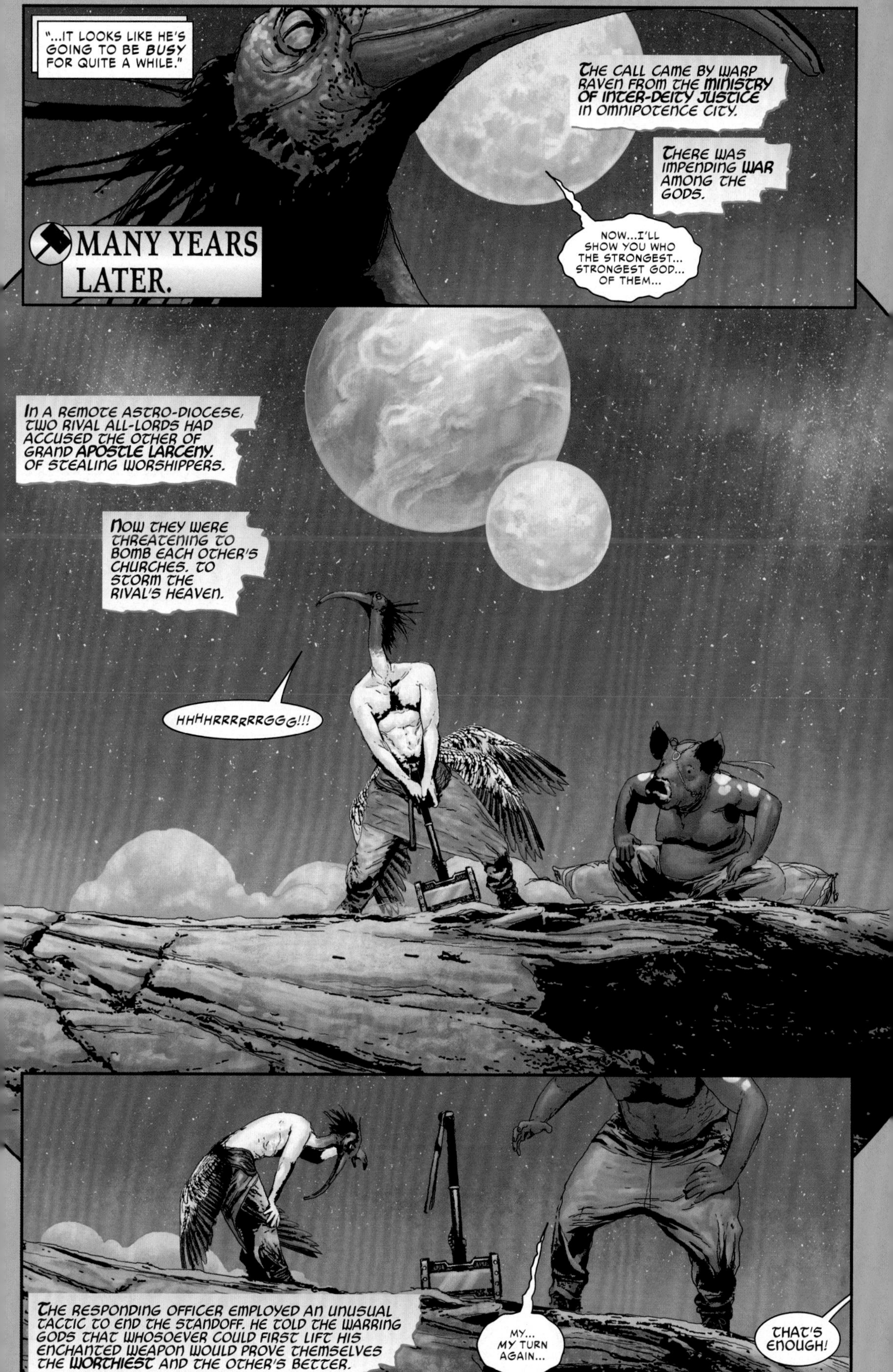

"...IT LOOKS LIKE HE'S GOING TO BE BUSY FOR QUITE A WHILE."
MANY YEARS LATER.
THE CALL CAME BY WARP RAVEN FROM THE MINISTRY OF INTER-DEITY JUSTICE IN OMNIPOTENCE CITY.
THERE WAS IMPENDING WAR AMONG THE GODS.
NOW...I'LL SHOW YOU WHO THE STRONGEST... STRONGEST GOD... OF THEM...
IN A REMOTE ASTRO-DIOCESE, TWO RIVAL ALL-LORDS HAD ACCUSED THE OTHER OF GRAND APOSTLE LARCENY. OF STEALING WORSHIPPERS.
NOW THEY WERE THREATENING TO BOMB EACH OTHER'S CHURCHES. TO STORM THE RIVAL'S HEAVEN.
HHHHRRRRRRGGG!!!
THE RESPONDING OFFICER EMPLOYED AN UNUSUAL TACTIC TO END THE STANDOFF. HE TOLD THE WARRING GODS THAT WHOSOEVER COULD FIRST LIFT HIS ENCHANTED WEAPON WOULD PROVE THEMSELVES THE WORTHIEST AND THE OTHER'S BETTER.
MY... MY TURN AGAIN...
THAT'S ENOUGH!

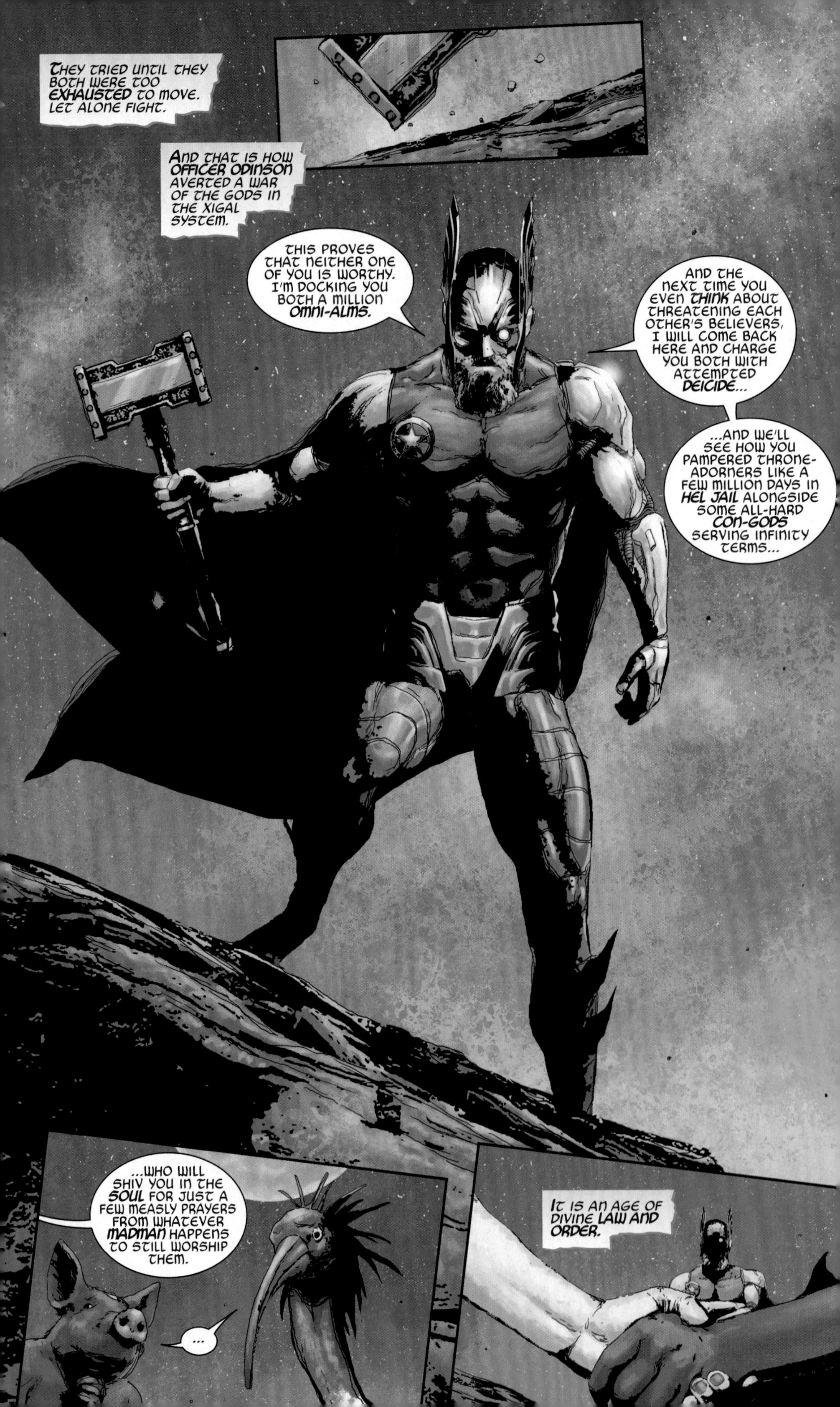

THEY TRIED UNTIL THEY BOTH WERE TOO EXHAUSTED TO MOVE. LET ALONE FIGHT.
AND THAT IS HOW OFFICER ODINSON AVERTED A WAR OF THE GODS IN THE XIGAL SYSTEM.
THIS PROVES THAT NEITHER ONE OF YOU IS WORTHY. I'M DOCKING YOU BOTH A MILLION OMNI-ALMS.
AND THE NEXT TIME YOU EVEN THINK ABOUT THREATENING EACH OTHER'S BELIEVERS, I WILL COME BACK HERE AND CHARGE YOU BOTH WITH ATTEMPTED DEICIDE...
...AND WE'LL SEE HOW YOU PAMPERED THRONE-ADORNERS LIKE A FEW MILLION DAYS IN HEL JAIL ALONGSIDE SOME ALL-HARD CON-GODS SERVING INFINITY TERMS...
...WHO WILL SHIV YOU IN THE SOUL FOR JUST A FEW MEASLY PRAYERS FROM WHATEVER MADMAN HAPPENS TO STILL WORSHIP THEM.
...
IT IS AN AGE OF DIVINE LAW AND ORDER.

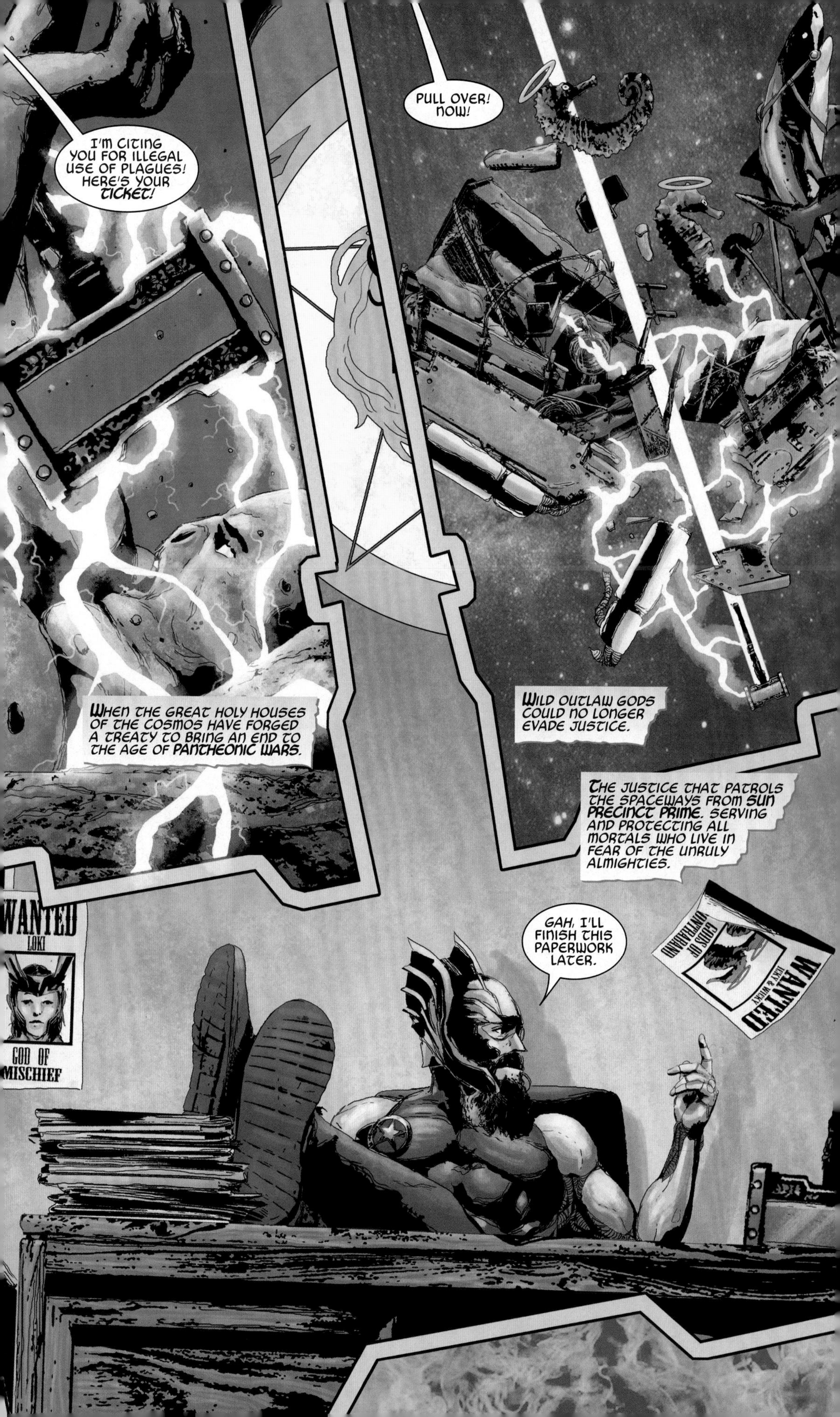
I'M CITING YOU FOR ILLEGAL USE OF PLAGUES! HERE'S YOUR TICKET!
PULL OVER! NOW!
WHEN THE GREAT HOLY HOUSES OF THE COSMOS HAVE FORGED A TREATY TO BRING AN END TO THE AGE OF PANTHEONIC WARS.
WILD OUTLAW GODS COULD NO LONGER EVADE JUSTICE.
THE JUSTICE THAT PATROLS THE SPACEWAYS FROM SUN PRECINCT PRIME. SERVING AND PROTECTING ALL MORTALS WHO LIVE IN FEAR OF THE UNRULY ALMIGHTIES.
WANTED
LOKI
GOD OF MISCHIEF
GAH, I'LL FINISH THIS PAPERWORK LATER.

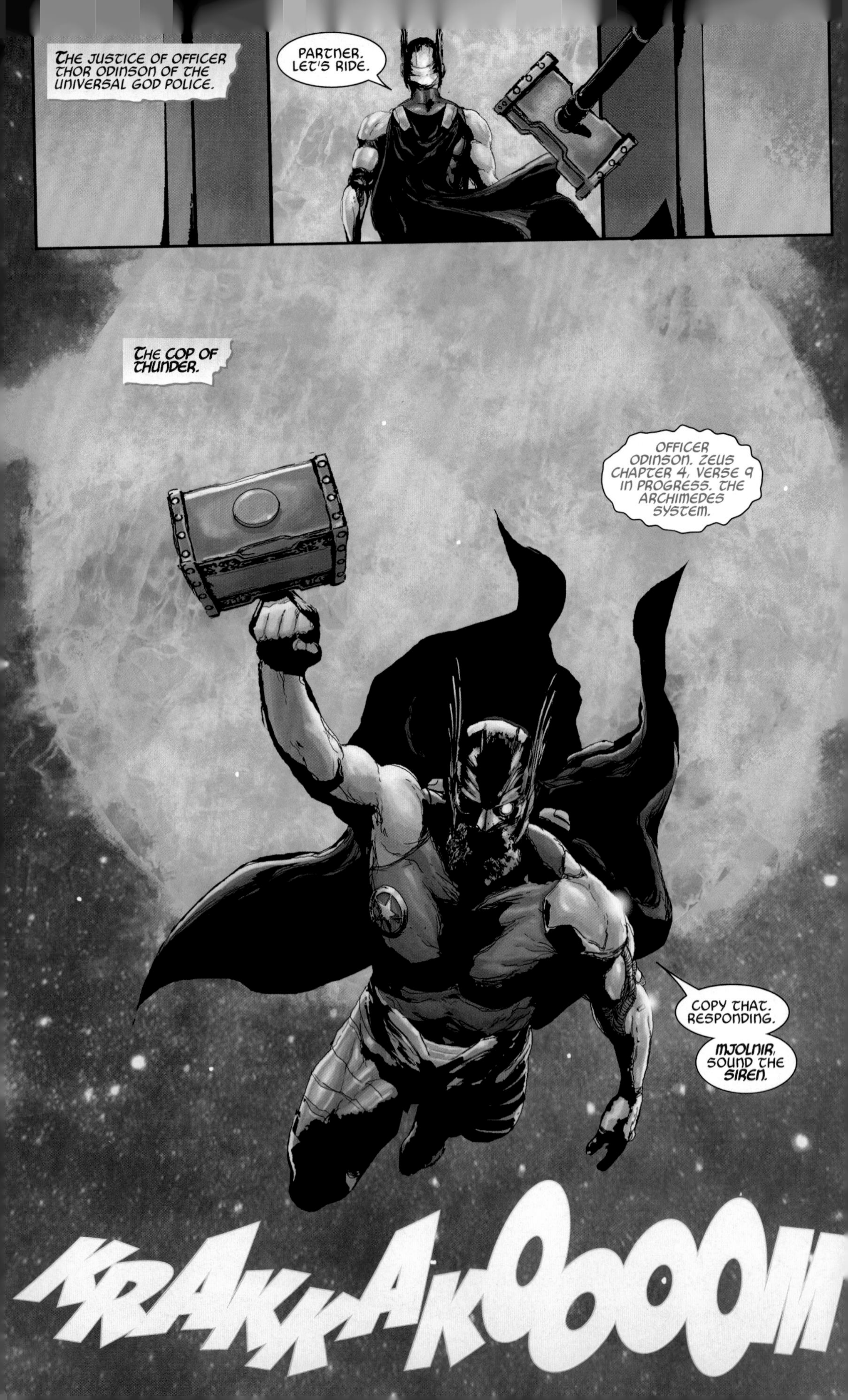
THE JUSTICE OF OFFICER THOR ODINSON OF THE UNIVERSAL GOD POLICE.
PARTNER. LET'S RIDE.
THE COP OF THUNDER.
OFFICER ODINSON. ZEUS CHAPTER 4, VERSE 9 IN PROGRESS. THE ARCHIMEDES SYSTEM.
COPY THAT. RESPONDING.
MJOLNIR, SOUND THE SIREN.
KRAKKAKOOOOM

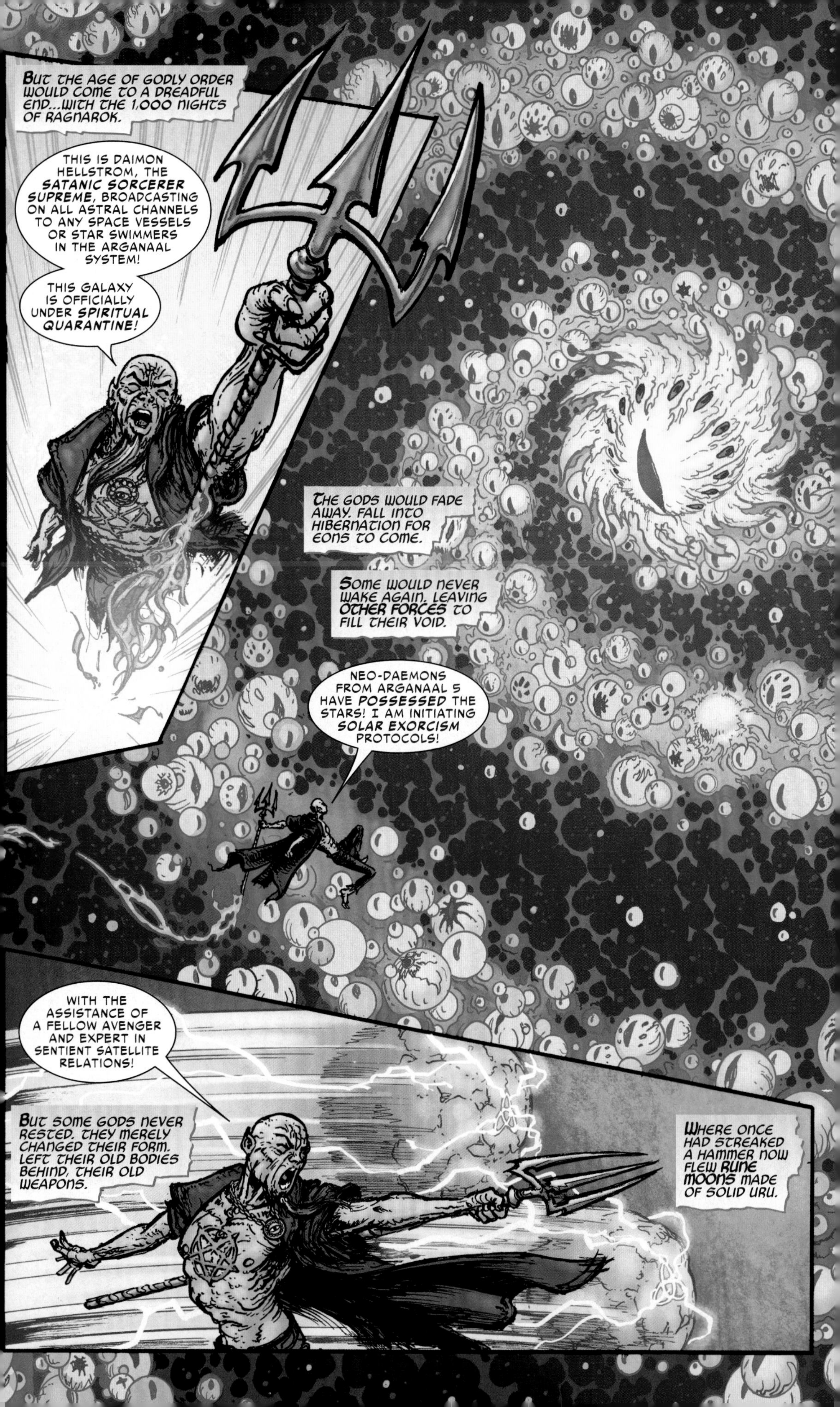

But the age of godly order would come to a dreadful end...with the 1,000 nights of Ragnarok.
This is Daimon Hellstrom, the satanic sorcerer supreme, broadcasting on all astral channels to any space vessels or star swimmers in the Arganaal system!
This galaxy is officially under spiritual quarantine!
The gods would fade away. Fall into hibernation for eons to come.
Some would never wake again. Leaving other forces to fill their void.
Neo-Daemons from Arganaal 5 have possessed the stars! I am initiating solar exorcism protocols!
With the assistance of a fellow Avenger and expert in sentient satellite relations!
But some gods never rested. They merely changed their form. Left their old bodies behind, their old weapons.
Where once had streaked a hammer now flew rune moons made of solid uru.

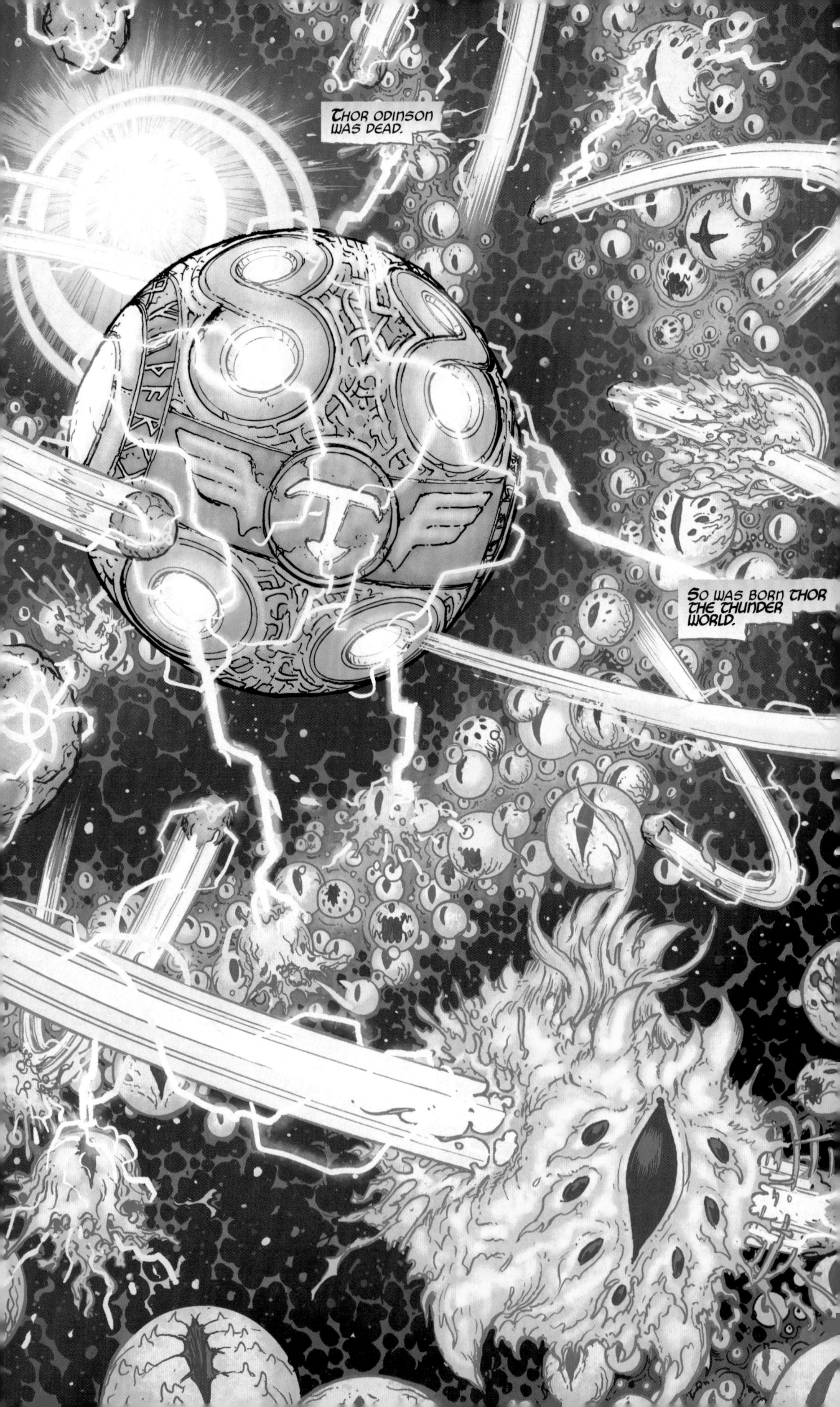
THOR ODINSON WAS DEAD.
SO WAS BORN THOR THE THUNDER WORLD.

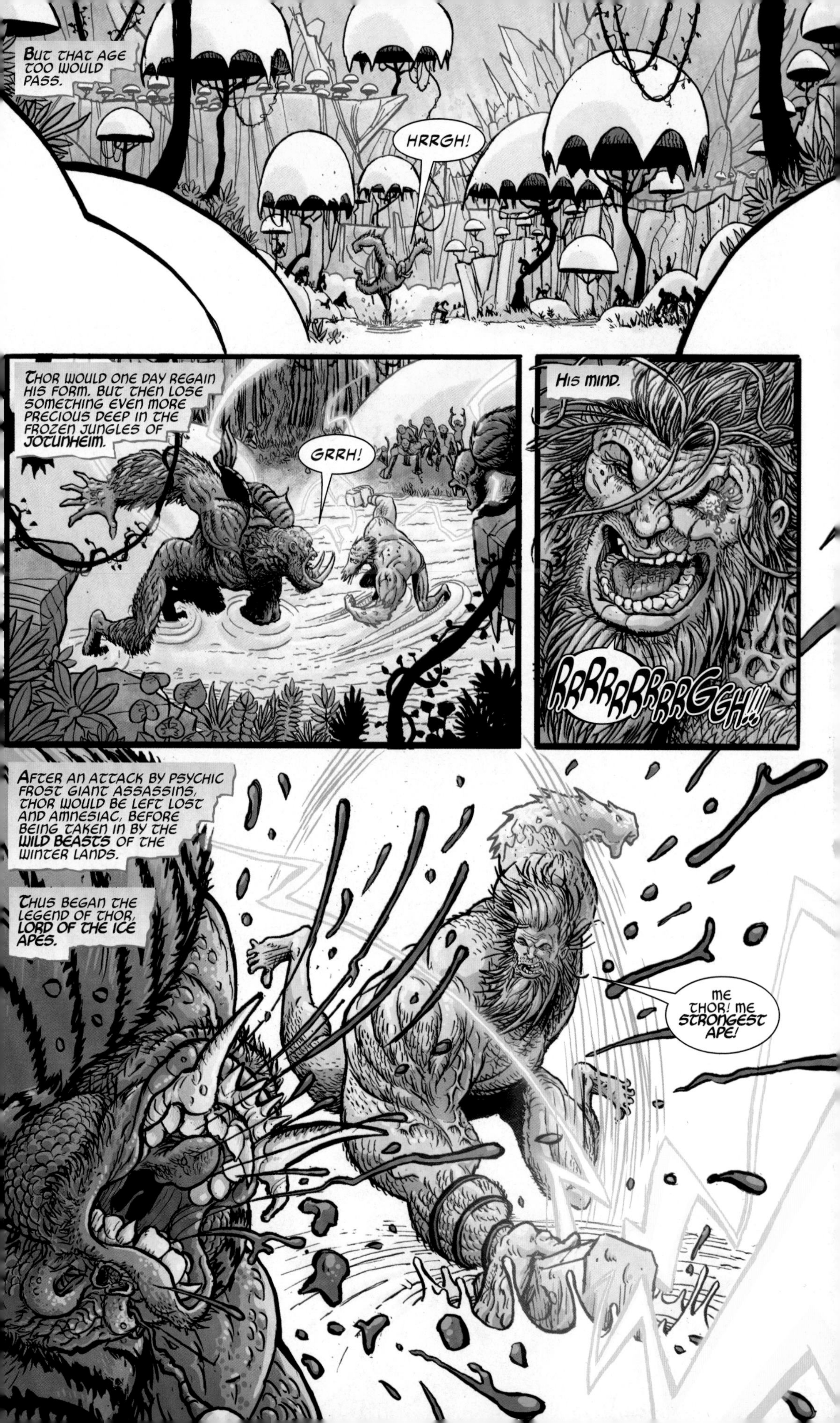
But that age too would pass.
HRRGH!
Thor would one day regain his form. But then lose something even more precious deep in the frozen jungles of JOTUNHEIM.
GRRH!
His mind.
RRRRRRRRRRGGH!!
After an attack by psychic frost giant assassins, Thor would be left lost and amnesiac, before being taken in by the WILD BEASTS of the winter lands.
Thus began the legend of Thor, LORD OF THE ICE APES.
ME THOR! ME STRONGEST APE!

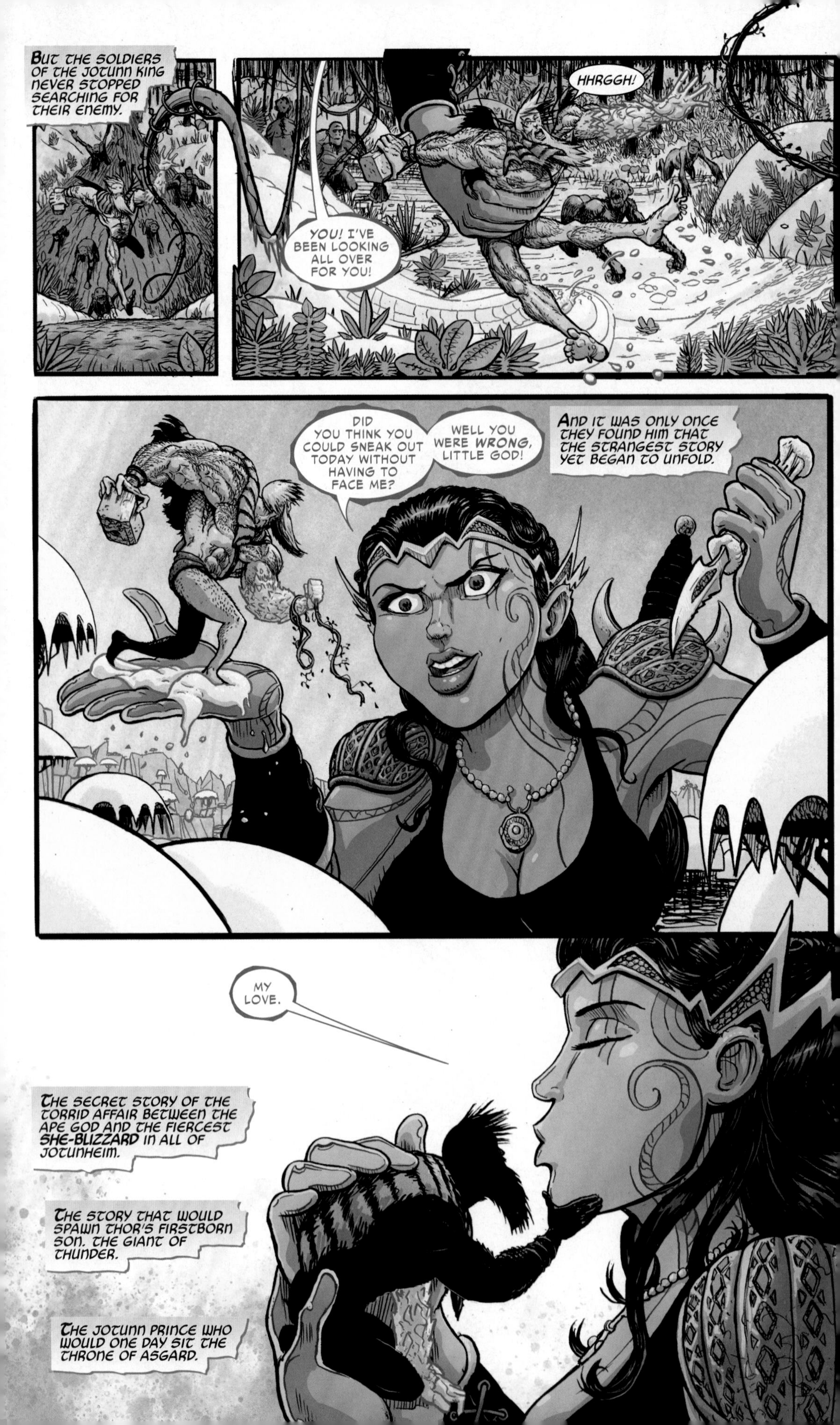

BUT THE SOLDIERS OF THE JOTUNN KING NEVER STOPPED SEARCHING FOR THEIR ENEMY.
HHRGGH!
YOU! I'VE BEEN LOOKING ALL OVER FOR YOU!
DID YOU THINK YOU COULD SNEAK OUT TODAY WITHOUT HAVING TO FACE ME?
WELL YOU WERE WRONG, LITTLE GOD!
AND IT WAS ONLY ONCE THEY FOUND HIM THAT THE STRANGEST STORY YET BEGAN TO UNFOLD.
MY LOVE.
THE SECRET STORY OF THE TORRID AFFAIR BETWEEN THE APE GOD AND THE FIERCEST SHE-BLIZZARD IN ALL OF JOTUNHEIM.
THE STORY THAT WOULD SPAWN THOR'S FIRSTBORN SON. THE GIANT OF THUNDER.
THE JOTUNN PRINCE WHO WOULD ONE DAY SIT THE THRONE OF ASGARD.

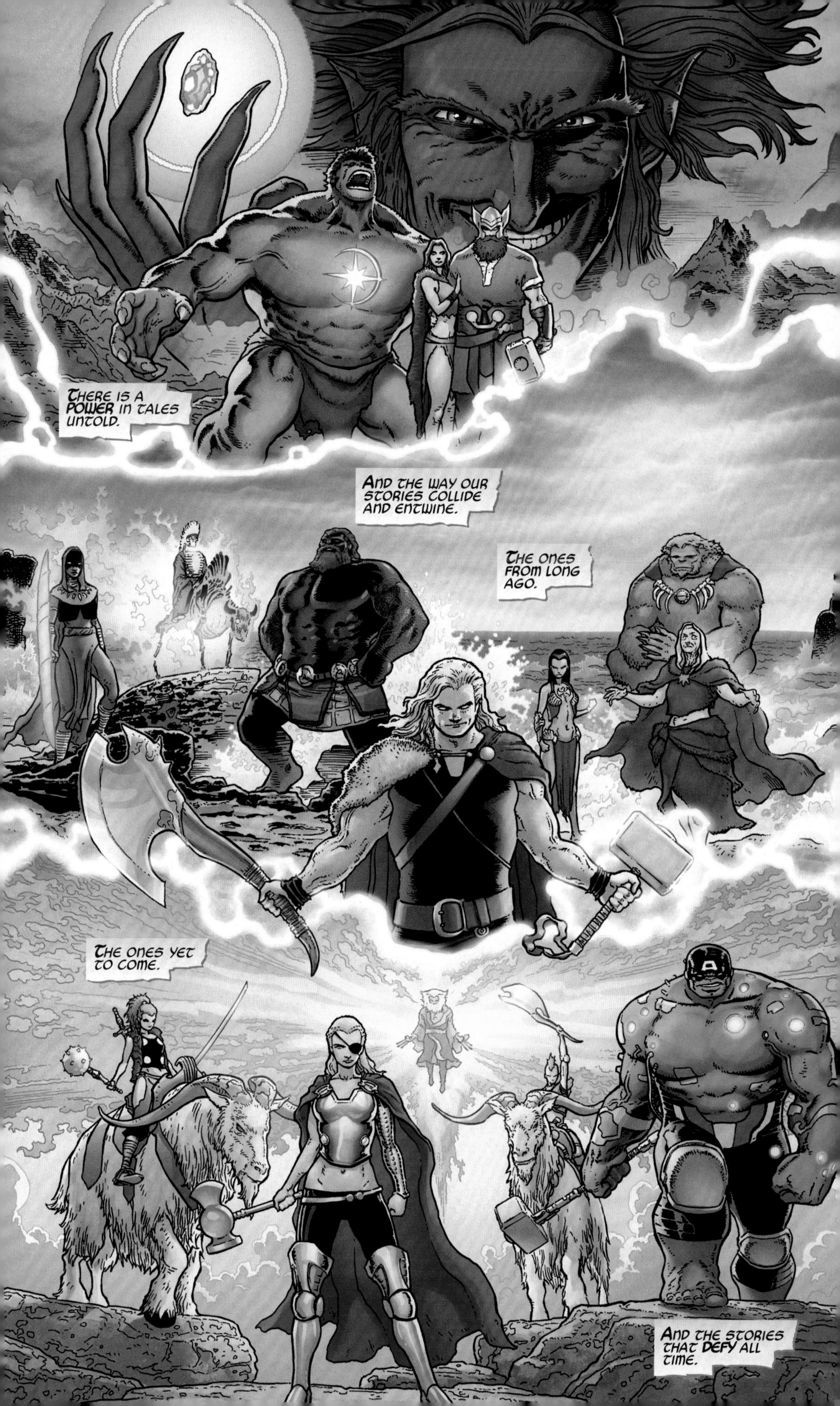
THERE IS A POWER IN TALES UNTOLD.
AND THE WAY OUR STORIES COLLIDE AND ENTWINE.
THE ONES FROM LONG AGO.
THE ONES YET TO COME.
AND THE STORIES THAT DEFY ALL TIME.

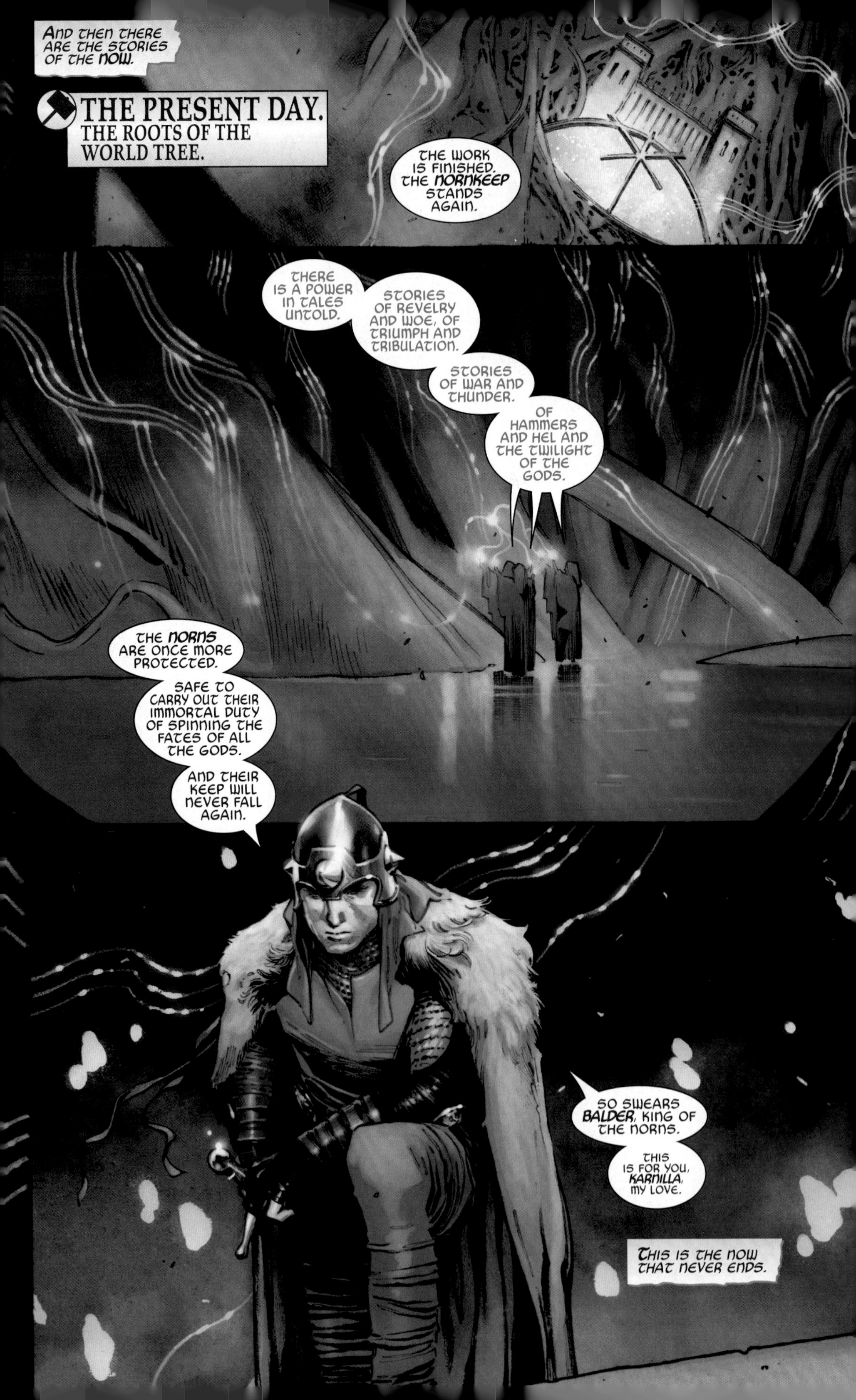

AND THEN THERE ARE THE STORIES OF THE NOW.
THE PRESENT DAY. THE ROOTS OF THE WORLD TREE.
THE WORK IS FINISHED. THE NORNKEEP STANDS AGAIN.
THERE IS A POWER IN TALES UNTOLD.
STORIES OF REVELRY AND WOE, OF TRIUMPH AND TRIBULATION.
STORIES OF WAR AND THUNDER.
OF HAMMERS AND HEL AND THE TWILIGHT OF THE GODS.
THE NORNS ARE ONCE MORE PROTECTED.
SAFE TO CARRY OUT THEIR IMMORTAL DUTY OF SPINNING THE FATES OF ALL THE GODS.
AND THEIR KEEP WILL NEVER FALL AGAIN.
SO SWEARS BALDER, KING OF THE NORNS.
THIS IS FOR YOU, KARNILLA, MY LOVE.
THIS IS THE NOW THAT NEVER ENDS.

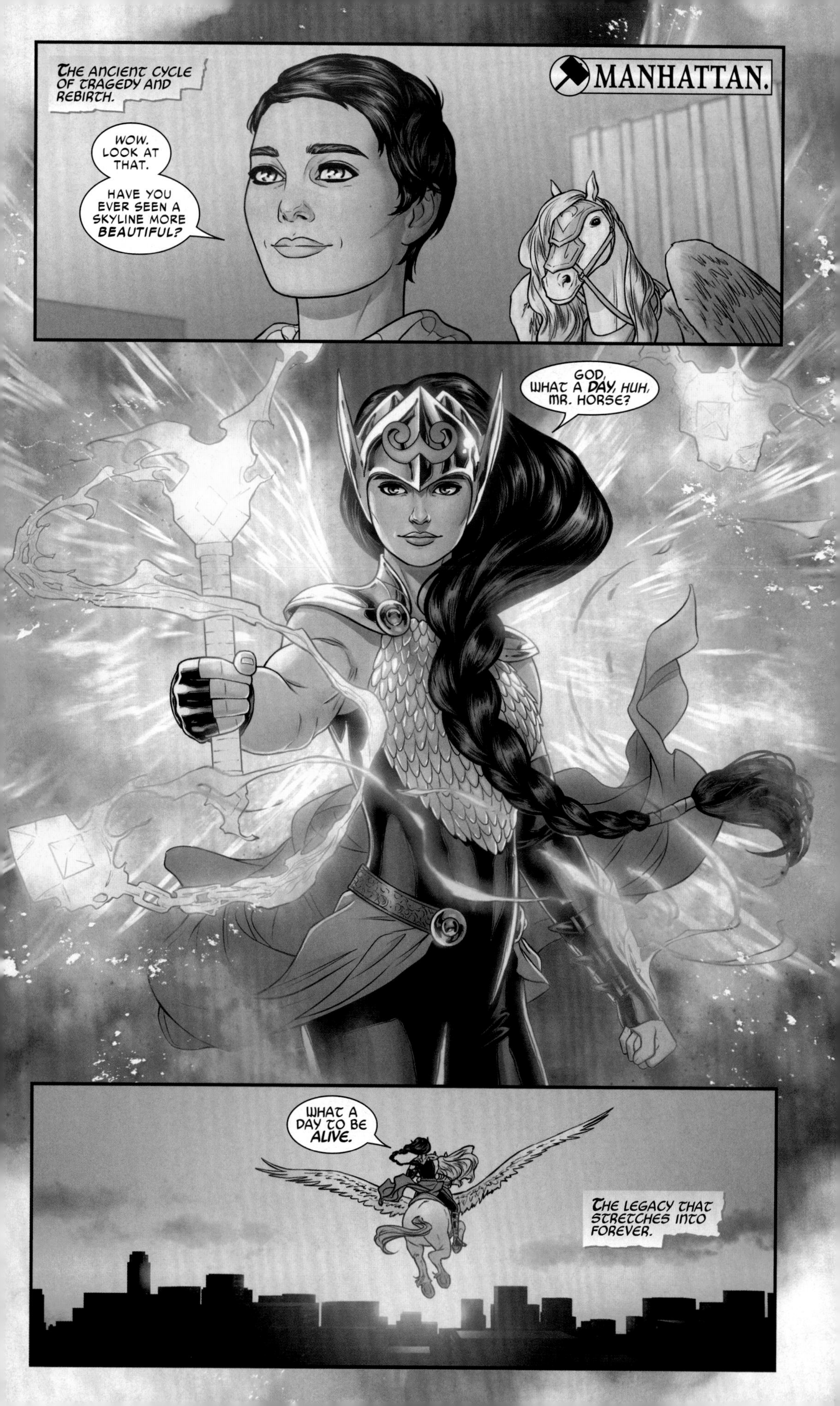
THE ANCIENT CYCLE OF TRAGEDY AND REBIRTH.
MANHATTAN.
WOW. LOOK AT THAT.
HAVE YOU EVER SEEN A SKYLINE MORE BEAUTIFUL?
GOD, WHAT A DAY, HUH, MR. HORSE?
WHAT A DAY TO BE ALIVE.
THE LEGACY THAT STRETCHES INTO FOREVER.

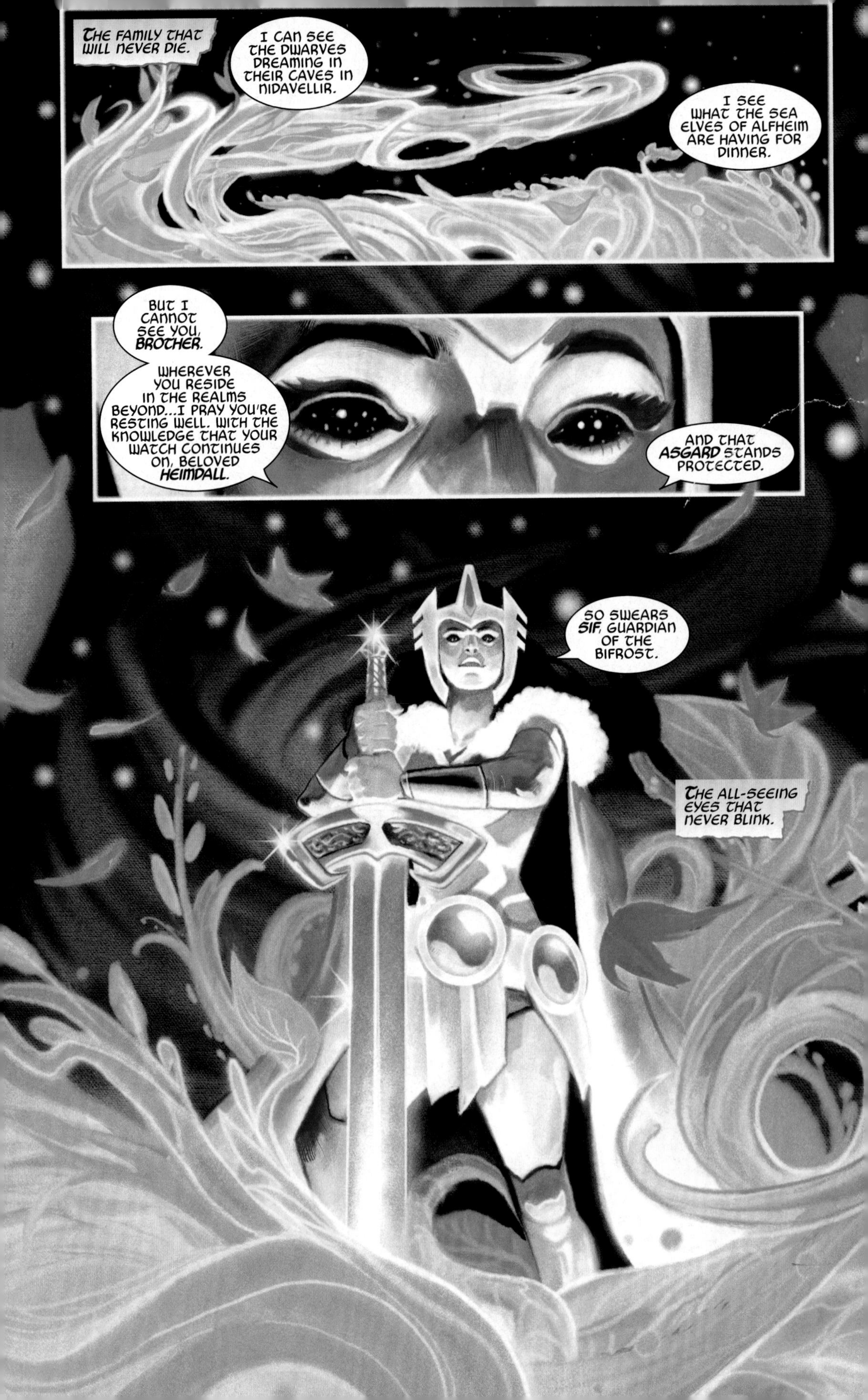

THE FAMILY THAT WILL NEVER DIE.
I CAN SEE THE DWARVES DREAMING IN THEIR CAVES IN NIDAVELLIR.
I SEE WHAT THE SEA ELVES OF ALFHEIM ARE HAVING FOR DINNER.
BUT I CANNOT SEE YOU, BROTHER.
WHEREVER YOU RESIDE BEYOND IN THE REALMS BEYOND...I PRAY YOU'RE RESTING WELL. WITH THE KNOWLEDGE THAT YOUR WATCH CONTINUES ON, BELOVED HEIMDALL.
AND THAT ASGARD STANDS PROTECTED.
SO SWEARS SIF, GUARDIAN OF THE BIFROST.
THE ALL-SEEING EYES THAT NEVER BLINK.

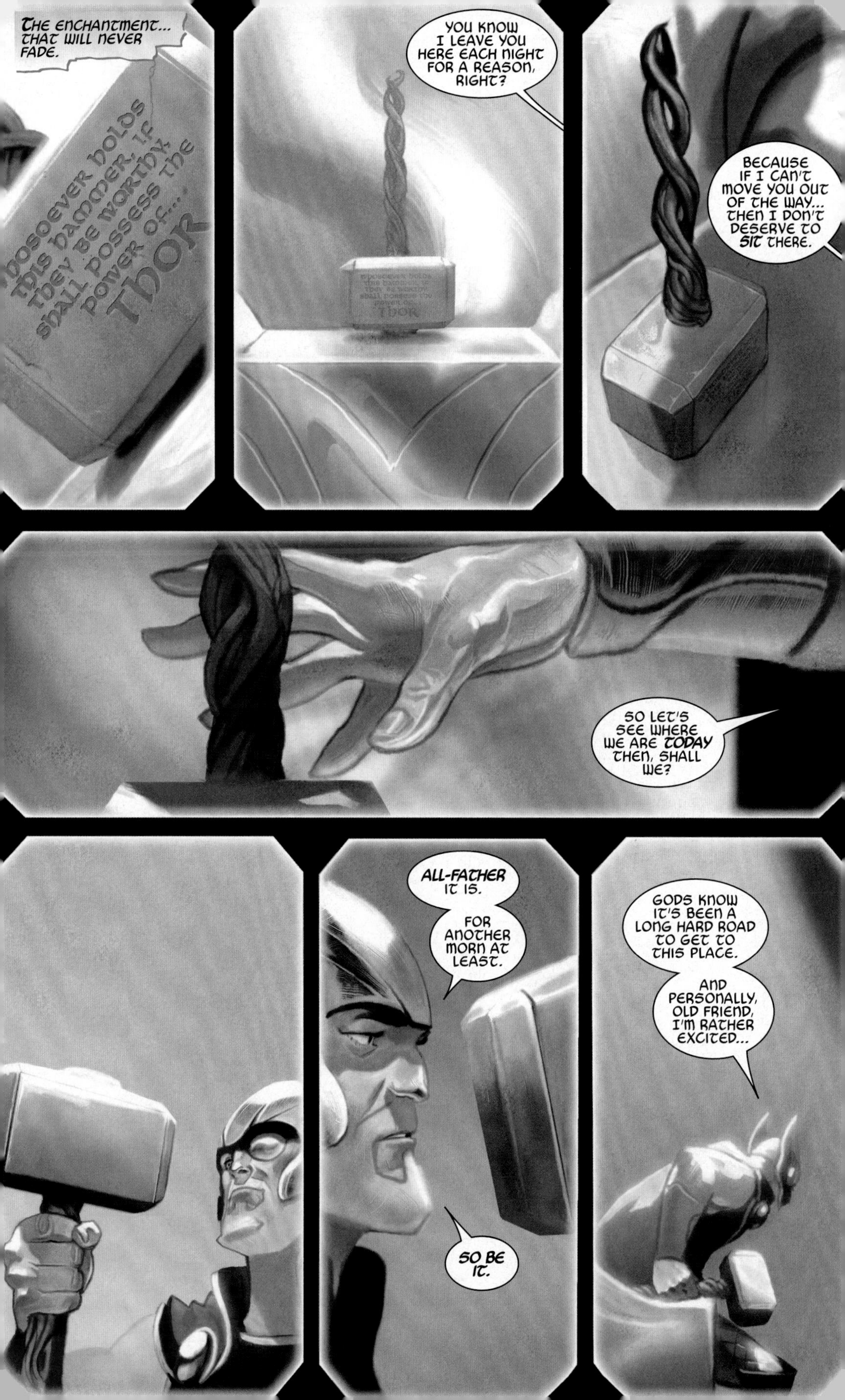
THE ENCHANTMENT... THAT WILL NEVER FADE.
WHOSOEVER HOLDS THIS HAMMER, IF THEY BE WORTHY, SHALL POSSESS THE POWER OF... THOR
YOU KNOW I LEAVE YOU HERE EACH NIGHT FOR A REASON, RIGHT?
BECAUSE IF I CAN'T MOVE YOU OUT OF THE WAY... THEN I DON'T DESERVE TO SIT THERE.
SO LET'S SEE WHERE WE ARE TODAY THEN, SHALL WE?
ALL-FATHER IT IS.
FOR ANOTHER MORN AT LEAST.
SO BE IT.
GODS KNOW IT'S BEEN A LONG HARD ROAD TO GET TO THIS PLACE.
AND PERSONALLY, OLD FRIEND, I'M RATHER EXCITED...

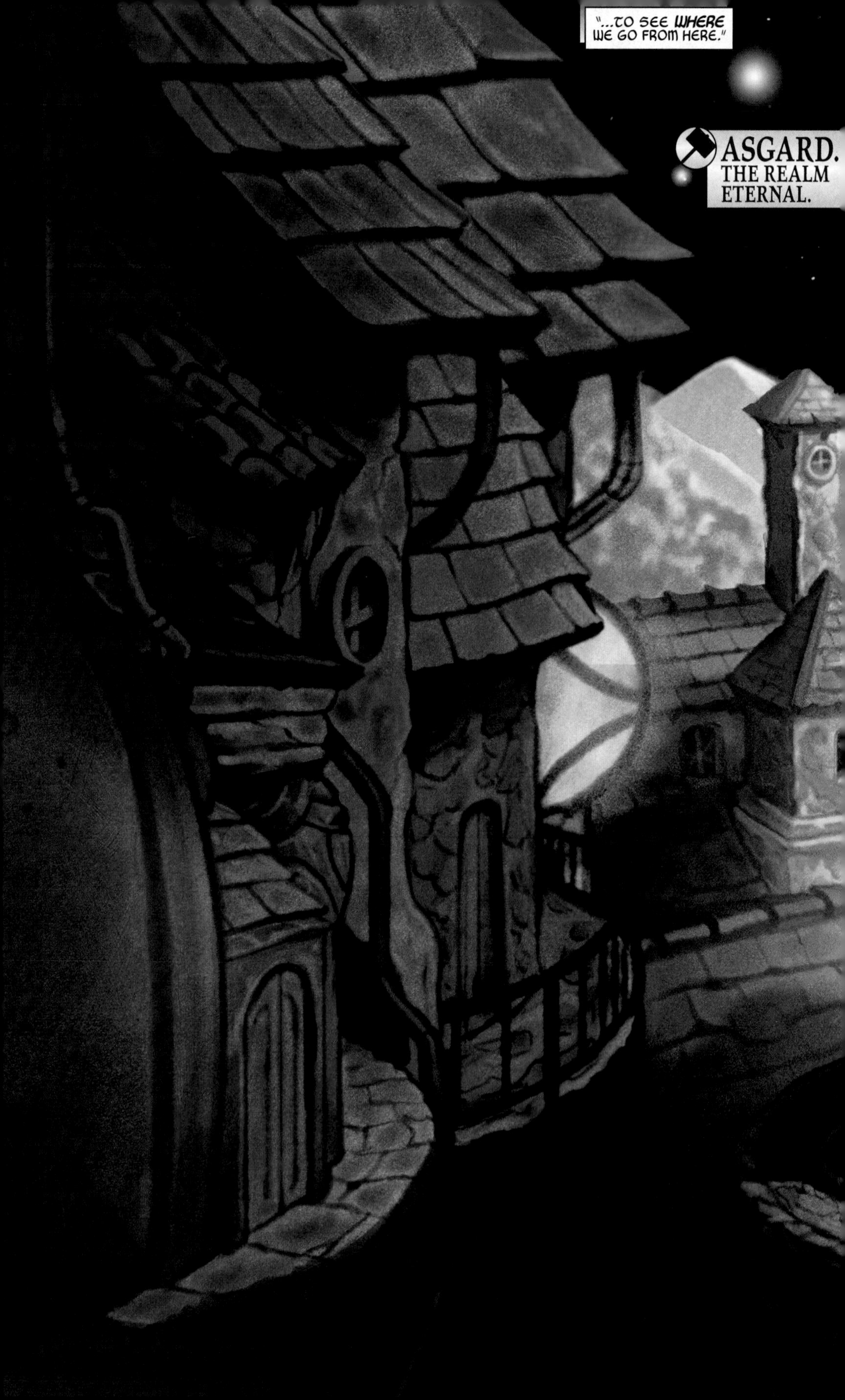
"...TO SEE WHERE WE GO FROM HERE."
ASGARD. THE REALM ETERNAL.

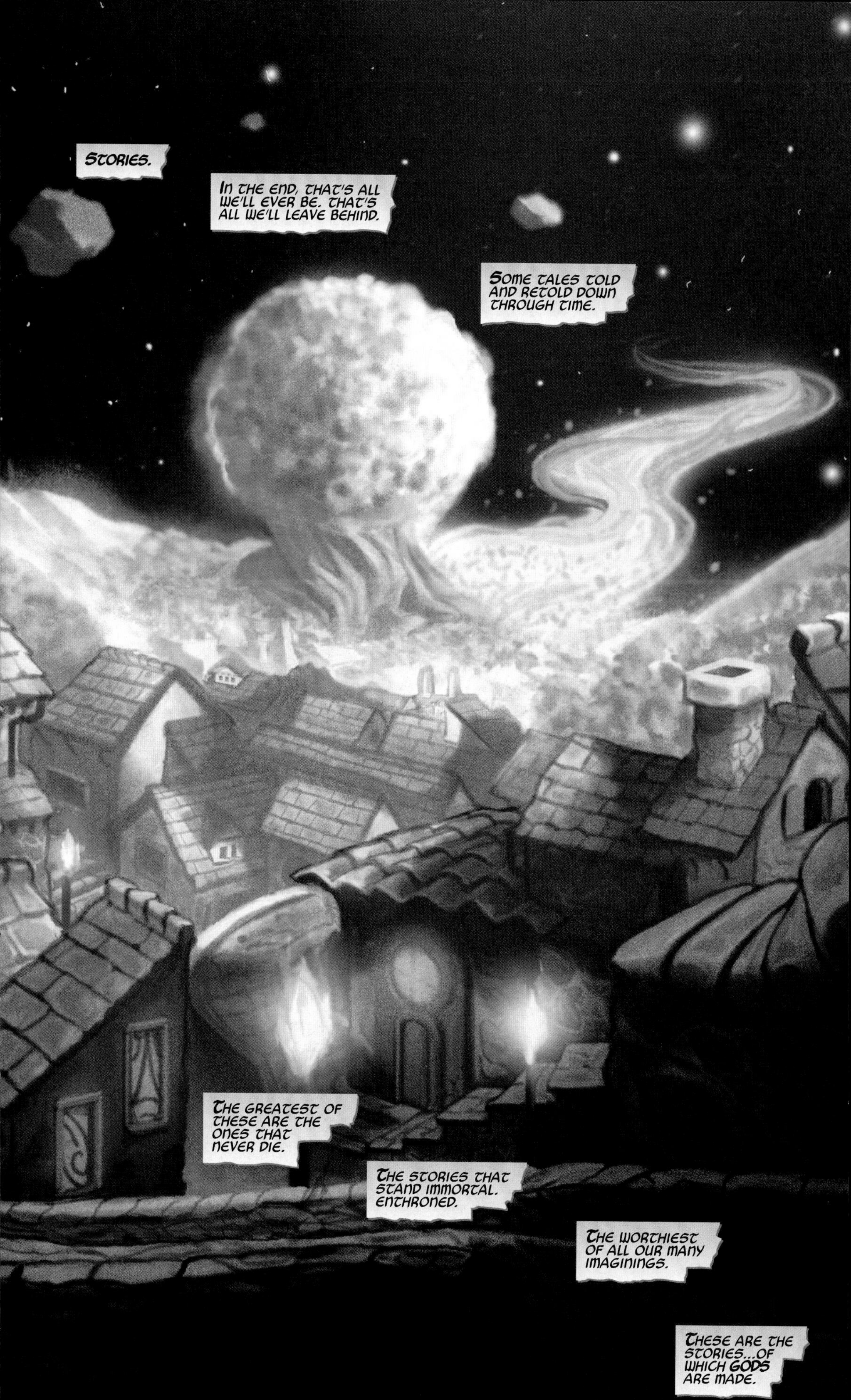
STORIES.
IN THE END, THAT'S ALL WE'LL EVER BE. THAT'S ALL WE'LL LEAVE BEHIND.
SOME TALES TOLD AND RETOLD DOWN THROUGH TIME.
THE GREATEST OF THESE ARE THE ONES THAT NEVER DIE.
THE STORIES THAT STAND IMMORTAL. ENTHRONED.
THE WORTHIEST OF ALL OUR MANY IMAGININGS.
THESE ARE THE STORIES...OF WHICH GODS ARE MADE.

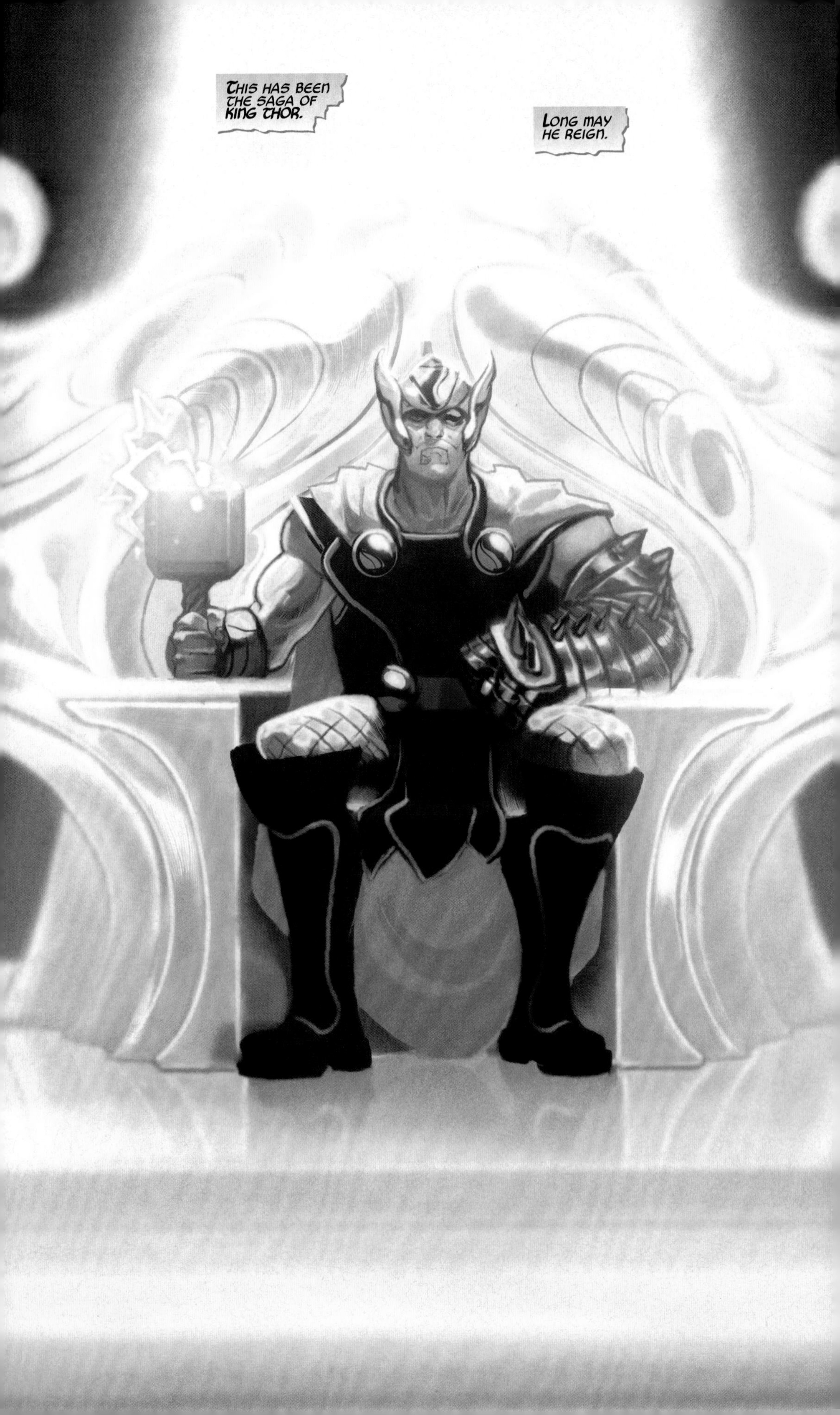
THIS HAS BEEN THE SAGA OF KING THOR.
LONG MAY HE REIGN.

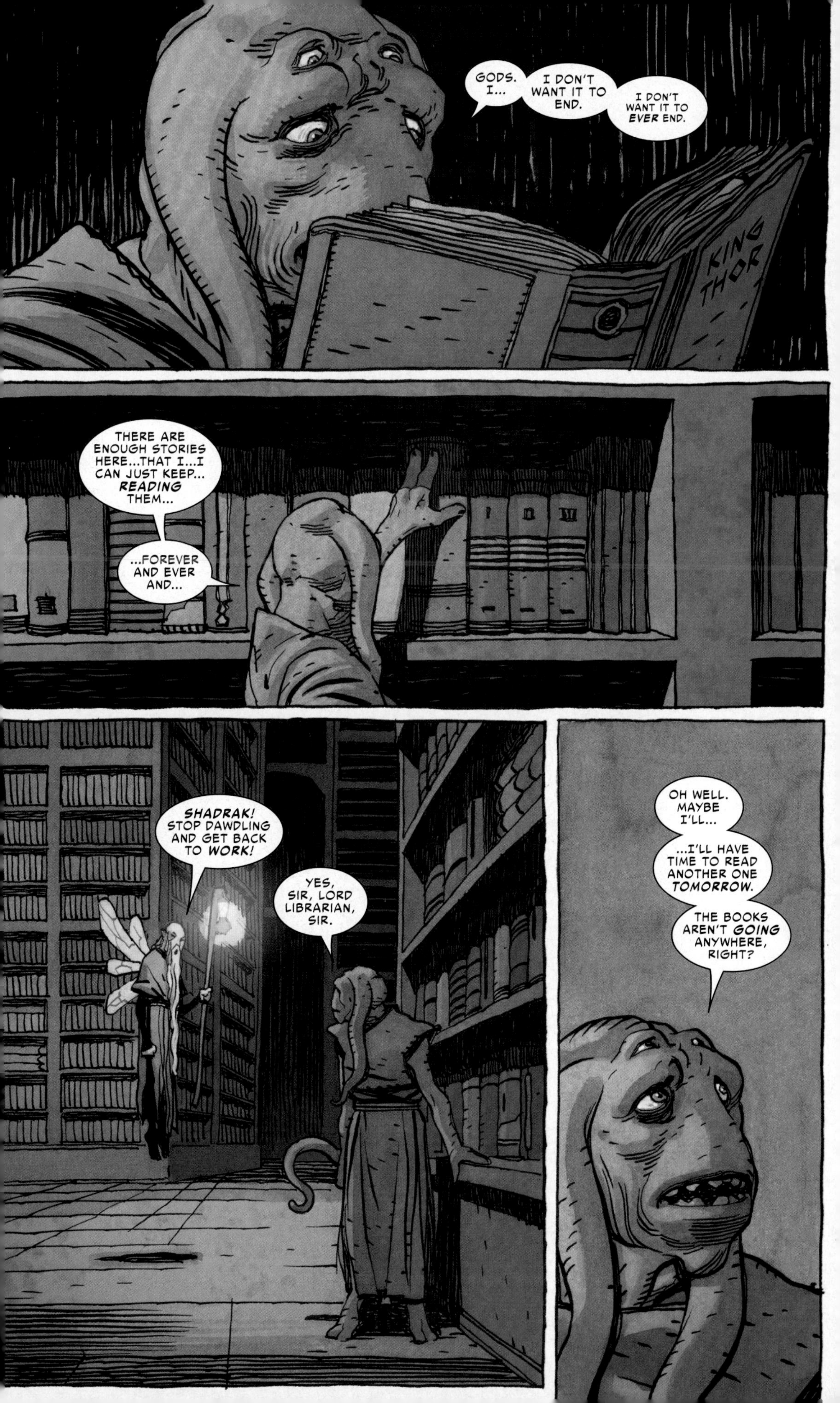
GODS. I...
I DON'T WANT IT TO END.
I DON'T WANT IT TO EVER END.
KING THOR
THERE ARE ENOUGH STORIES HERE...THAT I...I CAN JUST KEEP... READING THEM...
...FOREVER AND EVER AND...
SHADRAK! STOP DAWDLING AND GET BACK TO WORK!
YES, SIR, LORD LIBRARIAN, SIR.
OH WELL. MAYBE I'LL...
...I'LL HAVE TIME TO READ ANOTHER ONE TOMORROW.
THE BOOKS AREN'T GOING ANYWHERE, RIGHT?

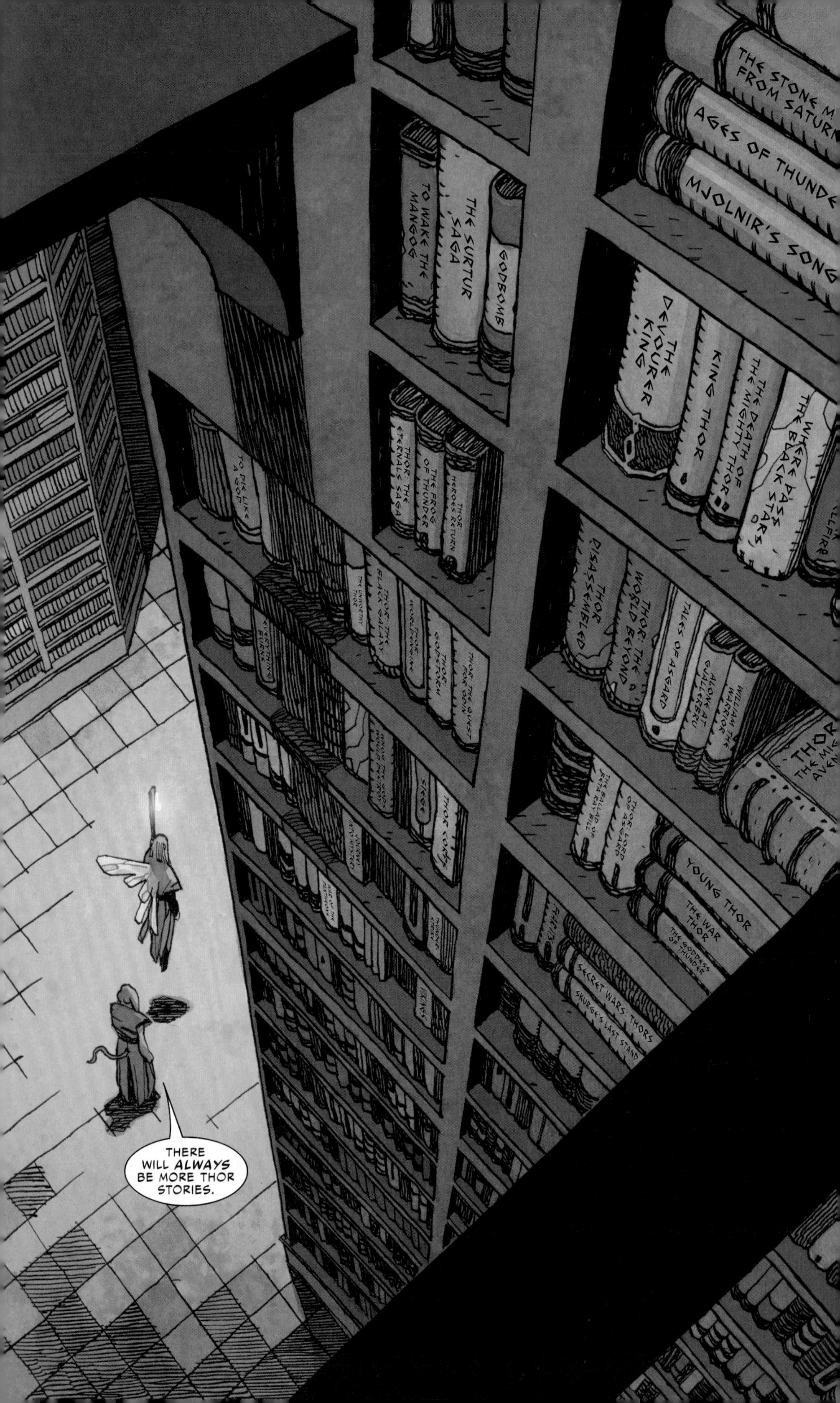
AGES OF THUNDER
MJOLNIR'S SONG
TO WAKE THE MANGOG
THE SURTUR SAGA
GODBOMB
KING THOR
THE DEATH OF THE MIGHTY THOR
TO DIE LIKE A GOD
THOR: THE ETERNALS SAGA
THE FROG OF THUNDER
THOR: HEROES RETURN
THOR DISASSEMBLED
THOR: THE WORLD BEYOND
TALES OF ASGARD
ALONE AT GJALLERBRU
WILLIAM THE WARRIOR
THE BALLAD OF BETA RAY BILL
THOR: LORD OF ASGARD
YOUNG THOR
THE WAR THOR
THE GODDESS OF THUNDER
SECRET WARS: THORS
SKURGE'S LAST STAND
SIEGE
THOR CORPS
THERE WILL *ALWAYS* BE MORE THOR STORIES.

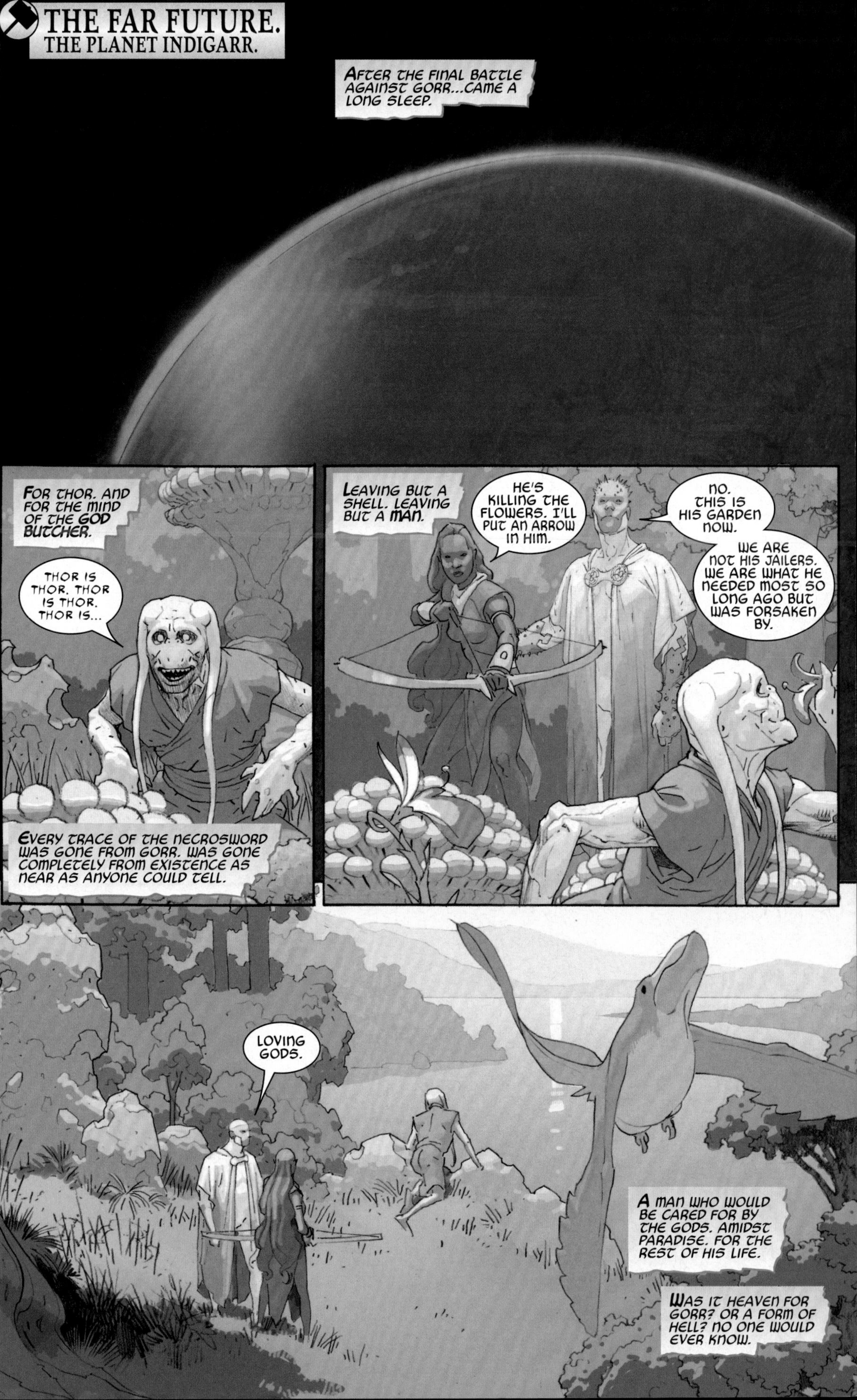
THE FAR FUTURE.
THE PLANET INDIGARR.
AFTER THE FINAL BATTLE AGAINST GORR...CAME A LONG SLEEP.
FOR THOR. AND FOR THE MIND OF THE GOD BUTCHER.
THOR IS THOR. THOR IS THOR. THOR IS...
EVERY TRACE OF THE NECROSWORD WAS GONE FROM GORR. WAS GONE COMPLETELY FROM EXISTENCE AS NEAR AS ANYONE COULD TELL.
LEAVING BUT A SHELL. LEAVING BUT A MAN.
HE'S KILLING THE FLOWERS. I'LL PUT AN ARROW IN HIM.
NO. THIS IS HIS GARDEN NOW.
WE ARE NOT HIS JAILERS. WE ARE WHAT HE NEEDED MOST SO LONG AGO BUT WAS FORSAKEN BY.
LOVING GODS.
A MAN WHO WOULD BE CARED FOR BY THE GODS. AMIDST PARADISE. FOR THE REST OF HIS LIFE.
WAS IT HEAVEN FOR GORR? OR A FORM OF HELL? NO ONE WOULD EVER KNOW.

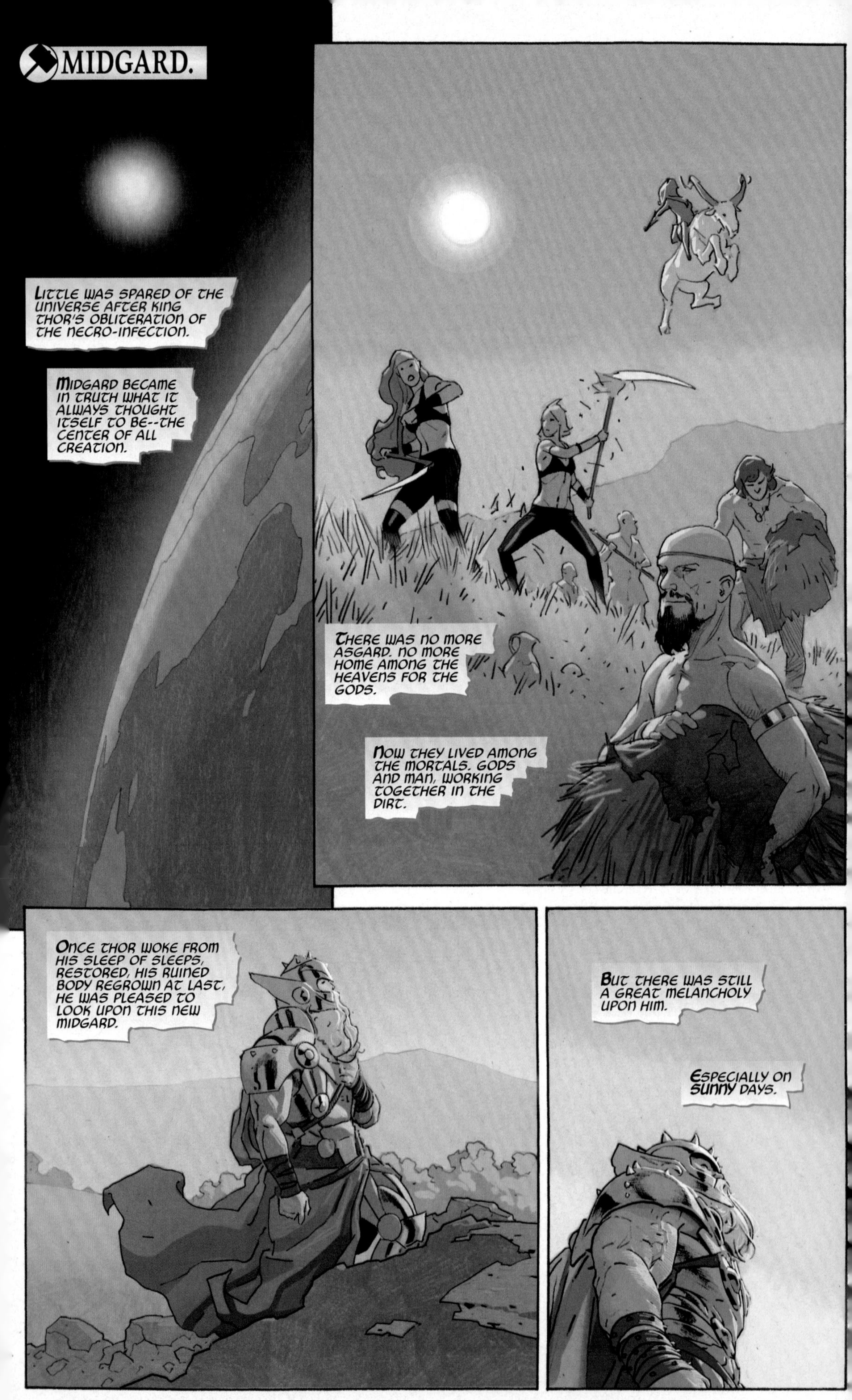
MIDGARD.
LITTLE WAS SPARED OF THE UNIVERSE AFTER KING THOR'S OBLITERATION OF THE NECRO-INFECTION.
MIDGARD BECAME IN TRUTH WHAT IT ALWAYS THOUGHT ITSELF TO BE--THE CENTER OF ALL CREATION.
THERE WAS NO MORE ASGARD. NO MORE HOME AMONG THE HEAVENS FOR THE GODS.
NOW THEY LIVED AMONG THE MORTALS. GODS AND MAN, WORKING TOGETHER IN THE DIRT.
ONCE THOR WOKE FROM HIS SLEEP OF SLEEPS, RESTORED, HIS RUINED BODY REGROWN AT LAST, HE WAS PLEASED TO LOOK UPON THIS NEW MIDGARD.
BUT THERE WAS STILL A GREAT MELANCHOLY UPON HIM.
ESPECIALLY ON SUNNY DAYS.

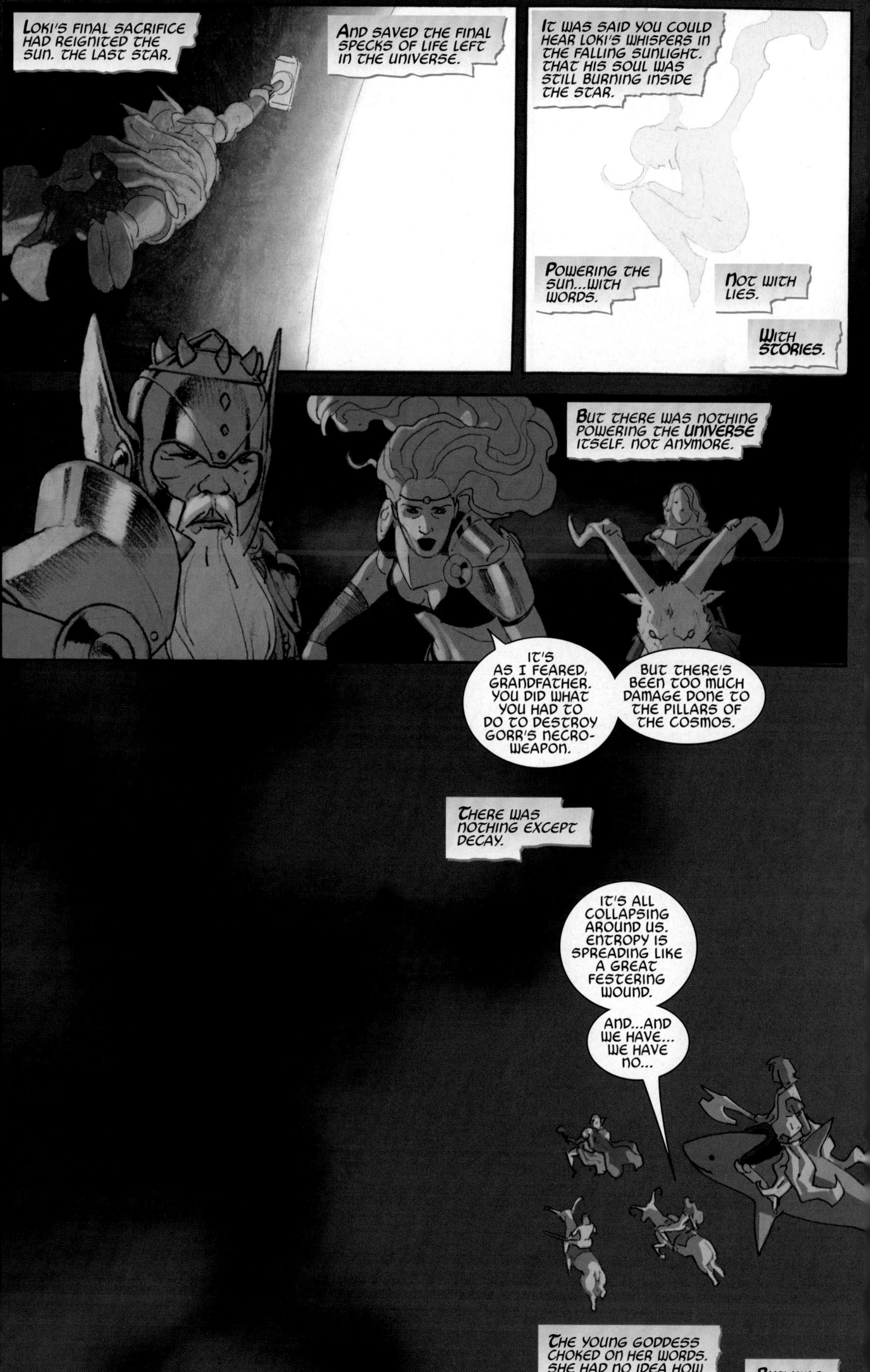
LOKI'S FINAL SACRIFICE HAD REIGNITED THE SUN. THE LAST STAR.
AND SAVED THE FINAL SPECKS OF LIFE LEFT IN THE UNIVERSE.
IT WAS SAID YOU COULD HEAR LOKI'S WHISPERS IN THE FALLING SUNLIGHT. THAT HIS SOUL WAS STILL BURNING INSIDE THE STAR.
POWERING THE SUN...WITH WORDS.
NOT WITH LIES.
WITH STORIES.
BUT THERE WAS NOTHING POWERING THE UNIVERSE ITSELF. NOT ANYMORE.
IT'S AS I FEARED, GRANDFATHER. YOU DID WHAT YOU HAD TO DO TO DESTROY GORR'S NECRO-WEAPON.
BUT THERE'S BEEN TOO MUCH DAMAGE DONE TO THE PILLARS OF THE COSMOS.
THERE WAS NOTHING EXCEPT DECAY.
IT'S ALL COLLAPSING AROUND US. ENTROPY IS SPREADING LIKE A GREAT FESTERING WOUND.
AND...AND WE HAVE... WE HAVE NO...
THE YOUNG GODDESS CHOKED ON HER WORDS. SHE HAD NO IDEA HOW TO STOP THE END.
BUT KING THOR DID.

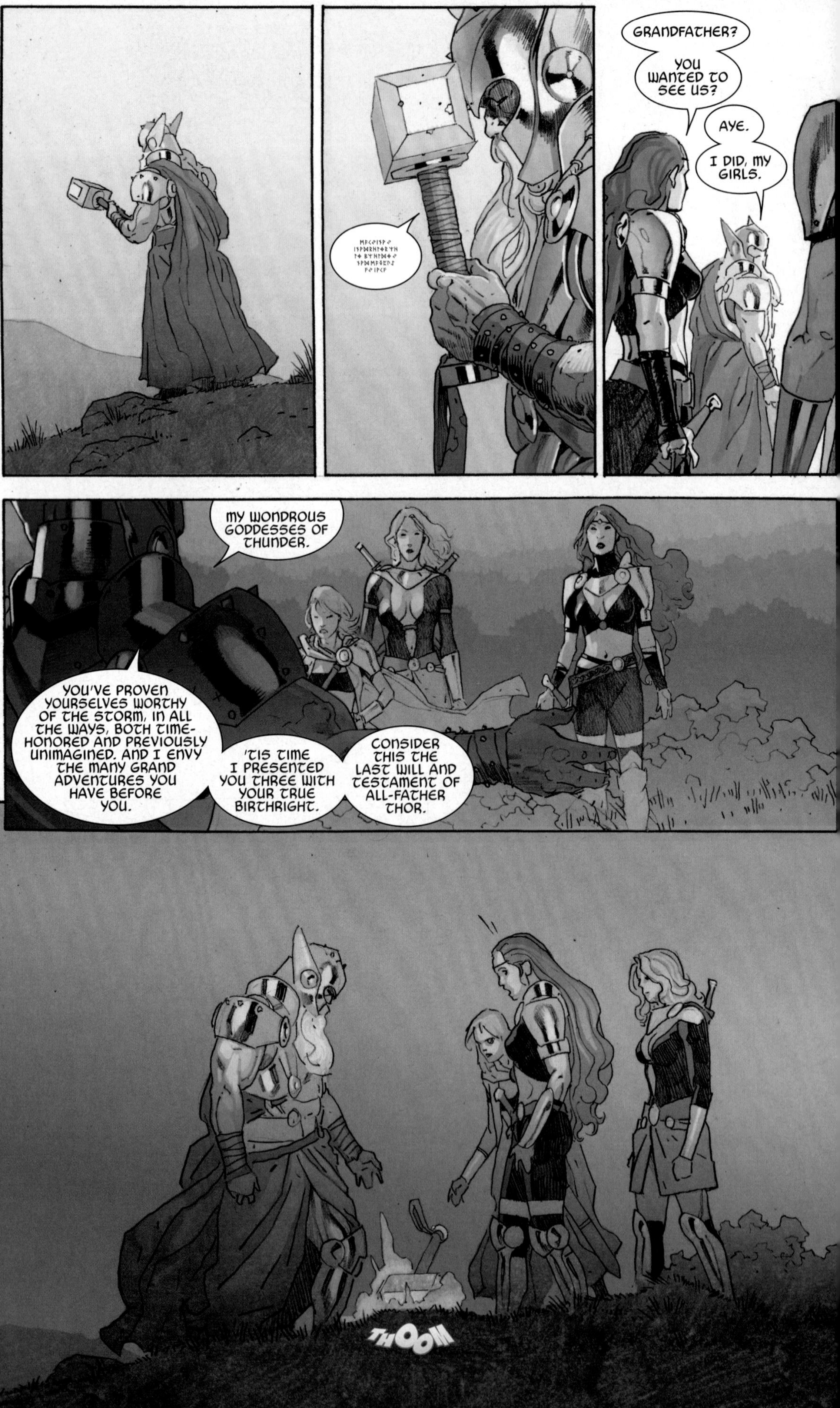
GRANDFATHER?
YOU WANTED TO SEE US?
AYE.
I DID, MY GIRLS.
MY WONDROUS GODDESSES OF THUNDER.
YOU'VE PROVEN YOURSELVES WORTHY OF THE STORM, IN ALL THE WAYS, BOTH TIME-HONORED AND PREVIOUSLY UNIMAGINED. AND I ENVY THE MANY GRAND ADVENTURES YOU HAVE BEFORE YOU.
'TIS TIME I PRESENTED YOU THREE WITH YOUR TRUE BIRTHRIGHT.
CONSIDER THIS THE LAST WILL AND TESTAMENT OF ALL-FATHER THOR.
THOOM

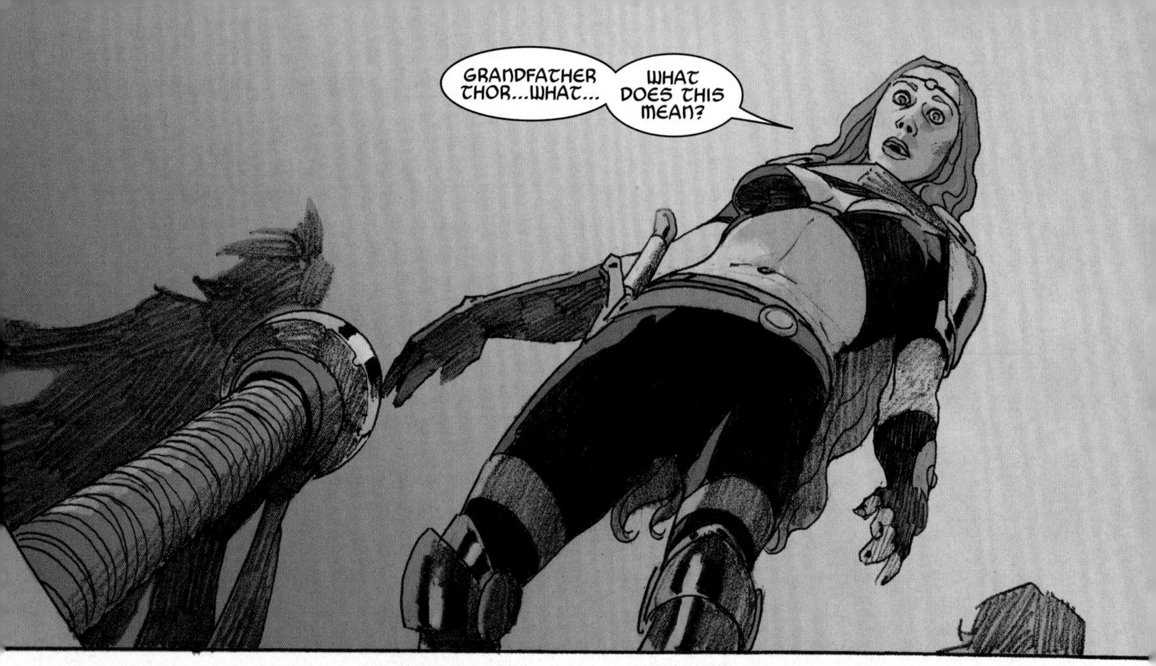
GRANDFATHER THOR...WHAT...
WHAT DOES THIS MEAN?

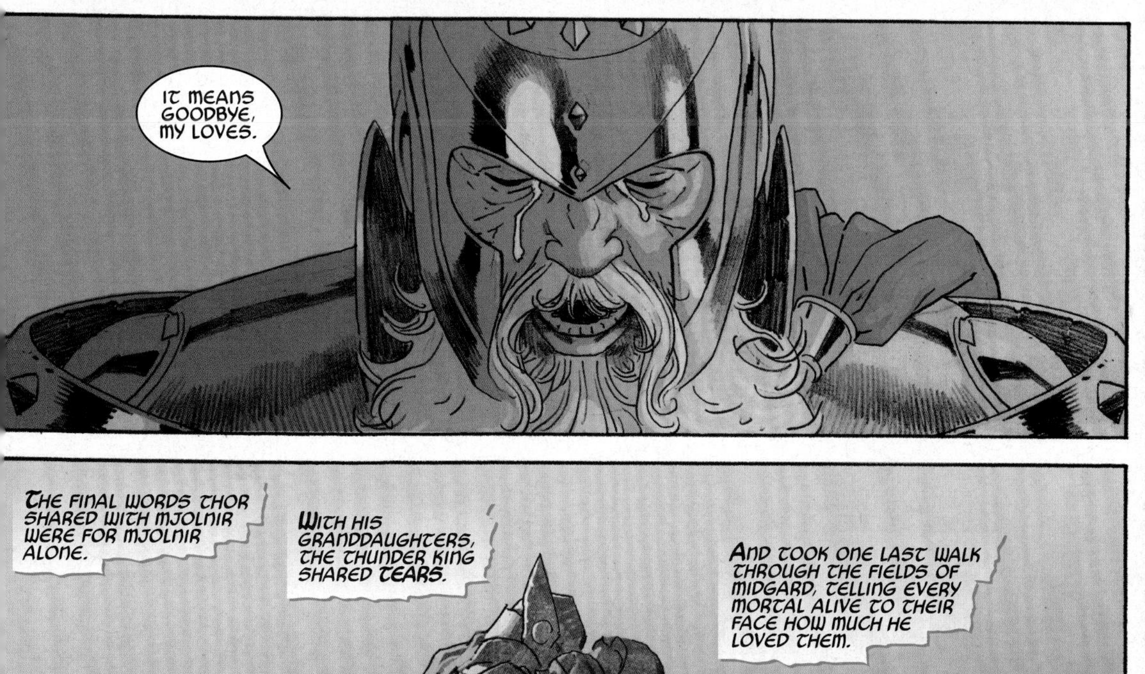
IT MEANS GOODBYE, MY LOVES.

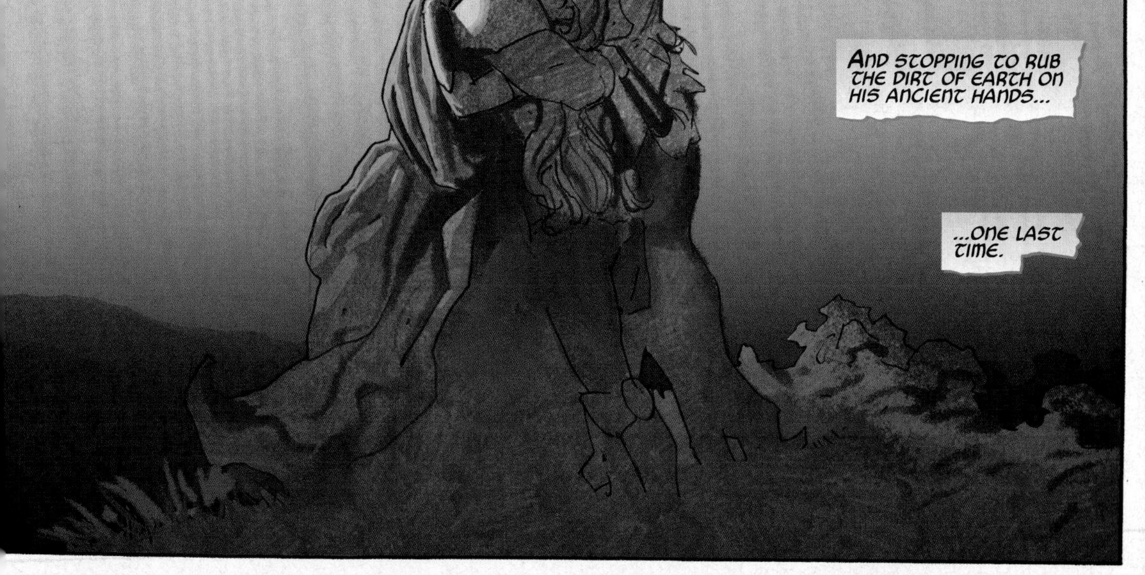
THE FINAL WORDS THOR SHARED WITH MJOLNIR WERE FOR MJOLNIR ALONE.
WITH HIS GRANDDAUGHTERS, THE THUNDER KING SHARED TEARS.
AND TOOK ONE LAST WALK THROUGH THE FIELDS OF MIDGARD, TELLING EVERY MORTAL ALIVE TO THEIR FACE HOW MUCH HE LOVED THEM.
AND STOPPING TO RUB THE DIRT OF EARTH ON HIS ANCIENT HANDS...
...ONE LAST TIME.

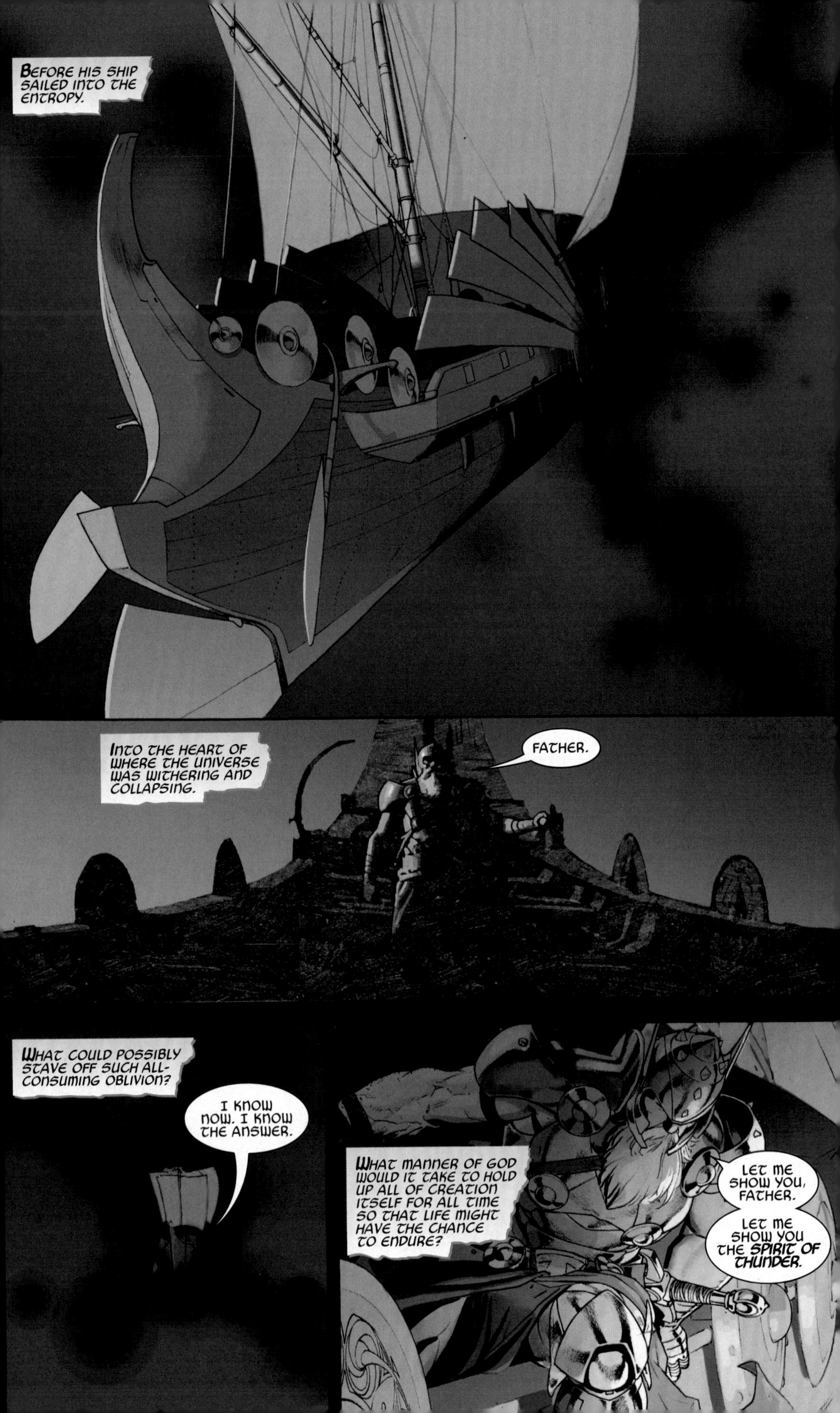
BEFORE HIS SHIP SAILED INTO THE ENTROPY.
INTO THE HEART OF WHERE THE UNIVERSE WAS WITHERING AND COLLAPSING.
FATHER.
WHAT COULD POSSIBLY STAVE OFF SUCH ALL-CONSUMING OBLIVION?
I KNOW NOW. I KNOW THE ANSWER.
WHAT MANNER OF GOD WOULD IT TAKE TO HOLD UP ALL OF CREATION ITSELF FOR ALL TIME SO THAT LIFE MIGHT HAVE THE CHANCE TO ENDURE?
LET ME SHOW YOU, FATHER.
LET ME SHOW YOU THE SPIRIT OF THUNDER.

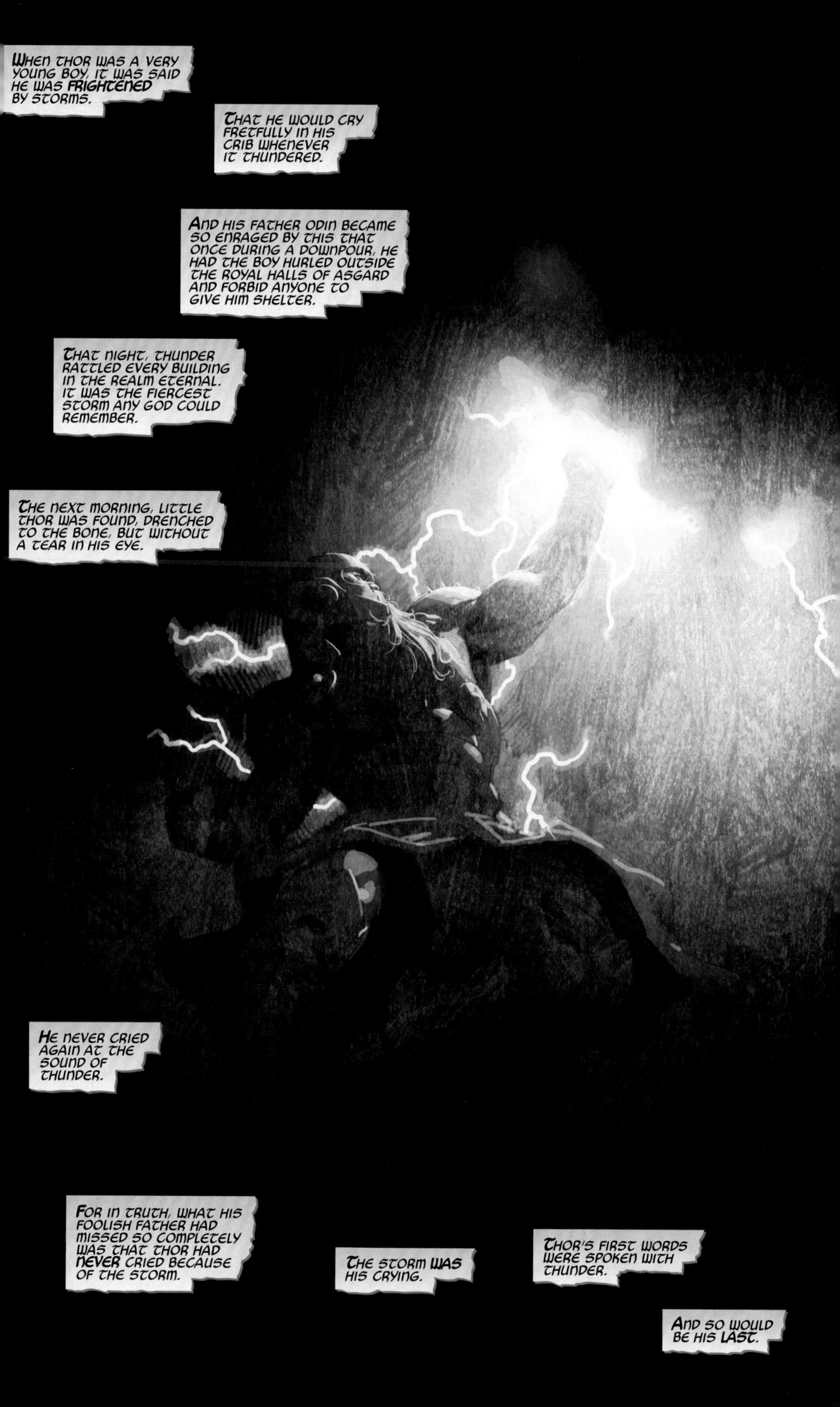

WHEN THOR WAS A VERY YOUNG BOY, IT WAS SAID HE WAS **FRIGHTENED** BY STORMS.
THAT HE WOULD CRY FRETFULLY IN HIS CRIB WHENEVER IT THUNDERED.
AND HIS FATHER ODIN BECAME SO ENRAGED BY THIS THAT ONCE DURING A DOWNPOUR, HE HAD THE BOY HURLED OUTSIDE THE ROYAL HALLS OF ASGARD AND FORBID ANYONE TO GIVE HIM SHELTER.
THAT NIGHT, THUNDER RATTLED EVERY BUILDING IN THE REALM ETERNAL. IT WAS THE FIERCEST STORM ANY GOD COULD REMEMBER.
THE NEXT MORNING, LITTLE THOR WAS FOUND, DRENCHED TO THE BONE, BUT WITHOUT A TEAR IN HIS EYE.
HE NEVER CRIED AGAIN AT THE SOUND OF THUNDER.
FOR IN TRUTH, WHAT HIS FOOLISH FATHER HAD MISSED SO COMPLETELY WAS THAT THOR HAD **NEVER** CRIED BECAUSE OF THE STORM.
THE STORM **WAS** HIS CRYING.
THOR'S FIRST WORDS WERE SPOKEN WITH THUNDER.
AND SO WOULD BE HIS **LAST**.

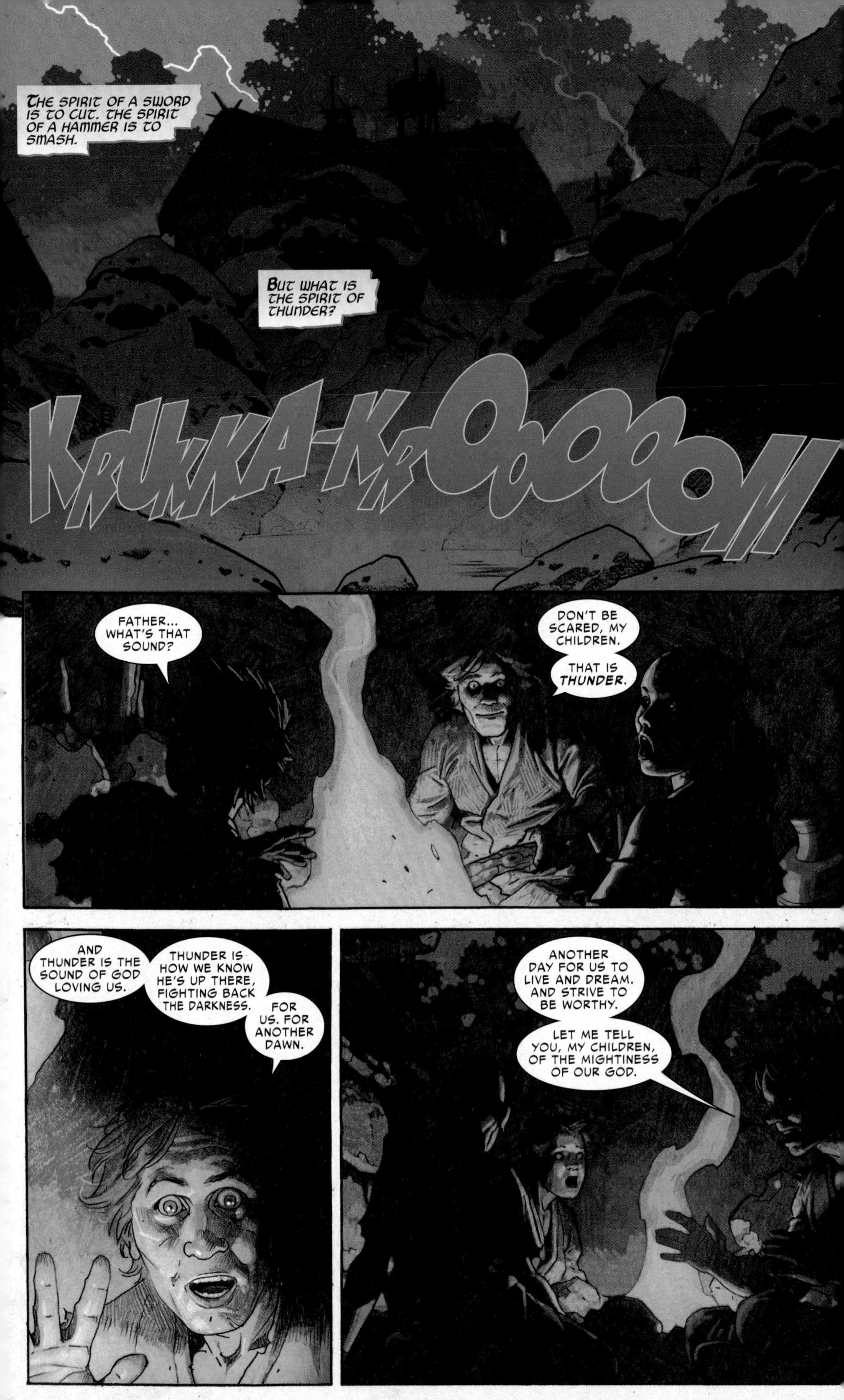
THE SPIRIT OF A SWORD IS TO CUT. THE SPIRIT OF A HAMMER IS TO SMASH.
BUT WHAT IS THE SPIRIT OF THUNDER?
KRUKKA-KROOOOOM
FATHER... WHAT'S THAT SOUND?
DON'T BE SCARED, MY CHILDREN.
THAT IS THUNDER.
AND THUNDER IS THE SOUND OF GOD LOVING US.
THUNDER IS HOW WE KNOW HE'S UP THERE, FIGHTING BACK THE DARKNESS.
FOR US. FOR ANOTHER DAWN.
ANOTHER DAY FOR US TO LIVE AND DREAM. AND STRIVE TO BE WORTHY.
LET ME TELL YOU, MY CHILDREN, OF THE MIGHTINESS OF OUR GOD.

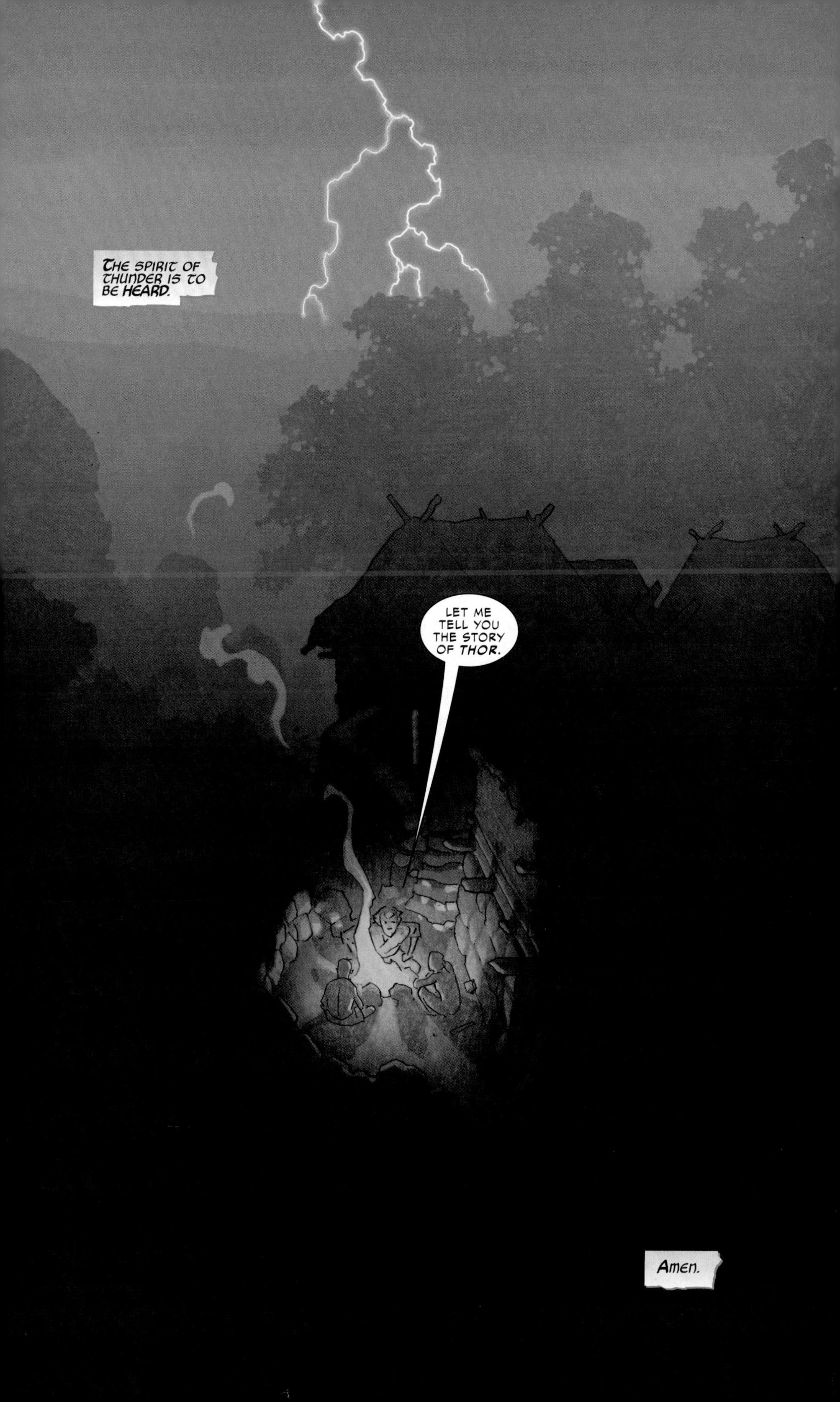
THE SPIRIT OF THUNDER IS TO BE HEARD.
LET ME TELL YOU THE STORY OF THOR.
Amen.

I'm not gonna lie. It was hard to let go.

I don't know that I'm very good at letting go in general. But especially after seven years and 100 or so issues of being the "Thor guy" at Marvel, I found it was really hard to put this final one to bed. I held on to those last few pages for as long as I possibly could. Even though that last scene had been sitting in my head, waiting to be written, for many years.

I put a lot of myself into those 100 issues. A lot of who I was growing up, playing alone in the woods of the Deep South, breathing in stories like the purest of pine-scented oxygen, dreaming my way in the roundabout direction of the life I wanted. And a lot of who I became when I grew up, lost religion, almost lost myself, moved away, found love, found fatherhood, found the man I wanted to be, a man I'm still working to more fully realize every day.

Thor helped with that. Thor literally changed my life. And I just hope I returned the favor in some way that mattered.

Personally, I haven't believed in God, in any gods, for a long time. Faith hasn't been a part of who I am for many years. But I still have ideas and values that are precious and fundamental to me in ways that feel almost religious in nature. Even as an atheist, I still have things I worship.

And I wrote about all of them with Thor.

Thor is truly the sort of god (or gods, I guess, as I wrote a whole bunch of Thors) that I would like to believe in. The god who wakes up every single day and looks at that hammer, with its worthiness enchantment, and doesn't know if they will be able to lift it. Who lives every day questioning their own worthiness, aspiring for it, while also embracing their unworthiness, their failings. The kind of god who delights and takes unbridled joy from the wild, unimaginable beauty all around them. A god who sometimes drinks too much, sometimes loves too recklessly, who thinks both too highly and too lowly of themselves, who laughs big, weeps bigger, who thunders and broods and feels things deeply, even through near-impenetrable flesh. Who would die a thousand times to save what's most precious to them, which is us. Like the Vikings of old weaving their sagas, I was fortunate enough to be able to dream that very god into being, while standing on the shoulders of god-spawning giants with names like Lee and Kirby and Simonson. And now Thor will always be very real to me. The God of Thunder will always be a profound presence in my life.

I wasn't a huge Thor fan growing up. This *Thor* run of mine was never really the plan. Until suddenly it was. Back in 2012, there was a moment when every major title at Marvel was up for grabs all at once. I'd already been penciled in to take over a different solo Avenger series. But for some reason, it didn't feel right. And something else did. I'd really loved Matt Fraction's *Thor: Ages of Thunder* one-shots. Something about them really resonated with me at that moment in time. And so I asked if I could take over *Thor*. I didn't have a story. Didn't have a direction. Didn't know who Thor was to me. But suddenly, he was mine. And if nothing else, I hope it still shows seven years later that I have thoroughly enjoyed our time together.

So if there's a lesson in there, I guess it's to be who you are and follow what feels right in the moment.

And dream your own gods.

Speaking of gods, there's a long list of the artistic variety whom I was lucky enough to collaborate with over the course of this run. It's too large a pantheon for me to list every single deified one of them here, but I would like to acknowledge a few. Before I ever had my first Thor story idea, I knew Esad Ribić was going to draw it, and that truly helped define everything to me. The scope, the power, the feel. Everything I've done with the character goes back to Esad's initial designs and the power of his opening pencils (along with Ive Svorcina's breathtaking colors). Esad was the spark, the fiery cosmic genesis, the jaw-dropping spectacle. And he was a tough damn act to follow. But Russell Dauterman still managed to swoop in and make the character and the world so completely and utterly his own. Along with the near-omnipotently talented colorist Matthew Wilson, Russell became the heart, the soul, the beauty and Uru-strong emotion of the series. I've never cried so much looking at a comic page as I still do with Russell and Matthew's work on the Jane Foster storyline. And I expect that will always be the case. And then the amazing Mike del Mundo took the reins for the last big series and brought his own unique, staggeringly imaginative and inventive style to Thor's world. Mike managed to weave together the spectacle and the heart, the power and the passion, in a way that felt like both a progression of what had come before and something wildly new and different. I will owe these artists free drinks for the rest of my life. And I look forward to them collecting.

I also owe unending thanks to everyone at Marvel who's helped make this happen, from former EiC Axel Alonso and my original editor Lauren Sankovitch to the current chief C.B. Cebulski and my longtime editorial collaborators and infinitely patient creative partners, editors Wil Moss and Sarah Brunstad. Those artists I mentioned before are the reason this run has looked so incredible for so long. But Wil and Sarah are the power behind that. It's been their eyes and impeccable tastes guiding the look of all these gorgeous series. So we all owe them free drinks for that.

And there's one other vitally important person who's been an even bigger part of my run than anyone else. And that's letterer Joe Sabino. Joe has brought his letters and creativity to every single issue of my time on *Thor*. And even more than that, he's been a part of Thor history for even longer, working on the character all the way back to the JMS days. And thankfully Joe will still be here after I'm gone.

Which I guess means it's time to pass the Mjolnir on to its new caretakers, Donny Cates and Nic Klein, so I can step aside and enjoy the cosmic epicness that I know for a fact they're about to bestow upon us.

And enjoy it; I will. Because I'll be right there with all of you now. The people I owe the most thanks to. The fans who read and supported this entire tale. I don't know how I could ever possibly convey to you just how deeply I've cherished and appreciated the connection we've forged from across the pages. If nothing else, I hope that connection has earned me the honor of standing alongside you. As a Thor fan. Eagerly awaiting the next issue. The next grand adventure. The next chance to spend a little more time with a dear old friend.

I love you, Thor. Most verily, I do. Thanks for the chance to share that love with the world.

I'll look for you in the storm clouds, friend.

Stay worthy.
Jason Aaron
KC, November 14, 2019

#4 VARIANT COVER
BY MIKE DEL MUNDO

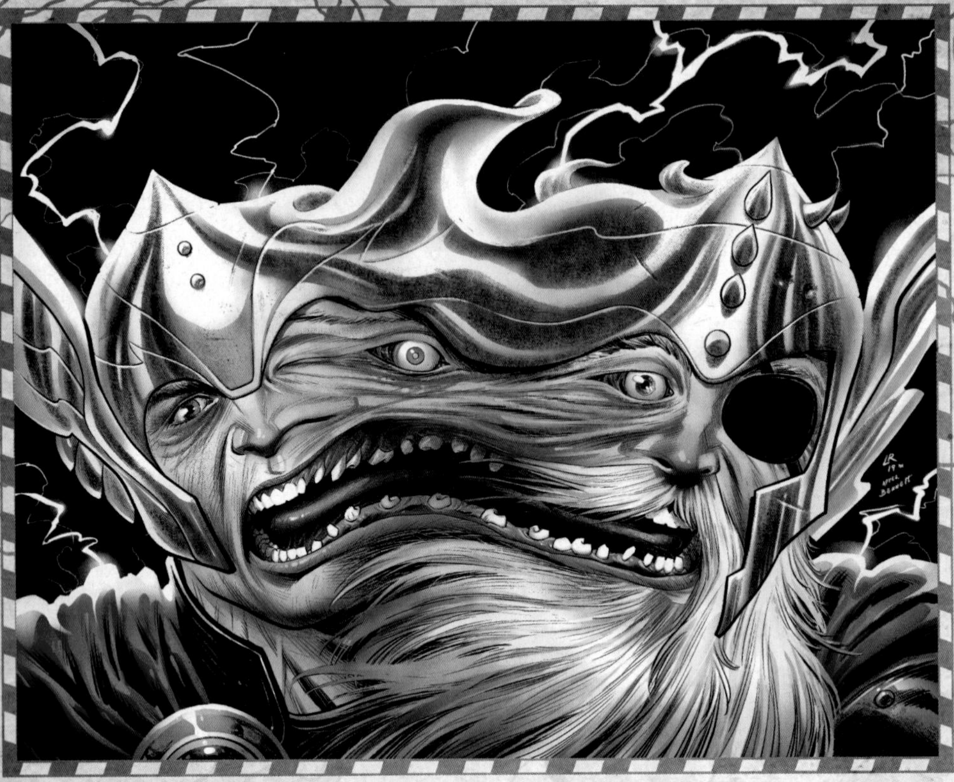

#1 IMMORTAL VARIANT COVER BY **GERARDO ZAFFINO**

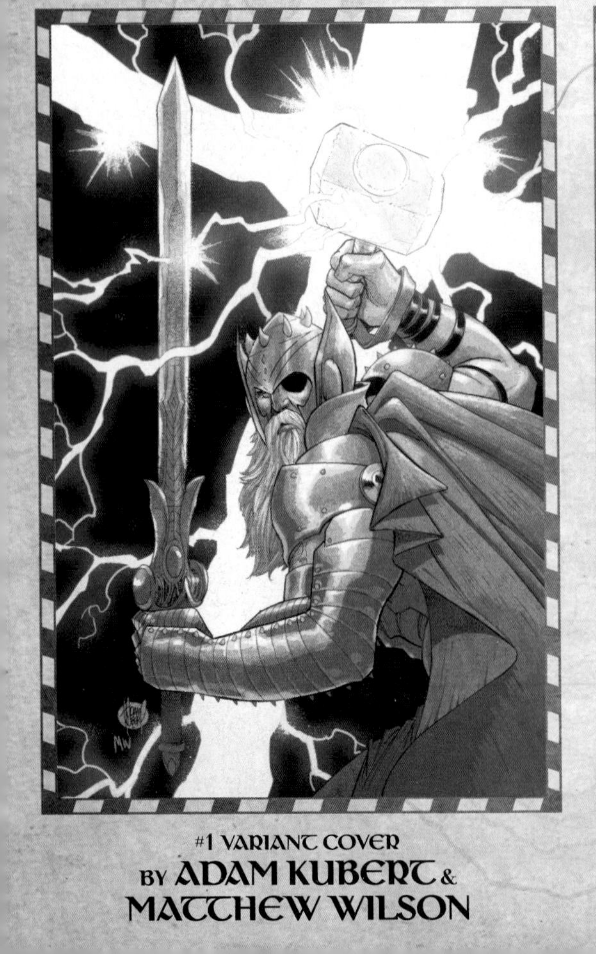

#1 VARIANT COVER
BY **ADAM KUBERT & MATTHEW WILSON**

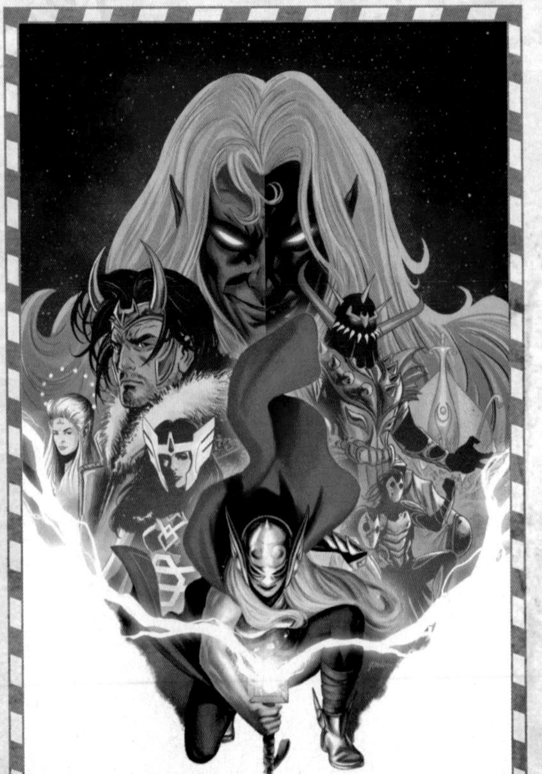

#4 VARIANT COVER
BY **STEVE EPTING**